How to Make Your Mark

A Manual for Evangelism and Discipleship

Printed in the United States of America.

Foreword

Jesus spoke, lived and died as has no other man of history. He was both perfect God and perfect man, and to Him all authority in heaven and earth was given. He commissioned the 11 men with whom He had worked for more than three years to go into all the world and make disciples of all the nations, baptizing and teaching what He had taught them.

The only reasonable explanation for that command is that our Lord did not expect these 11 men to accomplish this mission by themselves. Obviously, He expected the Holy Spirit to accomplish this task through movements of evangelism and discipleship. Throughout history God has raised up such movements. Through periods of revival and awakening, the very course of human history has been changed. Now the torch has been passed to us. This is our golden hour of opportunity.

The greatest spiritual advance in the history of man is now taking place throughout the world. More people are hearing the gospel, receiving Christ and being trained to serve Him than at any other time since the Great Commission was given nearly 2,000 years ago.

We have the manpower, the technology and the finances to fulfill the Great Commission now—in this generation. But if we are to learn from history, we must realize that this unprecedented opportunity for spiritual awakening, like other great awakenings—Pentecost, the Reformation, the Wesleyan revivals and campus revivals of the Student Volunteer era—will come to an end. We dare not miss this opportunity! If ever we plan to do anything for the Lord Jesus Christ and His kingdom, we must do it now!

Over 30 years ago I realized that the vision God had placed in my heart to help fulfill the Great Commission could never be accomplished through my own efforts, whether in personal or mass evangelism. For this reason, our goal from the very beginning has been to build movements of evangelism and discipleship. From these spiritual seedbeds, we have seen God produce thousands of laborers for the harvest. Now, a full-time and associate staff of more than 16,000 is discipling tens of thousands who are in turn reaching and training millions more for our Savior.

In large part these results are due to the fact that students are committed to making an eternal mark for the glory of God. They have made their mark by carrying the torch of the gospel, which had been passed down to them by previous generations of radically committed Christian students. I pray that you will join with us as we continue to carry the gospel to our nation's campuses. Together we can make a mark on the world for Christ that will never be erased. We can help fulfill the Great Commission on the campuses of America and of all other nations in *this* generation!

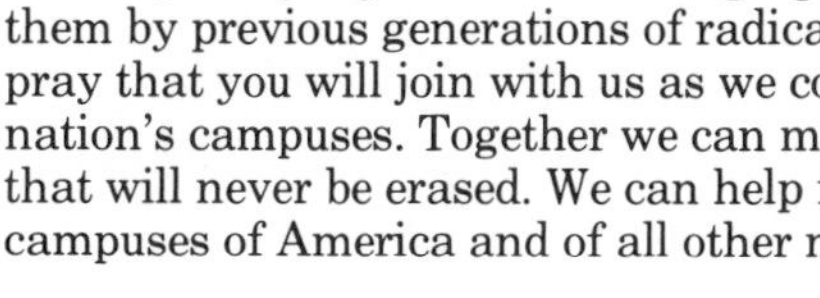

Bill Bright, Founder and President
Campus Crusade for Christ International

Introduction

Can you imagine one-third to one-half of a university's student body coming to Christ in a single year? Then can you imagine 50 percent of those new believers going into full-time Christian work following graduation? Could you envision more than 20,000 students eventually serving Christ overseas due to the influence of only a few of these students?

Hold on to your seat. All this happened! It began in the early 1800s at schools like Amherst, Dartmouth, Princeton, Williams and Yale, where up to half the students turned to Christ. By 1835, 1,500 students had committed their lives to Christ in 36 colleges. Impressive statistics—especially when you realize that in those days student bodies numbered only 100 to 250. Similar results continued to be seen from one generation of students to the next. In 1853, 11 New England colleges with a total enrollment of 2,163 reported that there were 745 active Christians on campus. Of this number, 343 planned to go into the ministry.

Then in the 1800s an unprecedented missionary enterprise, known as the Student Volunteer Movement, came into being. "The Evangelization of the World in This Generation" became its rallying cry. This spirit was evident in the movement's results—more than 20,000 serving in overseas mission fields within half a century. College students made their mark in this era of spiritual advance. You are invited as well to make your mark.

Trail West Agreement

The group of college and university staff workers from Campus Crusade for Christ, Inter-Varsity Christian Fellowship and The Navigators who assembled at Trail West Lodge agreed to teach the staff of their organizations the following principles about their relationships with other Christian groups.

1. We are all part of Christ's body.

2. None of us regards any campus as our exclusive field. We recognize that many more students may be helped through the various appeals and styles of the different organizations.

3. We will establish relationships with other Christian groups on campus, especially by taking the initiative in building bridges to our counterparts in the other organizations.

4. We will avoid criticism or censoriousness of any member of the body of Christ.

5. We will not take leadership from other groups.

6. When starting a new work on a campus, each organization should endeavor to select new leaders, not leaders of other groups already on campus.

7. Officers of one organization should not participate in functions of other organizations while they are holding office.

8. Students have complete freedom to choose which organization they will associate with, but once they have sampled the various organizations, we will all encourage them to make their selection and stick with one group rather than continuously shop them all.

9. We will endeavor to work out periodic cooperative ventures where all Christians can cooperate.

10. We will agree to share addresses and phone numbers of a contact man for each region and state (or equivalent) at least annually.

How to Use This Book

This book is written to help you.

It explains the philosophy, strategy and "how to's" of helping you reach your campus for Christ. It also explains how to develop in your knowledge and walk with God.

It contains the essence of 31 years of experience of nearly 3,000 Campus Crusade for Christ campus staff members and tens of thousands of students.

It is designed to be a resource. It is not a substitute for the Holy Spirit. Nor is it a substitute for developing your walk with God, increasing your knowledge of your campus or drawing upon the knowledge and experience of a staff member who keeps in contact with you.

Used as a complement to all those other sources of knowledge, and used in the power of the Spirit, it can help you be effective in seeing a movement of God begin and grow on your campus.

Part 1: Reaching Your Campus: The Goal of a Movement

This part gives you an overall framework in which to fit all the detailed pieces of your ministry. It defines a movement, and gives you a picture of what a movement can look like on your campus. It helps you think through what is unique about your campus. A movement most of all needs spiritual leadership, so we have included suggestions on how to develop in your walk with God in Chapter 6.

Part 2: Evangelism: The Cutting Edge of a Movement

Evangelism means that we are continually taking the initiative in talking to people about Christ and giving them the opportunity to receive Christ. Because it characterizes a movement of God and it is at the head of all that we're doing, we call it the "cutting edge." This part explains exactly how to share your faith one-to-one as well as why our Lord wants us to be involved daily in telling others about Him. You will learn how to reach groups and how to use evangelism in discipling others.

Part 3: Discipleship: Strengthening the Movement

This part explains the discipleship process: helping move a person who has received Christ to a point of spiritual maturity and spiritual multiplication (i.e., the point at which he can transfer his knowledge of the Christian life to others). These chapters explain how to follow up a new Christian, how to start and lead a new believers' Bible study and how to lead an intensive discipleship group.

Part 4: Ways to Accelerate a Movement

This part explains how to accelerate the development of your ministry by using conferences, weekly meetings and campus-wide evangelistic meetings. It tells you how to produce momentum in your ministry: the sense that God is at work and moving in people's lives.

Table of Contents

Table of Exhibits

PART I
REACHING YOUR CAMPUS: THE GOAL OF A MOVEMENT

Chapter 1
Student Movements That Made a Mark

Five ordinary students—not even Christians—had finally become disgusted with the blatantly immoral climate on their campus. As a last resort, they decided to hold a prayer meeting to ask for God's help. Fearing the reaction of other students, they locked themselves in a room and kept their voices down so they would not be found out.

However, other students discovered them and tried to break down the door. The president of the college heard the disturbance and came to find out who had started the latest riot. One of the students outside said, "Oh, sir, it's nothing important; there are just some fanatics in here holding a prayer meeting! Can you imagine? So we thought we'd teach them a lesson. We won't hurt them. We'll rough them up a little bit, but we won't hurt them."

The president rebuked them saying, "You don't mind cheating, you don't mind stealing from rooms, you don't mind the lying and the profanity you get on this campus, but you object to a prayer meeting. Well, I do not!" He then knocked on the door and said authoritatively, "This is the president of the college speaking. Will you please come out?" The students unlocked the door and came out, not knowing what to expect. President Smith said, "Gentlemen, come to my study; we'll pray there together."

This prayer meeting marked the beginning of American campus revivals during the Second Great Awakening of the 1790s and early 1800s. The revival experienced by students at Hampden Sydney College in Virginia had no relationship to the typical tent meeting people often picture in their minds when they hear the word *revival.* To revive something means literally "to bring it back to life." The first signs of new life on campus were seen in the life of the typical Christian students, whose previously broken relationships with God were now restored. Next, the non-Christians on campus were drawn to Christ as the general college community was "awakened" to the reality of spiritual issues. As a result of prayer, not only did half the students at Hampden Sydney College turn to Christ, but revival and spiritual awakening also spread to local churches and to other schools, having similar effects.

In college after college, students formed similar Christian fellowships. At Harvard, Bowdoin, Brown, Dartmouth, Middlebury, Williams and Andover, students began to meet together to pray. Three students at Brown formed the College Praying Society, which met in a private room "for fear of disturbance from the unpenitent." At Harvard in December 1802, seven students formed the Saturday Evening Religious Society, which also met secretly.

Certain characteristics were typical of these student prayer meetings:

1. The students asked the Holy Spirit to point out any unconfessed sin in their lives, whether attitudes or actions. "If I regard wickedness in my heart, the Lord will not hear" (Psalm 66:18).

2. They claimed the forgiveness that was theirs through Christ's death on the cross for them. "If we confess our sins He is faithful and righteous to forgive us our sins and to cleanse us from all unrighteousness" (1 John 1:9).

3. If restitution was appropriate, they took time to reconcile any differences they had with others. "Therefore, if you are offering your gift at the altar and there remember that your brother has something against you, leave your gift there in front of the altar. First go and be reconciled to your brother; then come and offer your gift" (Matthew 5:23,24, NIV).

4. By faith they experienced the fullness of the Holy Spirit.

   "And do not get drunk with wine, for that is dissipation, but be filled with the Spirit" (Ephesians 5:18).

   "This is the confidence which we have before Him, that, if we ask anything according to His will, He hears us. And if we know that He hears us in whatever we ask, we know that we have the requests which we have asked from Him" (1 John 5:14,15).

5. They believed God to supernaturally fulfill His primises in their lives and in the world. "For our struggle is not against flesh and blood, but against the rulers, against the powers, against the world forces of this darkness, against the spiritual forces of wickedness in the heavenly places" (Ephesians 6:12).

   ". . . for the weapons of our warfare are not of the flesh, but divinely powerful for the destruction of fortresses. We are destroying speculations and every lofty thing raised up against the knowledge of God, and we are taking every thought captive to the obedience of Christ" (2 Corinthians 10:4,5).

The prayers of students continued to cause Christians to proclaim the gospel more boldly. The accompanying results were nothing short of dramatic. At Yale, President Timothy Dwight began preaching apologetical messages in chapel. He hit the relativistic philosophy of the day head-on with such talks as "Are the New Testament Documents Reliable?" As a result of the Christians' prayers and Dwight's powerful presentations, one-third of Yale's student body indicated they received Christ as Savior and Lord in 1802!

A Student Organization Channels the Work of the Holy Spirit

At Princeton in 1975, a student Christian group known as the Philadelphia Society had 110 active members. Luther Wishard, who became the group's president in 1876, united the society with the growing YMCA movement

The objectives of the Intercollegiate YMCA, as framed by Wishard, included: "1) The importance of seeking the salvation of students for their own sake and their influence as educated men; 2) the importance of securing their salvation while in college; 3) the value of united work and prayer."

The methods for achieving these objectives included: "1) diligent study of the Word of God; 2) prayer; 3) personal work (one-to-one evangelism); 4) efficient organization."

Through Wishard's leadership and the students' prayers, evangelist Dwight L. Moody was persuaded to conduct a series of evangelistic meetings on campus. As a result, nearly one-third of the student body indicated they received Christ!

Among those working in the Princeton YMCA were some of the most outstanding campus leaders. One such student evangelist was Tommy

Wilson, who eventually became president of the university. Later still he became better known as T. Woodrow Wilson, 28th President of the United States.

A Supernatural Movement Sweeps the Continent

During the early 1900s dynamic student movements continued to flourish as a result of the nationwide awakening of 1905:

- At Cornell University, 350 of the school's 3,000 men were in Bible study groups in 1907.
- At Rutgers University, 111 of the school's 220 students were in Bible study groups, an increase of 400 percent within one year.
- At Princeton in late 1905, the average attendance at a weekly evangelistic meeting was more than 1,000 out of the school's enrollment of 1,384.
- At Juanita College in Huntingdon, Pennsylvania, in 1906, more than half the students were enrolled in missionary study classes, meeting voluntarily each week to prepare for service in the field.
- At Mississippi A&M College, probably every one of the 800 students on campus attended the student-run evangelistic meetings. Attendance averaged 360 at each meeting, and more than 60 decisions for Christ were reported.
- At Trinity College in Durham, North Carolina, only 25 students had not made decisions for Christ out of an enrollment of 200 men.
- At Berkeley in 1905, 10 percent of the student body of 1,450 were in Bible studies. In one fraternity Bible study, many key student leaders were won to Christ, including the star halfback, the private secretary to the university and the captain of the football team.
- In 1906 at Stanford University, 200 out of a student population of 1,000—20 percent—were part of the Student Christian Association, and more than 300—33 percent—attended weekly Bible studies.
- Of the 1,200 men at Iowa State College in Ames in 1905, 616 students attended Bible studies led by the 200 members of the Student Christians Association.
- At Northwestern University in Evanston, Illinois, two-thirds of the men enrolled were part of the Student Christian Association, and one-third were part of the Association's Bible studies.
- At Northwestern College in Naperville, Illinois, there was such a spiritual awakening that 80 percent of the school's student body of

200 became members of the Christian Association, 10 percent were in Bible studies and 104 were studying missions.

- As a result of the 1905 revival, the Christian Association at Drake University in Des Moines reported that one-third of the student body were attending Bible studies.
- At the University of Michigan in 1905, two-thirds (2,400 of the school's enrollment of 3,600 students) packed out University Hall in Ann Arbor to hear the gospel.

The Holy Spirit Causes Growth in Student Christian Associations

In 1902, the 642 collegiate YMCA groups across America were ministering to the total student population of 126,841. Of this number, 27,926 were members of these Student Christian Associations. An aggregate of 643,454 attended meetings sponsored by the YMCAs and other parachurch groups. Obviously the Holy Spirit was at work orchestrating a dramatic movement through the nation's colleges and universities.

After the awakening of 1905, however, the picture was even more positive. By then there were 667 YMCAs ministering to 169,945 students—an increase of almost 25 percent. Of this number, 29,660 were active members of the collegiate YMCAs. Attendance at meetings sponsored by the Student Christian Association jumped significantly to 929,539—more than a 23 percent increase!

The growth of these movements resulted in renewed evangelistic thrusts on college campuses. At the University of Michigan, for instance, John R. Mott held three meetings that drew 1,000 men to each. In a final meeting, 3,000 men and women attended, and nearly 200 remained behind afterward for further counsel.

The Movement Spawns Interest in Missions

As men and women were won to Christ, they answered God's call to invest their lives in the task of winning and building others for Christ. In 1896 more than 2,000 students were in missionary study groups. As revival swept America's campuses, this number jumped dramatically to over 11,000. This increased interest in missions is also seen in the attendance figures at the missions conferences sponsored by the Student Volunteer Movement. In 1891, 680 students attended the Cleveland SVM convention; in 1894, 1,325 attended in Detroit; in 1898, 2,221 went to Cleveland; in 1902, 2,597 gathered in Toronto; and in 1906, 4,188 met in Nashville.

Not only did students attend missionary conferences, but their inquisitiveness also led to further action. In 1902, 211 sailed for the mission fields; in 1903, 219; in 1904, 293; and in 1905, more than 300. Through the Student Volunteer Movement, more than 20,000 were eventually sent overseas to preach the gospel—most coming from the collegiate YMCAs on campuses scattered across America.

The Movement Continues Today

God raised up key students, faculty and laymen during the 18th and 19th centuries to spearhead a great spiritual awakening. Through ministries of evangelism and discipleship, they were responsible for reaching several generations of collegians for Christ. As part of the continuing work of God on America's colleges and universities, Campus Crusade for Christ was born in 1951. Its story is a powerful testimony of the grace of God. "For it is God who is at work within you, giving you the will and the power to achieve His purpose" (Philippians 2:13, Phillips).

Campus Crusade's strategy—to help fulfill the Great Commission in this generation by winning, building and sending students and laymen to the world for Christ—was not something fabricated by men. It was a commission of God, as has been demonstrated by His blessing on the ministry since its inception.

Campus Crusade for Christ Begins as One Man Is Reached

Bill Bright, founder and president of Campus Crusade for Christ International, tells about the events that led to the beginning of the ministry: "When I was a student in college, many honors came my way: editor of the college year book, student body president, 'Who's Who in American Colleges and Universities,' and others. I knew hundreds of students personally, and counted many members of the faculty as special friends. Yet, I look back on my college career with such regret. Had I known the Lord Jesus Christ then, so much more of lasting and eternal significance could have been accomplished for Him during my college days.

"Following my college graduation, I joined the faculty of Oklahoma State University Extension Department. Later I pursued an active business career until, through my mother's prayers and the ministry of Dr. Henrietta C. Mears, Dr. Louis Evans Sr. and others, the Lord Jesus Christ became my personal Savior. Immediately, I was impressed to share this thrilling new life in Christ with others. For approximately five years, I was chairman of deputation work at the First Presbyterian Church of Hollywood where, with more than 100 other college students and adults, it was my regular practice to witness individually and with teams in other churches, as well as to 'down and outers' on skid row, in the jails and in road camps. Then one day I was awakened to the fact that, while thousands of Christians were giving their time to reaching these unfortunates for Christ, I knew only a few whose ministries were designed to reach the 'up and outers,' especially college students.

"I remember well our first attempt to do something about reaching the students. We organized a special student deputation team which visited a number of the fraternity and sorority houses in the Los Angeles area. There we met with a gratifying response. However, in our inexperience, we did not know how to turn the interest of the students into commitments to Christ or how to encourage them to grow in the Christian faith.

"Various experiments to reach the students were tried, and with each attempt we found ourselves closer to our objective of reaching the collegiate world for our Savior. In the meantime, while continuing my business interests, I enrolled in Princeton Theological Seminary and later transferred to Fuller Theological Seminary in an effort to learn as much as possible about Christ and to prepare myself to serve Him as a layman. It was during my last year of seminary that something unusual happened in my life.

Campus Crusade for Christ Is Born Out of Revival

"There are certain sacred experiences of life which one is reluctant to share. However, this story would not be complete without at least a reference to that unforgettable experience with God in which Campus Crusade for Christ was born . . .

"So it was a spring night, 1951, in our home in the Hollywood hills. The hour was late. A seminary classmate and I were studying together for a Greek examination. Then, without warning, God spoke to me in a most illuminating way. It should be explained that God did not speak in audible words, but in a very real way He showed me that I was to start working on the college campus and that, through developing the campus emphasis, the world could be reached for Christ. That night, the plan for helping to reach the collegiate world for Christ was given to me, and Campus Crusade for Christ International was born.

"It is not easy to share such an experience, for there is always the danger of being misunderstood. Further, there is always the chance that other Christians may seek such an experience for themselves. To do so would be most unwise, for the Christian is to live by faith, and the very act of seeking an experience denies the principle of faith. However, it is only for the glory of God that this is being told. For several weeks I prayed for guidance and met daily with seminary classmates Dan Fuller, Hugh Brom and Bill Savage to pray concerning this commission of God to reach the universities of the world with the gospel. Though lacking only a few units for graduation, I felt compelled to leave seminary to launch the ministry of Campus Crusade for Christ."

The Movement Continues on Your Campus Today.

We live in a period of history increasingly characterized by loneliness, fear and uncertainty. While computer chips have speeded up and increased the flow of data, feelings and human relationships remain unprogrammable. True joy, peace and security are to be found only in the person of Jesus Christ and the hope of His message.

Students are hungry for the life-changing promises of Christ: "The Son of Man has come to seek and to save that which was lost"; "I came that they might have life, and might have it more abundantly"; "I am the way, and the truth, and the life; no one comes to the Father, but through Me"; "Peace I leave with you; My peace I give to you; not as the world gives, do I give to you. Let not your heart be troubled, nor let it be fearful"; "I will never desert you, nor will I ever forsake you."

Christ spoke, lived and died as has no other man of history. He was both perfect God and perfect man, and to Him all authority in heaven and earth has been given. With this authority, He commissioned us to go into all the world and make disciples of all nations (Matthew 28:19,20).

As Christians we can no longer remain apathetic to the needs of others—seeking first our own comfort and pleasure. God has always used people to reach people with the good news of new life in Christ. That God will use someone to reach the students on your campus with the gospel is certain. He is simply waiting for someone to step forward to lead the charge. Why not let that someone be you? If you make your self available to God, you can be part of the greatest spiritual awakening since Pentecost. You can help usher in the fulfillment of the Great Commission in this generation.

A Ministry on Every U.S. Campus by 1990

From the time we awaken each day until our last conscious thought or act at night, we should be involved in winning and building individuals for Christ. We should do so as an expression of our love and gratitude to God for all the benefits and blessings that are ours by His grace, and as an act of obedience to His command.

C.T. Studd was a famous Cambridge athlete and heir to a great fortune. As he turned from all the promises of fame and wealth to follow Christ to Asia and to Africa as a missionary, he said, "If Jesus Christ be God and died for me, then no sacrifice can be too great for me to make for Him."

The objective of the Campus Ministry of Campus Crusade for Christ is to help reach every college student in America with the gospel, to build disciples through movements of impact and to send as many of these men and women as possible to the United States and the world as witnesses for Christ. This task involves ministering to more than 11.3 million students on more than 3,200 campuses.

Over one-third (3.7 million) of our nation's college population attends schools where our ministry is present. However, many schools can be reached only by students and lay volunteers. We are believing God to raise up at least one person on each U.S. campus by 1990 who will make it his personal responsibility to help reach his school for Christ. The scope of this dream is so great that only through a supernatural outpouring of the Holy Spirit will the job be accomplished. Never before have the opportunities for involvement in the harvest been as challenging as they are today. We invite you to shoulder the burden of this task with us.

The Next Step Is Yours . . . To Be Empowered for Action

This training manual includes many lessons learned through personal contacts with thousands of individuals and in hundreds of meetings, large and small. It has been designed and written to help you be more effective in your personal witness for Christ and in your walk with Him.

In a unique way throughout history, God has chosen to use college students just like you as catalysts for revival and for furthering the cause of Christ. What an honor and awesome responsibility it is to be in the vanguard of such a tradition! As you are available to God, you can be a significant part of His plan for fulfilling the Great Commission in this generation.

Our prayer is that you, like your predecessors, will experience a relationship with Christ that is characterized by the power of the Holy Spirit. Then, as you apply the tools and strategies in this book, God may use you as the catalyst for fulfilling the Great Commission on your campus.

Chapter 2
The Holy Spirit: Our Power Source

Jesus promised His disciples that even though He would no longer be with them after the cross, He would not leave them alone:

> "But now I am going to Him who sent Me; and none of you asks Me, 'Where are you going?' But because I have said these things to you, sorrow has filled your heart. But I tell you the truth, it is to your advantage that I go away; for if I do not go away, the Helper shall not come to you, but if I go, I will send Him to you" (John 16:5-7).

The common denominator running through those spiritual movements of history that have made a mark has been the promised Holy Spirit. After the Holy Spirit came, it was said of the believers in Jerusalem, "And everyone kept feeling a sense of awe; and many wonders and signs were taking place through the apostles. And all those who had believed were together, and had all things in common" (Acts 2:43,44).

> "And Peter said to them, 'Repent, and let each of you be baptized in the name of Jesus Christ for the forgiveness of your sins; and you shall receive the gift of the Holy Spirit. For the *promise* is for you and your children, and for all who are far off, as many as the Lord our God shall call to Himself.' And with many other words he solemnly testified and kept on exhorting them, saying, 'Be saved from this perverse generation!' So then, those who *had received* his word were baptized; and there were added that day about three thousand souls" (Acts 2:38-41, italics added).

As you appropriate the power of the Holy Spirit, as explained in this chapter by Bill Bright, you will be prepared to make an eternal mark for Christ. As you are empowered by the Holy Spirit, God can use you to help develop a movement on your campus today.

You Shall Receive Power
by Bill Bright

Has it ever occurred to you that there is much more to the Christian life than what you are now experiencing?

Jesus said, "I came that they [you and I and all Christians] might have life, and might have it abundantly" (John 10:10). Yet, if you are an average professing Christian, you are undoubtedly thinking, "There is certainly nothing abundant about my life. I try to witness, but no one is interested in what I have to say. I experience nothing but doubts, fears, frustrations and defeat. Surely there must be something more to this Christian life, but I have never found it."

Because of the evangelistic emphasis of Campus Crusade, we have found it absolutely imperative that each member of our staff, as well as the student leaders with whom we work, be filled with the Holy Spirit if we are to have an effective ministry for Christ on the college campus.

There was a time in my own Christian ministry when I challenged Christians to witness and live holy lives for Christ, but the results were so discouraging that I began to devote most of my time and energies to evangelism, where God blessed with much more apparent results. However, as the years have passed, the Holy Spirit has helped me to see the great potential power in lukewarm Christians, if only they are awakened and harnessed for Christ. I am now convinced that the lukewarm, carnal Christian can be changed into a vital, dynamic, witnessing Christian, if he will surrender his will to Christ and be filled with the Holy Spirit. Again and again I am reminded of the great contrast between the church of Jesus Christ today and His church of the first century.

What is the difference? What is that strange quality that sets one man apart from another when both are Christians? Some theologians would say that it is the degree of commitment. Yet there are many people all over the world who are crying out to God, dedicating their lives to Christ day after day, and yet are continuing to be impotent and defeated. Why? Are we not told in Matthew 5:6, "Blessed are those who hunger and thirst for righteousness, for they shall be satisfied"?

Did not John, the beloved disciple, quote Jesus (1 John 1:5-7) as saying that God is light, and in Him is no darkness at all, and that if we walk in the "light" we have fellowship with the Father and the Son?

Christians need not live in spiritual poverty. The many thousands of promises recorded in the Word of God apply to every Christian. These promises include: assurance of God's love (1 John 3:16); eternal life (Romans 6:23); forgiveness of sin (1 John 1:9); provision of material needs (Philippians 4:19); the ordering of one's steps (Psalm 37:23); the secret of successful prayer (John 15:7); the promise of an abundant life (John 10:10b); God's promise to honor a holy life (2 Chronicles 16:9); assurance that everything that happens is for our own good (Romans 8:28); deliverance from temptation (1 Corinthians 10:13); victory over fear (1 John 4:18); as well as thousands of others.

The Bible promises that every Christian should possess love, joy, peace, faith and many other beneficial qualities. What is wrong? Dr. Billy Graham has stated that at least 90 percent of all Christians in America are living defeated lives. Others who are in a position to know the spiritual pulse of America have made similar statements. It is quite likely that, according to the law of averages, you are among the 90 percent. You may have a heart for God. You read your Bible faithfully, you pray, you witness, you are active in your church; yet year after year you continue to fight a losing battle. Temptations come! Half-heartedly you resist, then yield, surrender and are finally defeated. For months you journey in the slough of despondency with Mr. Christian in Bunyan's *Pilgrim's Progress*. Then you attend a spiritual retreat and you are back on the Alpine heights for a brief time. Up, down, victories, defeats! Soon you cry out with Paul in Romans 7:24, "Wretched man that I am! Who will set me free from the body of this death?"

As president of Campus Crusade for Christ, I have the privilege of speaking to thousands of students each year. At the conclusion of a message which I once gave at Princeton University, a devout young man approached me in great concern over his lack of "fruit" in witnessing. "I have tried to witness," he said, "but I have had no results. I read my Bible daily and pray and memorize Scripture. I attend every Christian meeting on campus. Yet, I have never been able to introduce another to Christ. What is wrong with me?" In counseling with him, I gently probed for the answer to his problem. I knew that he meant business. He wanted to please God. He sincerely wanted his friends to know his wonderful Savior, and according to his conduct and Christian activities, he was a model Christian.

Jesus promises in John 14:26 and 16:13 that the Holy Spirit will teach us all things and will guide us into all truth. As I counseled with this young man, we were directed to some very important passages of Scripture. When he claimed these, by faith, they unlocked the door to victory and to unspeakable joy. He left the counseling room rejoicing and with an expectant heart. At that point, he began to experience a fruitful life in Christ such as he had never before known. He knew that something had happened in his life. He was a new man—no longer afraid, impotent and defeated. Now he was bold and had power and faith to believe God. He could hardly wait to see what God was going to do through Him. "Lord," he prayed, "who will be the first to whom You will lead me today?"

In the course of the day, the Holy Spirit led this young Christian to a fellow student to whom he had previously witnessed without apparent success. But today was different. God had prepared the heart of the other student and soon these two were bowed in prayer as the student's friend received Christ. The next day this marvelous experience was repeated with another student responding as if drawn by an invisible hand. This is not strange, for the Word of God tells us, "No one can come to Me, unless the Father . . . draws him" (John 6:44). Through the power of the Holy Spirit, this Princeton student continued to lead fellow students to Christ day after day. His own life was so wonderfully changed and empowered, so used of God, that he eventually became a Christian minister.

The story of this Princeton student is typical of hundreds of others who have sought counsel on campus after campus across the nation and around the world. There was a young minister who had earned his bachelor's and master's degrees in one of the finest theological seminaries of America, but was ineffective in his witnessing. Upon learning how he could appropriate the power of the Holy Spirit by faith, he experienced a new spirit of expectancy and joy that resulted in a victorious and fruitful life. There was the shy, timid student at a college retreat who expressed his concern for the lost, but was utterly frustrated and defeated by his fear of man. When God's power, victory, love and faith took possession of him, he experienced joy and fruit such as he had never believed possible. Fear and defeat gave way to courage, radiance and victory. Another faithful witness who heard, believed and received, discovered that witnessing was no longer a duty, but a joy! "It is just like being released from prison," he later exclaimed.

Countless additional examples such as those just cited could be given of others whose fruitless and frustrated lives became fruitful and victorious when they received by faith the power of the Holy Spirit and discovered that the promises of Jesus were for them: "Follow Me, and I will make you fishers of men" (Matthew 4:19); "By this is My Father glorified, that you bear much fruit" (John 15:8); "You did not choose Me, but I chose you, and appointed you, that you should go and bear fruit, and that your fruit should remain, that whatever you ask of the Father in My name, He may give to you" (John 15:16); "And without faith it is impossible to please Him, for he who comes to God must believe that He is, and that He is a rewarder of those who seek Him" (Hebrews 11:6).

Through the centuries there have been followers of Christ who were just ordinary Christians. Nothing spectacular ever happened to them or through them. Then, as happened to Peter and the disciples, something changed their lives. They were no longer ordinary or average. They became men and women of God, instruments of power. Their defeat turned to victory. Doubts and fear turned to assurance, joy and faith. They were the ones who "turned the world upside down" (Acts 17:6). Cowardly Peter, who denied Jesus three times (you and I have denied Him many more), became the bold Peter of Pentecost who preached fearlessly. On separate occasions, 3,000 and 5,000 believed in Christ and were added to the church. The early disciples possessed a strange new quality of life, a life of power which transformed the heart of a wicked Roman Empire during the first century. Their boldness led every one of the 12 to a martyr's grave—except John, who died in exile on the Isle of Patmos.

The change in the lives of those to whom I have just referred all began at Pentecost when those who were gathered together were filled with the Holy Spirit. Through this same power of the Holy Spirit, millions of others through the centuries have been changed into vital, dynamic Christians.

What do you know about the Holy Spirit? What does the Holy Spirit mean to you personally?

Jesus promised in His apostolic commission that the Holy Spirit would give us power to be His witnesses. "But you shall receive power when the Holy Spirit has come upon you; and you shall be my witnesses both in Jerusalem, and in all Judea and Samaria, and even to the remotest part of the earth" (Acts 1:8).

It is the purpose of this brief article to explain how to be filled with the Holy Spirit as it relates to the fulfillment of the Great Commission of our Lord. Therefore, we shall not dwell on the many truths concerning the role of the Holy Spirit in the life of every Christian except as they contribute to our major objective.

Let us now consider briefly some of the spiritual truths as they relate to the filling of the Holy Spirit.

A. What is the Spirit-filled life?

The Spirit-filled life is the Christ-filled life. The Spirit-filled Christian is one who, according to Romans 6:11, has considered himself to be dead to sin, but alive to God in Christ Jesus. Christ is now on the throne of the life. He is Lord! The Holy Spirit came to exalt and glorify Jesus Christ. In order to be filled with the Holy Spirit a Christian must be dead to self. When he is dead to self, the Lord Jesus Christ, who now has unhindered control of his life, can begin to express His love through him. The one to whom "all power in heaven and in earth is given," and, "in whom dwells all the fullness of the Godhead bodily," can now express that power through the Spirit-filled Christian. The one who came to seek and to save the lost now begins to seek the lost through the Christian. He directs the Christian's steps to those who are lost and to those who are in need. He begins to use the Christian's lips to tell of His love. His great heart of compassion becomes evident in the Spirit-filled life.

Actually, in a very real sense, the Christian gives up *his* life, *his* impotence and defeat for the power and victory of Jesus Christ. This is what the great missionary statesman Hudson Taylor referred to as the "exchanged life." When a Christian is filled with the Holy Spirit, he is filled with Jesus Christ. He no longer thinks of Christ as one who helps to do some kind of Christian task, but rather, Jesus Christ does the work through the Christian. He does not want us to work for Him. He wants us to let Him do His work through us. This is that glorious experience that the apostle Paul knew when he said in Galatians 2:20, "I have been crucified with Christ; and it is no longer I who live, but Christ lives in me." The Christian's body now becomes Christ's body to use as He wills; the mind becomes His mind to think His thoughts; the will is now controlled by His will; the total personality, time and talents are now completely His.

The beloved apostle goes on to say, ". . . and the life which I now live in the flesh I live by faith in the Son of God, who loved me, and delivered Himself up for me." Whose faith? The faith of the Son of God, the one who loved us and gave Himself for us, the one to whom "all power in heaven and earth is given." Think of it! Can you grasp what this means? If you can, and if you yield your will to God the Holy Spirit and acknowledge that Jesus Christ is in your life moment by moment, you are in for a great adventure. The Lord Jesus Christ will begin to draw scores of lost men and women to Himself through your yielded, Spirit-filled life.

B. Why are so few Christians filled with the Holy Spirit?

Basically, the problem involves the will. Man is a free moral agent. He was created by God with a mind and will of his own.

God would be breaking His own spiritual laws if he *forced* man to do His bidding. At the time of conversion the will of man is temporarily yielded to the will of God. In Romans 10:9, Paul tells us that, if we confess with our mouths Jesus as Lord, and believe in our hearts that God has raised Him from the dead, we shall be saved. Man must be willing to "repent," which means to turn from his own way to go God's way, before he can become a child of God. However, after conversion, the heart frequently loses its "first love." The radiance and glow that accompanied the spiritual birth experience are gone, and many Christians no longer walk in "the light as He Himself is in the light" (1 John 1:7). They no longer seek to do the will of God, but for various reasons, have chosen to go their own way. They have chosen to work out their own plan and purposes for life. Believing themselves to be free, they become servants of sin and finally they say with the apostle Paul in Romans 7:19,20,24: "For the good that I wish, I do not do; but I practice the very evil that I do not wish. But if I am doing the very thing I do not wish, I am no longer the one doing it, but sin which dwells in me. Wretched man that I am! Who will set me free from the body of this death?" There is no one more miserable than a Christian out of fellowship with Christ.

In this spiritual condition there is no longer any joy in the Christian walk, no longer any desire to witness for Christ, no concern for those who are desperately in need of the forgiveness and love of our Savior.

What are the reasons, then, that one who has experienced the love and forgiveness that only Christ can give, one who has experienced the joy of His presence, would reject the will of God and choose to go his own way? Why would a Christian sacrifice the power and dynamic of the Spirit-filled life in order to have his own way?

There are several reasons:

1. Lack of knowledge of the Word of God: God's Word contains glorious truths concerning the relationship that the Christian has with the Lord Jesus Christ, God the Father and the Holy Spirit. This lack of information has kept many from appropriating the fullness of the Holy Spirit. Think of it—every Christian is a child of God (1 John 1:12). His sins have been forgiven and he may continue to be cleansed from all sin (1 John 1:7) as he continues in fellowship with Christ. God the Father, Son and Holy Spirit actually dwell in the heart of every Christian, waiting to empower and bring each child of God to his full maturity in Christ.

2. Pride: Pride has kept many Christians from being filled with the Holy Spirit. Pride was the sin of Satan (Isaiah 14:13,14). Pride was the first sin of man as Adam and Eve wanted to be something they were not. Pride is at the root of most of man's self-imposed estrangement from God. The self-centered, egocentric Christian cannot have fellowship with God: "For God is opposed to the proud, but gives grace to the humble" (1 Peter 5:5).

3. Fear: Fear of man keeps many Christians from being filled with the Holy Spirit. "The fear of man brings a snare" (Proverbs 29:23). One of the greatest tragedies of our day is the general practice among Christians of conforming to the conduct and standards of a non-Christian society. Many are afraid to be different; ashamed to witness for the one "who loved us and gave Himself for us." Remember, in 1 Peter 2:9 we are told: "But you are a chosen race, a royal priesthood, a holy nation, a people for God's own possession, that you may proclaim the excellencies of Him who has called you out of darkness into His marvelous light." "The Lord favors those who fear [reverence which leads to obedience] Him" (Psalm 147:11). Jesus said, "For whoever is ashamed of Me and My words, of him will the Son of Man be ashamed" (Luke 9:26).

   Many Christians are fearful of being thought fanatical by their fellow Christians and others should they be filled with the Holy Spirit.

4. Secret sin: Unconfessed sin keeps many Christians from being filled with the Holy Spirit. Perhaps God has reminded you of a

lie you have told that has damaged someone's reputation; or stolen merchandise or money that has not be returned; or an unethical transaction; or cheating on an exam, or any number of acts that He wants you to confess to Him. He may lead you to make restitution to those whom you have wronged (Matthew 5:23,24). If so, be obedient to His leading. We may be able to hide these things from our friends and others, but we cannot hide them from God. "Would not God find this out? For He knows the secrets of the heart" (Psalm 44:21). Is there anyone whom you have not forgiven? If so, God will not forgive you (Mark 11:24-26). However, if we confess these sins to God as the Lord directs us, we are forgiven and cleansed (1 John 1:9).

5. Worldly mindedness: A love for material things and a desire to conform to the ways of a secular society keep many Christians from being filled with the Holy Spirit. "Do not love the world, nor the things in the world. If any one loves the world, the love of the Father is not in him. For all that is in the world, the lust of the flesh, and the lust of the eyes and the boastful pride of life, is not from the Father, but is from the world. And the world is passing away, and also its lusts; but the one who does the will of God abides forever" (1 John 2:15-17). Man lives a brief span of years and is gone from this earthly scene. Every Christian should make careful and frequent evaluation of how he invests his time, talents and treasure in order to accomplish the most for the cause of Christ. "Only one life, will soon be past; only what's done for Christ will last."

   "No one can serve two masters; for either he will hate the one and love the other, or he will hold to one and despise the other. You cannot serve God and mammon. But seek first His kingdom, and His righteousness; and all these things shall be added to you" (Matthew 6:24,33).

6. Lack of trust in God: This keeps many Christians from making a full surrender of their wills to Him and from being filled with the Holy Spirit. Many Christians have a fear, that amounts almost to superstition, that, if they surrender themselves fully to God, something tragic will happen to test them. They may fear that they will lose a loved one. Some fear that God will send them to some remote section of the world as a missionary to some savage tribe against their wills.

   I remember well a young lad who had such fears—he was afraid that God would change his plans. As we reasoned together, I reminded him that God's love was so great that He sent His only begotten Son to die for his sins. We spoke of a Savior who loved him so much that He gladly gave His life on the cross and shed His blood for his sins. Then I asked the question, "Can you trust a God like that?" He replied, "I had never thought of it that way—I can and will trust Him." Today this young man has finished seminary and is a member of our Campus Crusade staff. He is one of the most fruitful and victorious Christians I know.

You can trust God with your life, your loved ones, your money, your future, everything! Not only is He a loving Father, but God's love is wiser than that of any earthly father and is more tender than that of any earthly mother. So do not be afraid to trust God with your whole life, every moment of every day, and He will fill you with His Holy Spirit.

I have two sons whom I love dearly. Suppose, for the sake of illustration, that they were to come to me and say, "Dad, we love you and have been thinking about how we can show our love for you. We have decided that we will do anything that you want us to do." Now, how would I respond? Would I say, "Boys, I have ben waiting for just this moment. Now that you have relinquished your wills to mine, I am going to lock you in your rooms, give away all your favorite possessions, and make you do all of the things that you most dislike to do. You will regret the day you were born. I will make you the most miserable boys on this block."

How ridiculous! I would respond by trying to demonstrate my love for them in an even greater way. In the same way, our heavenly Father is ready to bless and enrich our lives the moment we yield our wills, our all, to Him.

These and many other experiences of defeat have kept Christians from experiencing the joy of the Spirit-filled life. For example, do any of the following apply to you:

—An exalted feeling of your own importance
—Love of human praise
—Anger and impatience
—Self-will, stubbornness, unteachability
—A compromising spirit
—Jealous disposition
—Lustful, unholy actions

—Dishonesty
—Unbelief
—Selfishness
—Love of money, beautiful clothes, cars, houses and land

Some of you may wonder, "Is it necessary for me to gain victory over all of my defeats and frustrations before I can be filled with the Holy Spirit?" Absolutely not! Just as Jesus Christ is the only one who can forgive your sins, so the Holy Spirit is the only one who can give victory and power.

. How can a Christian be filled with the Holy Spirit?

First, we need to know that just as there are many different experiences of receiving Jesus Christ as Lord and Savior, so are there different experiences of being filled with the Holy Spirit. For example, one man responds to the invitation to receive Christ in an evangelistic campaign, another kneels quietly in the privacy of his home and receives Christ. Both are born again, and their lives are changed by the power of Christ. Of course, there are scores of other circumstances and experiences through which sincere men meet the Savior and become "new creatures in Christ."

In like manner, and in different ways, sincere Christians are filled with the Spirit. It should be made clear at this point that to be "filled with the Spirit" does not mean that we receive more of the Holy Spirit, but that we give Him more of ourselves. As we yield your lives to the Holy Spirit and are filled with His presence, He has greater freedom to work in and through our lives, to control us in order to better exalt and glorify Christ.

God is too great to be placed in a man-made mold. However, there are certain spiritual laws that are inviolate. Since the Holy Spirit already dwells within every Christian, it is no longer necessary to "wait in Jerusalem" as Jesus instructed the disciples to do, except to make personal preparation for His empowering. The Holy Spirit will fill us with His power the moment we are fully yielded. It is possible for a man to be at a quiet retreat and become filled with the Holy Spirit. It is likewise possible for a man to be filled with the Holy Spirit while walking down a busy street in a great city. Such was the experience of Dwight L. Moody. It is even possible for a man to be filled with the Holy Spirit and know something wonderful has happened, yet be completely ignorant at the time of what has actually taken place, provided he has a genuine desire to yield his will to the Lord Jesus Christ.

I do not want to suggest that the steps which I am about to propose are the only way in which one can be filled with the Holy Spirit. This spiritual formula is offered, first, because it is scriptural, and second, because I know from experience that it works.

Do you want to be filled with the Holy Spirit? What are your motives? Are you looking for some ecstatic experience, or do you sincerely desire to serve the Lord Jesus Christ with great power and effectiveness? Do you want, with all of your heart, to help others find Christ?

This is the spiritual formula that I urge you to prayerfully consider:

1. *We are commanded to be filled with the Spirit*

   "And to not get drunk with wine, for this is dissipation, but be filled with the Spirit" (Ephesians 5:18). This is an admonition of God. Do you think that He would ask you to do something beyond that which you are able to experience?

2. *We shall receive power for witnessing when we are filled.*

   "But you shall receive power when the Holy Spirit has come upon you; and you shall be My witnesses both in Jerusalem, and in all Judea and Samaria, and even to the remotest part of the earth" (Acts 1:8). If you have no desire to be Jesus Christ's witness, or if you have no power in your witness, you may be sure that you are not filled with the Holy Spirit. The Holy Spirit came in order for the disciples—and for you and for me—to receive power. Why do we need power? To be Christ's witnesses right where we are and in the remotest part of the earth. Can you sincerely say that this is your motive for wanting to be filled with the Spirit?

3. *If any man is thirsty, let him come to Me and drink.*

   "Now on the last day, the great day of the feast, Jesus stood and cried out saying, 'If any man is thirsty, let him come to Me and drink. He who believes in Me, as the Scripture said, "From his innermost being shall flow rivers of living water."' But this He spoke of the Spirit, whom those who believed in

Him were to receive; for the Spirit was not yet given, because Jesus was not yet glorified" (1 John 37:39). "Blessed are those who hunger and thirst for righteousness, for they shall be satisfied" (Matthew 5:6).

When a Christian is ready to respond to the gracious invitation of our blessed Savior, "If any man is thirsty, let him come to Me and drink," he is ready to relinquish his will for the will of God. Therefore, this third step involves a complete surrender of your will, without reservation, to the will of God. You have come to the place where you joyfully anticipate knowing and doing His will because you know God is loving and trustworthy and that His will is best.

Up until this moment the Holy Spirit has been just a "guest" in your life, for He came to live in you the moment you became a Christian. Sometimes He was locked up in a small closet, while you used the rest of the house for your own pleasure.

Now you want Him to be more than a guest—as a matter of fact, you want to turn over the title deed of your life to Him and give Him the keys to every room. You invite the Holy Spirit into the library of your mind, the dining room of your appetites, the parlor of your relationships, the game room of your social life. You invite Him into the small hidden rooms where you have previously engaged in secret, shameful activities. All of this is past. Now, He is the Master! The challenge of Romans 12:1,2 has become clear and meaningful to you and you want to ". . . present your bodies a living and holy sacrifice, acceptable to God, which is your spiritual service of worship." And you no longer want to be conformed to this world, but you want to be transformed by the renewing of your mind, "that you may prove what the will of God is, that which is good and acceptable and perfect."

Now you know that your body is the temple of the Holy Spirit who lives within you. You are not your own any more for you were bought with the precious blood of the Lord Jesus; therefore, you now want to glorify God in your body and in your spirit, which are God's (1 Corinthians 6:19,20).

Now, with all of your heart, you want to seek first the kingdom of God (Matthew 6:33).

Now you want to seek "the things above, where Christ is, seated at the right hand of God. For you have died, and your life is hidden with Christ in God" (Colossians 3:1,3).

Now you can say with joy unspeakable, as Paul did, "I have been crucified with Christ; and it is no longer I who live, but Christ lives in me; and the life which I now live in the flesh I live by faith in the Son of God, who loved me, and delivered Himself up for me" (Galatians 2:20). You have exchanged your life for the life of Christ.

If you can say these things and mean them with all of your heart, you are ready for the fourth step. However, before we take up the discussion of this next step, I feel constrained to call your attention to the words of our Savior found in John 15:18,20. "If the world hates you, you know that it has hated Me before it hated you . 'A slave is not greater than his Master.' If they persecuted Me, they will also persecute you."

The Spirit-filled Christian life is not an easy one, though it is a life filled with adventure and thrills, the likes of which one cannot possibly experience in any other way. Whether or not we are Christians, we are going to have problems in this life. Christians or not, we will one day die. If I am going to be a Christian, I want all that God has for me and I want to be all that He wants me to be. If I am to suffer at all, and one day die, why not suffer and die for the highest and best, for the Lord Jesus Christ and His gospel!

Before we leave this thought, let me ask you a question. Have you ever heard of one of God's saints who has suffered for the cause of Christ express any regrets? I never have! I have heard only praise, adoration and thanksgiving to God for the privilege of serving Christ, no matter how difficult the task. On the other hand, I have heard many who have received Christ late in life tell how sorry they are that they waited so long. Do not develop a martyr's complex, but do not expect a "bed of roses" either.

Now for the next step in receiving the fullness of the Holy Spirit.

4. *We appropriate the filling of the Holy Spirit by faith.*

Remember that, if you are a Christian, God the Father, Son

and Holy Spirit are already living within you. Great spiritual power and resources are available to you. Like a miser starving to death with a fortune in boxes and jars about his cluttered room, many Christians are starving spiritually, living in defeat, failing to utilize the spiritual fortune that is their heritage in Christ.

In Ephesians 5:18, Paul admonishes, "And do not get drunk with wine, for that is dissipation, but be filled with the Spirit."

Further, in 1 John 5:14,15, we are assured, "And this is the confidence which we have before Him, that, if we ask anything according to His will, He hears us. And if we know that He hears us in whatever we ask, we know that we have the requests that we have asked from Him." We know that it is God's will that we be filled with His Spirit. Therefore, as we ask the Holy Spirit to fill us, we can know according to the Word of God that our prayer is answered.

Like our salvation, the filling of the Holy Spirit is a gift of God—we do not and cannot earn either. Both are received by the complete yielding of our wills, in faith.

Here is a review of the steps that we have discussed in preparation for the filling of the Holy Spirit:

1. We are admonished to be filled.
2. We are promised power for service when we are filled.
3. We are to yield our wills to God's will and seek first the kingdom of God.
4. We are to appropriate the filling of the Holy Spirit by faith.

We must expect to be filled.

"And without faith it is impossible to please Him, for he who comes to God must believe that He is, and that He is a rewarder of those who seek Him" (Hebrews 11:6).

Do you believe God wants you to be filled with the Holy Spirit?

Do you believe God has the power to fill you with the Holy Spirit?

In Matthew 9:28,29, Jesus talked to the blind men and asked of them, "Do you believe that I am able to do this?" They said to Him, "Yes, Lord." Then He touched their eyes, saying, "Be it done to you according to your faith."

Find a quiet place where you can be alone and read again the portions of Scripture given in this booklet. You do not have to wait for the Holy Spirit. He is waiting for you to allow Him to fill you. Remember, "Be it done to you according to your faith." "He is a rewarder of those who seek Him."

Have you honestly yielded your life to Christ, your will to His will?

Do you believe that you are filled with the Holy Spirit at this moment? If so, thank Him that you are filled. Thank Him for His indwelling presence and power. Thank Him by faith for victory over defeat, for effectiveness in witnessing. Praise God and give thanks continually (Ephesians 5:20, 1 Thessalonians 5:18).

D. How can a Christian know when he is filled with the Holy Spirit?

There are two very good ways of knowing when you are filled with the Holy Spirit.

First, by the promises of the Word of God. And second, by personal experience.

If you have faithfully yielded to the will of God and sincerely surrendered your way to Him in accordance with the steps outlined in this presentation, if you have asked Him to fill you—He has done it! "And this is the confidence which we have before Him, that, if we ask anything according to His will, He hears us. And if we know that He hears us in whatever we ask, we know that we have the requests which we have asked from Him" (1 John 5:14,15). Is it His will that you be filled, according to Ephesians 5:18? Then, can you believe that He has heard you? Now, can you know that you have the petitions that you desired of Him?

God's Word promises us that we can know. Therefore, on the basis of His Word you can know that you are filled, if you have met the conditions which are given in His Word.

What about feelings? You may or may not have an emotional response at the time you kneel in prayer and ask for the filling of the Spirit. In counseling with many students, as well as adults, I have found that the majority experience calm assurance that they are filled, and with this assurance comes a spirit of expectancy that God is going to use them in a way they have never been used before to introduce others to Christ. Great faith in God and His Word is born in the hearts of those who have been filled with the Holy Spirit. Results? Greater faith, power, boldness and effectiveness in witnessing.

First, there is the fact of God's promise in His Word. Then there is the exercise of faith in the trustworthiness of God and His promises. Faith in the fact is followed by feeling. Remember: fact, faith and feelings—in that order.

E. What results can one expect from being filled with the Holy Spirit?

Now comes the real test that will determine if you are truly filled with the Holy Spirit. Do you have a new and greater love for Christ? Are you concerned for those who do not know His love and forgiveness? Are you experiencing a greater faith, boldness, liberty and power in witnessing? If so, you are filled with the Spirit. Jesus Christ is beginning to express His life and love through you and in you.

Remember, Jesus promised that we would receive power after the Holy Spirit has come upon us. After receiving power we will naturally want to be His witnesses wherever we are (Acts 1:8).

It is definitely true that you will have a greater love for Christ, for your fellow man and for the Word of God when you are filled with the Holy Spirit. Also, the fruit of the Spirit, as described in Galatians 5:22,23, will become more evident in your life.

However, we must remember that there is a difference between the fruit of the Spirit and the gifts of the Spirit.

The filling of the Holy Spirit is given for power and boldness in witnessing for Christ. Many Christian leaders agree with Dr. R.A. Torrey, who said, "I have gone through my Bible time and time again checking this subject and I make this statement without the slightest fear of successful contradiction that there is not one single passage in the Old Testament or the New Testament where the filling with the Holy Spirit is spoken of, where it is not connected with testimony for service.'

We hasten to add that, as a Christian abides in Christ, living in the fullness of the Spirit, the fruit of the Spirit—love, joy, peace, patience, kindness, goodness, faithfulness, gentleness and self-control, listed in Galatians 5:22,23—is developed and the Christian becomes more mature spiritually. The maturing of the fruit of the Spirit is a lifetime process which goes on continually as the image of Christ is being formed in the life of the Christian. Some Christians give greater evidence of the fruit of the Spirit than do other Christians because of a greater degree of yieldedness to His working. The more we acknowledge ourselves to be dead to sin and give allegiance to the Lord Jesus Christ and His life within us, and the more we allow Him, through the power of the Holy Spirit, to live out His life through us, the more evident will be the fruit of the Spirit.

The development and maturing of the fruit of the Spirit is a long process, but the gifts of the Holy Spirit are given at the time a person becomes a Christian. Though every Christian who is filled with the Spirit receives power for witnessing, not every Christian receives the same gift, according to 1 Corinthians 12. Some are called to be apostles, some prophets, others evangelists, pastors and teachers (Ephesians 4:11). Therefore, we must let the Lord direct us into His place of service for us.

Do not try to imitate the ministry of someone else. Be patient. Do not try to decide what you should do with your life or where you should serve Christ. He will express His life in and through you as you continue to study His Word and remain obedient and sensitive to the leading of the Holy Spirit. Through God's Word and the leading of the Holy Spirit, you will discover what God's will is.

F. Is there more than one filling of the Holy Spirit?

Yes, there are many fillings of the Holy Spirit for the yielded Christian. We should be filled for each new opportunity for Christian service. The admonition to be filled with the Holy Spirit in Ephesians 5:18 literally means, in the original Greek, to be filled with the Spirit constantly and continually—to keep on being filled. The Scriptures record several instances where Peter and the disciples were filled with the Spirit.

G. How can a Christian continue to be filled with the Holy Spirit?

The Christian is utterly and wholly dependent upon the Holy Spirit for all spiritual victory and power. Therefore, the more yielded he is, the more liberty the Holy Spirit will have in working through his life in bringing others to Christ and bringing him to spiritual maturity in Christ.

Here are some practical suggestions that will assist you to live in the fullness of the Spirit:

1. Meditate on these glorious truths: Jesus Christ literally dwells within you. You are dead to self and sin and to all personal and selfish desires. You are alive to God through Jesus Christ (Romans 6:11). Remember, you have exchanged your life with all of its sin, frustrations and defeats, for the victorious and triumphant life of Christ, in whom "all the fullness of Deity dwells in bodily form, and in Him you have been made complete" (Collossians 2:9,10). Just think, the one who dwells in your heart is the one who claims all power in heaven and in earth! This is why the apostle Paul said, "I can do all things through Him who strengthens me" (Philippians 4:13). You have buried "Old Adam," screwed the lid down on the coffin and covered him over with six feet of sod. Jesus Christ is not helping you to live the Christian life with your old sin nature. Rather, He is now using your body as His temple, your mind to think His thoughts, your heart to express His love and compassion, your lips to speak His truths.

   His will has become your will. At first you may find it necessary to acknowledge and confirm many, many times during the day that this transaction has taken place. You may find it necessary to change your whole way of thinking and praying. Don't think, "What can I do for Christ?" or pray, "God, use me to do this or that for You." Pray rather, "Lord Jesus, I am Yours totally and completely without reservation. Use me as You wish. Send me wherever You will, for I am dead and my life is hidden with Christ in God." Seek to abide in Christ (1 John 2:6). What is involved in abiding in Christ? Jesus said, "If you keep My commandments, you will abide in My love" (John 15:10a).

   To abide is to keep His commandments. To keep His commandments is to obey. The abiding life is an effortless life. How slowly we arrive at this simple fact, that true New Testament living is effortless.

A branch does not try to produce fruit, any more than the electric light bulb tries to shine. Neither has any need to try; they simply draw upon an inexhaustible supply of life and energy. In doing so they scarcely touch the fringe of their resources. The Christian has infinitely greater resources. The one who created vegetable life and electric energy is the one who lives in us. Why do we need to try? Only because we are not abiding. The truest test of Christian living is, am I trying, or am I abiding? If I find myself still trying, I am not as yet an unchoked channel through which His life may flow.

Meditate on the following portions of Scripture: John 14-16; Matthew 6; Colossians 3; Ephesians 5; Romans 6,8,12 and 14; 1 Corinthians 13; 1 John 1; Hebrews 11; Galatians 5; and Psalm 37:1-7,23,24.

I suggest that you secure a notebook and make an outline of each of these chapters, listing especially those suggestions that you feel will aid you in abiding in Christ. Continue to use your notebook for outlining other portions of Scripture and for recording key verses you would like to memorize. There are many other portions of Scripture that will help you to abide in Christ.

2. Make a practice to spend definite time each day in prayer for God's guidance of your life and for the souls of men. Make a list of people whom you would like to have find Christ. Pray for them daily (Ephesians 6:18 and 1 Samuel 12:23).

3. Spend time daily reading and studying the Word of God. Make a practice of memorizing key portions of Scripture (Hebrews 4:12; 1 Corinthians 2:9-12; Psalm 119:4,9,15,16,97,98, 103,105,130).

4. Do not grieve the Holy Spirit. Confess and turn from sinful practices. 1 John 1:9 says, "If we confess our sins, He is faithful and righteous to forgive us our sins and to cleanse us from all unrighteousness." The moment you do something that you know is wrong, you will grieve the Holy Spirit if you do not confess it. What do we mean by grieving the Holy Spirit? The Spirit is holy, and He is grieved and displeased when a Christian commits sin and continues its practice. Therefore, if you want to continue to be filled with the Holy Spirit, to have power in witnessing for Christ, live a yielded, holy life.

5. Do not quench the Holy Spirit. Be sensitive to the leading of the Holy Spirit for He is omniscient. He has infinite wisdom and knowledge and will lead us into all truth (John 16:13). Never say "no" to Him. As you grow accustomed to the Spirit-filled, Christ-directed life, you will have many wonderful experiences such as Philip had (Acts 8:26-39) when the Holy Spirit led him to speak to the Ethiopians; and as Paul had (Acts 16:9) when he was called to Macedonia to preach the gospel.

The most thrilling experiences of my entire life have been those when the still, small voice of the Spirit spoke to my heart, telling me to speak to people about Christ, and, as I have talked with them in obedience to the Spirit's leading, I have always discovered that the Holy Spirit had prepared their hearts for my witness. Many times I have been told, "Bill, the Lord sent you to me." Or "Everything you have said has been for me. Someone must have told you of my problem." The Spirit knows all things, and if you and I are filled with His presence and power, we will always have the right thing to say to those who are in need.

There have been many such thrilling leadings of the Spirit, but I shall share only one. One day my wife, Vonette, and I were driving to the Forest Home Christian Conference Center for a session of the College Briefing Conference that has been so greatly used of God in the lives of thousands of collegians. It was an extremely hot day late in August, and our car developed a vapor lock and refused to run as we started up the mountain. We waited for the motor to cool and finally, after a considerable delay, we got the car started.

We drove into the yard of a nearby rural home to ask for water to fill the radiator. The man of the house was very generous and gracious. He helped me fill the radiator with water, but even though we were there five or ten minutes, I did not speak to him about Christ. My mind was on an important meeting up the mountain that we wanted badly to attend. As I leaned over to pick up the radiator cap, which had blown off, my New Testament fell out of my shirt pocket. Still I did not hear that still, small voice of the Spirit. We had thanked the man for his kindness and were driving out of his yard when suddenly I felt a strong compulsion to return to talk with this man about Christ. "But," I argued as we discussed it, "we are late for the meeting now. Anyway, he would think we are crackpots if we were to go back. Besides, if I were going to witness to him

> about Christ, I should have done it when he was helping me fill the radiator with water."
>
> Human arguments are futile against the insistent voice of the Spirit, and after we had driven a couple of miles, we turned around and headed back. As an added precaution we pulled over to the side of the road for prayer. "Lord, don't let us make a mistake—this seems so foolish. Give us the words to say. May Your will be done."
>
> As we drove into the yard, the man came out on the porch to greet us. "Did you forget something?" he asked. "Yes, we did forget something, sir. I know this may sound a little strange, but we are Christians and we felt that the Lord wanted us to come back to talk to you about Christ." There was no need to say more for, as I spoke, tears began to gather and trickle down his cheeks. His chin began to tremble as he told us that he knew the Lord had sent us. He asked us to come inside, and as we went in, he called his wife.
>
> He said, "I used to go to church years ago, but I fell into sin and I haven't been back in many years. This week my wife has been attending a revival meeting here in town and more and more, with each passing day, I have been burdened with the weight of my sins. I want to get right with God." We all knelt there in his living room and both he and his wife committed their lives and their home to Christ. We went on our way, praising God for the leading of His Holy Spirit and for another opportunity to witness for our blessed Savior.

As you ask God to fill you with the Holy Sprit, you are about to begin the greatest adventure of your life. Remember that you are asking to be filled with the Holy Spirit rather than filled with self. As He takes control of your life, you will become more like Christ. The Holy Spirit is not the author of confusion and emotional extremes. He has come to exalt and glorify Jesus; therefore, when you are filled with the Holy Spirit, it will be your constant desire to do the will of God and that which will please and honor Jesus Christ.

Why did Jesus come into this world? "To seek and to save that which was lost" (Luke 19:10).

What will please Him most? We shall please Him most as we help fulfill His Great Commission, by going into all the world and preaching the gospel to every creature and letting Him live His life through us.

How is this to be accomplished? By the power of the Holy Spirit.

Think of it—you and I are privileged to be used by our Savior in helping to reach a lost world with the glorious "good news"!

We dare not sin against the Lord and against those who are waiting to hear by hesitating another moment.

For a fuller discussion on the role and ministry of the Holy Spirit, see Transferable Concept #3, *How to Be Filled With the Spirit*, and the Holy Spirit booklet, Exhibit #10.

Chapter 3

What? A Movement on My Campus? What Is a Movement?

In the fall of 1970, several Christians at Clemson University in South Carolina began praying for their campus. Two years after starting their first small prayer and Bible study group, 200 students were involved. How did it happen? They had an attitude of expectancy: They were willing to believe God for spiritual awakening on their campus. What's more, they were willing to get involved, in the power of the Holy Spirit, and leave the results to God.

And, as they began to plan and pray for ways to reach their campus for Christ, they discovered their need for training in how to accomplish their goal.

These students attended several Campus Crusade for Christ conferences where they received training and heard of what God was doing through students on other campuses. They also were given a manual similar to this one. They returned to Clemson and began a weekly evangelistic meeting.

Did they experience any failures? Yes! Bible studies sometimes fizzled, campus-wide meetings were sometimes less than exciting.

But the Lord honored their desire to reach others with the gospel, and He took care of them at each point of failure or frustration. People came to know Christ even when evangelistic meetings were not as smoothly run as desired. Young Christians grew in their faith even when they were folowed up by untrained students.

These Christian students were seeing their prayers answered. The Lord was reaching their campus through them!

Those students who gathered to pray and trust God at Clemson didn't just establish a new club on campus. They helped start something bigger than their combined efforts. It ultimately affected the entire campus. *They helped start a movement.*

"Movement" may seem out of place when describing what can occur on your campus. We usually associate "movement" with political groups: civil rights, nuclear freeze, Solidarity labor.

But "movement" also describes what happened at Clemson: *A movement is the collective activity of committed, multiplying disciples as they band together and trust God for an impact greater than their own individual ministries.*

That's what a movement is all about. It's not just me leading my own group. It's being a part of something that is not only bigger than my little prayer group, it is bigger than the total effect of all the combined groups. A movement has a synergistic effect. (Synergism is a combined action which is greater in total effect than the sum of the individual effects.) A movement is what God produces.

To understand what a movement is all about, you need to understand some traits or characteristics of movements, and understand the three aspects that govern their functioning.

A. What characterizes a movement?

1. Organized action.

   It is not random action. It is deliberate, and it elicits involvement.

2. Differing levels of commitment.

   There are committed leaders, followers and sometime-followers.

3. Dedication.

   Members are highly dedicated, and thus are able to deal with opposition.

4. Unity.

   Division, criticism and antagonism from within eat at a movement's heart until people are no longer involved in organized action. It's essential to maintain unity.

5. Redeveloping leadership.

   Unity may initially be built around a leader, but to be self sustaining, there must be a constant development of new leadership.

   A movement only expands as fast as leadership is developed.

6. Purpose.

   There is a corporate commitment to a goal that is reflected by the goals of the individual members.

B. What controls a movement's growth?

1. Momentum.

   Brings the idea of excitement because the movement is going somewhere. It is the result of activities sparked by people who are enthusiastic about a common goal and are willing to become actively involved. It attracts new people because they want to be part of something that is going somewhere.

2. Multiplication.

   It is the continued expansion and reproduction of disciples who are producing other disciples.

   A group of students teach by word and example all that they know about the Christian life to a group of younger Christians. These younger ones in turn go on to teach others. This continual transfer of knowledge through the lives of people causes a "spiritual multiplication" effect.

3. Management.

   It is essential for a movement to have leadership that controls momentum and multiplication. A loss of management results in a loss of common goals, a breakdown in unity and loss of enthusiasm.

C. Benefits of a movement.

1. Expand your vision.

   There is often a great deal of isolation between Christians; they feel all alone in their convictions. Being part of a movement allows us to be encouraged by others who share our commitment.

   Like-minded people help us continue in the right direction even when we don't feel like it. That helps us stand firmly in our convictions.

2. Establishes credibility.

   A movement with a good public image allows individuals within that movement to do more because they represent that movement. It might be hard for you as an individual to speak about Christ at a fraternity dinner. But as a representative of Campus Crusade for Christ, which is involved with many Greek systems, you would be more likely able to speak.

3. Constant training

   Many Christians want to share their faith in an evangelistic meeting or have a personal ministry, but they simply do not know how. So they either do it in a way that is ineffective or they become frustrated and quit.

   In a movement, they first learn to share their faith individually with others. Later, they are trained to lead a group, share their testimonies and speak to larger groups.

4. Breaks faith barriers.

   People involved with a movement seldom feel qualified or ready to do what is asked of them. But when they stand up in front of 50 people to share their testimony, coordinate a large scale evangelistic program (a "classic"), or lead a new believers' follow-up Bible study for the first time, they break faith barriers.

If we only do those things that we are comfortable with, our faith stagnates. But doing what we aren't completely self-confident in causes us to trust God; we break a faith barrier.

5. Exposure to godly leadership.

   We tend to become like those with whom we spend time and those we admire. A movement's leadership is often mature and visionary.

6. Exposure to ministry situations.

   We have opportunities to try doing many types of ministry when we are involved in a movement because its scope is so wide. This can mean working with different types of people than we normally associate with.

Conclusion:

To have the greatest impact on our campus, we need to be involved in a spiritual movement that allows us to multiply our time, talents and resources most effectively. Associating with like-minded, highly-committed Christians will help us generate momentum that multiplies and produces a movement glorifying to God.

Chapter 4
Objectives and Goals of a Movement

Our objective is to *help* reach the *world* for Christ. We are not the only Christian group with that goal, and we do not pretend that we can reach the world for Christ by ourselves. It is only as thousands of churches and organizations become involved that the Great Commission will be fulfilled.

But the goal is the *world*. Karl Marx wrote in his "Theses on Feuerbach": "Philosophers have only interpreted the world differently; the point, however, is to change it." We believe the world can be changed through the changed lives of people brought to Christ. Our faith in this revolution is based not upon the uncertainties of economic or class theory, but upon the certainty of God's Word.

A. But why reach the world (and thus the campus) for Christ?

1. *Christ commanded us to take the gospel to the world.*

   Matthew 28:18-20, commonly known as the Great Commission, records Jesus' command to "make disciples of all the nations." Other verses (Mark 16:15; Luke 24:46,47; John 20:21; Acts 1:8) also tell us that we are to preach the gospel to every creature.

2. *Telling others about Christ glorifies God.*

   We bring glory to God by being obedient to Him. God's glory is the ultimate reason for doing all that we do (John 17:4; Colossians 3:23,24).

3. *People are spiritually dead and separated from God apart from Christ* (John 3:16-18).

4. *People are living purposeless lives apart from Christ.*

   We have the truth they need to hear. We should be motivated to tell them by our love for the lost (John 10:9,10).

5. *Christ died for the sins of the world.*

   The very reason that Christ came was that the world might be saved through Him (Luke 19:10).

B. The Bible doesn't literally say "Reach your campus!" So why be involved in reaching my campus when there are many other places I could be reaching for Christ?

1. *It is strategic.*

   Most of the United States' future leaders—as well as many international leaders—are now in college (there are several hundred international students currently studying in the United States).

2. *The college years are a key time in people's lives for making decisions.*

   Students are gaining knowledge, shaping values and making decisions that will affect the rest of their lives. Also, they have the time to be involved in Bible study and discipleship; there will be far less time available after graduation.

3. *Your campus is your Jerusalem.* (Acts 1:8)

   Our greatest ministry will occur with those who can see the example of our lives and can spend time with us. God has you in your sorority, fraternity or dormitory for a reason. You can reach many people now whom no one else could reach as easily.

Involved in our own movement's part in the overall effort to reach the world is our strategy to *win, build* and *send.*

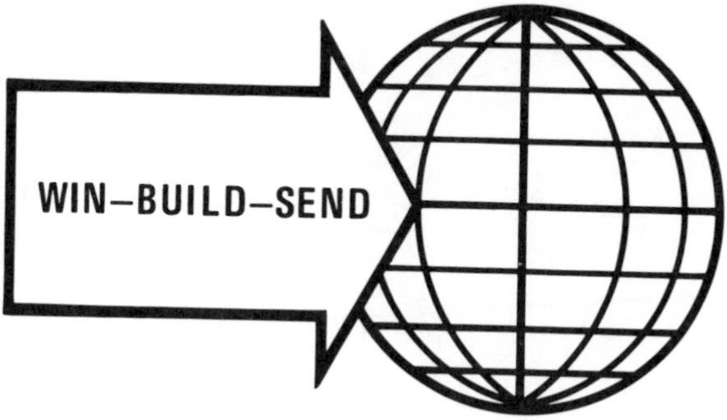

1. Winning.

Winning means exposing people continually to the Gospel, and seeing *God* "win" people to Himself.

We want to make sure everyone in the academic community is confronted with Christ as Savior and is given a chance to make a personal decision for Him.

2. Building

Building means to equip people with principles of Christian living and to motivate and train people for a lifetime of ministry.

The building of disciples has always been at the heart of our ministry. We want to encourage every Christian to become a "spiritual multiplier" and to make his life count for Him.

3. Sending.

Sending means directing students that are being built spiritually onto their campuses as Christians committed to reaching it; and directing graduates into a lifetime of ministry through their secular profession or through full-time Christian work.

Chapter 5

A Strategy for Our Movement

It is not only important to understand the objectives and goals of Campus Crusade for Christ; you also need to know how to translate them into a strategy for reaching your campus. You need to think through what kind of campus you are on and the developmental level of your movement.

You probably know your campus fairly well. You know what students generally think about being involved in school activities (are they all involved in some group, or are they apathetic?). You know how they spend their time (they major in parties or they all have part-time jobs or they study constantly because of the competition).

You also need to know the developmental stage of your movement: how far the movement has progressed toward the goal of winning, building and sending. Understanding the movement's development will help you decide when to begin a weekly meeting, when to concentrate your efforts on building disciples, and when to begin expanding your efforts to reach more diverse groups in the campus population.

To help you in assessing the progress of a movement, Campus Crusade for Christ has developed a four-phase strategy: *penetration, concentration, saturation,* and *continuation.* Using this strategy will help you diagnose a movement and know what tools you should use to keep the movement going and growing.

A. The four-phase strategy.

FOUR PHASE STRATEGY
TO REACH THE CAMPUS

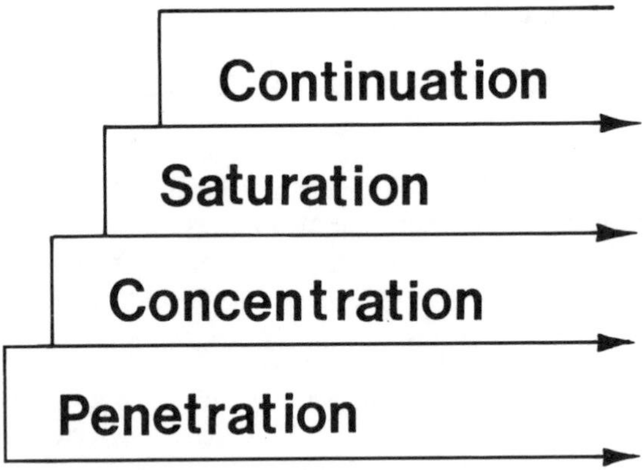

1. **Phase #1: Penetration.**

   a. In this initial stage, the objective is to find and gather students. You want to develop a nucleus of 25 to 40 students who will eventually become the framework for helping to reach the entire campus. Without this nucleus, you will not be able to build a movement.

   b. This stage involves a lot of evangelism.

   c. Locate Christians who are ready to accept the challenge of discipleship, or are at least willing to grow spiritually.

   d. Identify and seek out the campus leaders. We need to go to people who will influence others.

   e. Use group evangelistic meetings. It is easier to gather people if you are exposing many to the gospel. If you limit yourself to presenting the gospel one-to-one, gathering will take much longer.

f. Remember your image. People remember first impressions, so make your first impression sharp!

g. The amount of time your movement remains in phase #1 will be influenced by the number of Christians on your campus and the openness of students to the gospel. But don't let these factors keep you from trusting God for big things! Movements can start small and grow very quickly.

2. **Phase #2: Concentration.**

a. At this stage, you are directing the efforts of the movement's leaders.

b. Saturate a segment of the campus that is capable of producing leaders. These leaders will in turn carry the movement into Phase #3.

c. In nearly all cases, the *freshmen class* should be the segment to saturate.

They will be in school four years and will have time to develop as leaders. Their free time will be less scheduled, and they will be freer to participate in more activities. Also, freshmen are often more open than upperclassmen who have developed intellectual arguments against the gospel.

d. As in Phase #1, look for leaders in the freshmen class.

Freshmen involved in student government, Greek systems and on athletic teams will exert future influence on key campus groups.

e. A ministry to minorities, faculty and international students should begin during this phase. Each of these groups has strategic value.

3. **Phase #3: Saturation.**

a. Phase #1 and #2 continue to be carried on concurrently with this phase. Therefore, a large manpower source is needed before this phase can be launched.

b. Your movement will be in Phase #3 when 70 percent of the student body is hearing the gospel each year through individual and group activities.

c. Two percent to three percent of the student body is involved in small groups.

d. In addition to personal evangelism, large-scale evangelistic meetings, affinity group meetings ("team" meetings) and evangelistic classroom lectures are taking place.

4. Phase #4: Continuation

a. All other phases are now in operation simultaneously.

b. Leadership is being built each year to maintain campus saturation.

c. The "send" emphasis now becomes a more dominant theme.

This sending involves not only the campus itself, but also other segments of society while students are undergraduates: nearby campuses, high schools and churches.

d. The campus has become a "sending agency" and is thus fulfilling one of our movement's main goals: supplying manpower to help fulfill the Great Commission in this generation.

NOTE: The above model is based upon a residential campus with much of the campus life focusing on a strong set of affinity groups: the Greek system, athletic teams and other extracurricular groups.

B. Using the four-phase strategy on different campuses.

1. The multiversity campus.

"Multiversity" refers to a university so large and diverse that reaching only one segment of the campus would not lead to opening the entire campus to Christ. There is not one unique "multiversity" strategy, but rather a composite strategy involving elements from each of the following strategies.

2. **The commuter campus.**

Commuter campuses are characterized by decentralization and depersonalization.

Students do not live on campus nor do they identify primarily with the campus in terms of their social life or extracurricular activities. Affinity groups (groups with a common interest, such as the soccer club or sororities) are not strong on cummuter campuses.

There are two types of commuter schools: 1) the four-year campus; and 2) the two-year, or community, campus.

a. Phase #1—Penetration: find and develop the leadership.

1) A movement needs "movers" (those with a heart for God and teachable spirit). In the initial phase, the objective is to find and develop this leadership.

2) The primary need is to *determine where the students are gathered.*

Unlike the residential campus, many commuter campuses do not have the traditional living units that provide a captive audience for exposing the students to the gospel. *If there are any residents on campus, we need to start with them first,* since they are the most accessible and can provide momentum.

3) Some of the unique considerations:

It is difficult to make an initial contact with commuter students by phone. Students are usually at work, not at home.

Since students spend few hours on the campus outside of class, it may be difficult to arrange an appointment time.

Their schedules are generally fuller (part-time work on top of studies). It may be harder to motivate them to meet.

4) Suggestions:

The best hours to catch a student at home when you call are suppertime or later evening (8 to 10 p.m.).

Make early morning appointments. Many commuter students eat breakfast on campus.

A good initial source of contacts is the registration line. Set up a literature table and take surveys, ask interested students to sign up, etc. (See Exhibit #12 for a sample questionnaire to be taken in registration lines.)

5) Keys in *building* commuter students into disciples:

Use weekend retreats and outings extensively. They provide one of the only places where they can spend a good deal of time with the other Christians on campus. Take them to church with you, too.

Remember that with commuters, Discipleship Groups will come together more on the basis of available hours than on natural affinity.

Parents have more of an influence on commuters since most commuters see them everyday.

6) Create momentum on a commuter campus.

The apathetic atmosphere on campus and the presence of competing activities in the city surrounding most commuter schools can stifle the momentum of most movements on campus.

You will have to use more highly visible activities, such as literature saturation and campus classics, than would otherwise be suggested for the penetration phase.

b. Phase #2—Concentration: Direct the efforts of the leaders.

1) Saturate that segment of the campus which will most effectively produce the leaders capable of executing Phase #3. In nearly all cases, this will be the freshman class.

2) An important "group" to concentrate on, in addition to whatever affinity groups may exist on campus, is the *classroom*. The classroom is a vast source of potential contacts, and one of the few such sources on a commuter campus.

3) The building of disciples can be further accelerated by encouraging staff and students to rent apartments in the same complex, to establish student prayer teams and to continue to emphasize weekend socials, retreats or outings.

c. Phase #3—Saturation: Saturate the entire campus with the gospel.

You may want to move your saturation program into the community during this phase in order to reach commuters where they live: at home and in near-campus apartments. Continue your emphasis on classroom evangelism and on saturating existing affinity groups (Greeks, athletes, clubs, etc.)

d. Phase #4—Continuation: Maintain total saturation continually.

The activities on a commuter campus during the continuation phase are the same as those listed previously in the model for Phase #4.

3. The low-momentum campus.

A potentially low-momentum campus is one that has no obvious central interest upon which to build momentum for a movement. Many community colleges fall into this category.

a. Guard against lack of confidence in your own experience and training. While the immediate problems on this type of campus are tough, it is wrong to conclude that the tools

God has provided for Campus Crusade will not work. If Satan convinces you of this, you are unarmed for battle. *An important step in seeing God win students on a low-momentum campus is to have confidence in our tools of evangelism and disciple building.*

b. Seek out the campus leaders and use the various evangelistic tools to tell them the claims of Christ. Leaders should be challenged individually. The places you find them might change, but the methods of winning and building them remain the same.

c. While looking for leaders, never overlook areas of the campus that might seem to have been de-emphasized, such as Greeks and athletes.

On one campus this statement was overheard: "Athletics are so unpopular on our campus of 20,000, that only 500 showed up for our last football game."

It is not important if athletics in general is not highly thought of on the campus; the fact remains that sharp athletes can often provide a movement with the confident, assertive leadership that Peter probably gave the disciples.

Conclusion:

We must remember that our vision should encompass helping to reach the entire world for Jesus Christ.

Our campus movement is not an end in itself. It is a means toward helping to fulfill the Great Commission. As you help reach your campus, the movement will produce disciples who are sent to help reach other areas of the world. In other words, if our campus ministries are not producing men and women to go to the world, we are missing our objective.

". . . God was in Christ reconciling the world to Himself, not counting their trespasses against them, and He has committed to *us* the word of reconciliation" (2 Corinthians 5:19, italics added).

Chapter 6
Spiritual Leadership for a Movement

Today's world needs trained Christians like you—dynamic believers equipped to lead others and to make an impact on America's campuses. This book provides tools to train you. But tools are not enough. You also need a deep, daily walk with Christ.

The succes of your ministry is not determined by training; it is dependent on your walk with Christ and what He does through you in His power.

In John 7, Jesus says, "Whoever believes in me, as the Scripture has said, streams of living water will flow from within him" (NIV). It is the overflowing life of Jesus within us that produces a life-giving ministry. Don't try to produce water from a dried up river; make sure the river stays connected to the source. Only Jesus can produce the water that becomes your ministry.

We hope this section will help you see the secret of successful spiritual leadership: that Jesus is always the source.

Quiet time

Essential to our ministry is time alone with God daily. Jesus demonstrated that our public work for God is preceded by our private time with God. He spent an entire night in prayer before choosing His disciples; He spent much time in prayer before performing important tasks. He left growing crowds and anxious disciples to depart to a lonely place to commune with the Father (Mark 1:35ff.).

Begin your ministry with your most essential appointment. Schedule a daily time to meet with God. Choose a time of the day when you are alert and will not be interrupted. And then keep it your priority!

Exhibit #1 gives further suggestions on how to have a quiet time.

Bible study

A spiritual leader also needs a growing knowledge of the Word. The more you study the Scriptures, the more you will know and understand God—His attributes, His power, His promises and His relationship to you. You will also develop strong biblical convictions that will shape your values and behavior and allow you to speak out for Christ with confidence.

Studying the Word also gives you a life model: the life of Christ. His leadership can help you balance accomplishing a task with loving and building people.

Learn to look to the Bible for the answers to questions people ask. It gives the basis for making objective decisions because it is God's Word, not man's.

Exhibit #2 gives suggestions for help in systematic Bible study.

Prayer

If you want to learn to pray, begin by praying. Then pray more. Prayer demonstrates our dependence on God as we follow Jesus' example and pray continually. Prayer also unleashes God's power and brings us in contact with our Father.

Learn to praise God as you pray. Instead of griping, pray. Our critical mood and bitterness will be removed as we give thanks. "Praise the Lord. How good it is to sing praises to our God, how pleasant and fitting to praise Him!" (Psalm 147:1, NIV).

Blanket your activities in prayer. When you go to speak at a dormitory meeting, pray before going, during the introduction, as you speak and afterward. Develop a lifestyle of prayer.

Follow the guidelines in this simple acrostic to help you experience a rich and meaningful time of prayer.

A - Adoration: Praise God for who He is and what He has done and will do.

C - Confession: Agree with God concerning any sin He reveals to you, and thank Him for His forgiveness.

T - Thanksgiving: Thank God in every situation, knowing that He works all things together for good.

S - Supplication: Make all your requests—big or small—known to God, who cares for all your needs.

Obedience: Our response to God's grace.

"The world has yet to see what God can do in and through and for one individual who is completely yielded to the Lord Jesus Christ." This was the challenge that inspired Chicagoan D.L. Moody to say, "I want to be that man." God used an "ordinary" man to evangelize multitudes.

The true test of our love for Christ is obedience. Jesus said, "He who has My commandments and keeps them, he it is who loves Me; and he who loves Me shall be loved by My Father, and I will love him, and will disclose Myself to him" (John 14:21).

The more we know of God and His love for us, the more we want to please Him. And knowing that His love is unconditional and constant gives us security about the future. There is nothing I can do to cause God to love me more tomorrow than He loves me today. And, there is nothing that I can do that will make Him love me any less.

But, to experience the benefits of that love, I must walk in obedience to Him.

Witnessing

The only thing many people associate with their first witnessing experience is fear. People forget their names, lose their voices or start shaking. Afterward, they think of all the clever things that they should have said.

Witnessing is a joy when we are led by the Spirit. Witnessing forces us to break out of our complacency and trust God. Just as a muscle becomes stronger with exercise, so does our faith become stronger as we tell others about Jesus Christ.

A student who does not witness eventually begins to stagnate spiritually. People develop a self-centered faith and grow critical of those who do witness. They forget that they are in a spiritual battle; they become deceived into sitting on the sidelines.

Remember that we don't witness to be spiritual or to earn God's favor. We witness out of the overflow of Jesus' life in us. Make sure you are filled with the Spirit each day and are ready for God to use you.

Fellowship

"If we walk in the light, as He is in the light, we have fellowship with one another," John wrote in his first epistle (1:7, NIV). Fellowship means to be in harmony with other Christians as we follow the pure light of Christ's Spirit.

As a leader, you need the fellowship of other believers just as you need fellowship with the Lord. Don't be a spiritual "Lone Ranger" (even *he* had Tonto).

Spend time with like-minded Christians and be willing to be vulnerable with them; you can encourage each other as you become "real people."

Stewardship of time

As a leader, time is a precious commodity. It can't be stopped, stored or reversed. Learning to manage your time can greatly enhance your life and ministry. Begin by developing your goals. Use the goal and planning sheet listed in Exhibit #3.

Once you have formulated goals, make a "TO DO" list. List the activities that are suggested by your goals. For example, assume that your goal is to make a "B" in organic chemistry. Your "TO DO" is to study one hour each day. You then write in your schedule "from 2 p.m. to 3 p.m. daily" and designate that time to study.

Exhibits 3-6 explain use of time and scheduling.

Conclusion

Leading a spiritual movement requires more than good methods or training. You need to become a spiritual leader, and that means letting the Spirit of God develop your heart and character as well as your activities.

Prayer: Essential to Our Movement

For more than a year before Campus Crusade for Christ began, Bill Bright led church deputation teams into college dormitories, fraternities and sororities in the Los Angeles area. Yet during that time, not a single person committed his life to Christ during any of those meetings.

After launching Campus Crusade for Christ in 1951, Dr. Bright held this ministry's first evangelistic meeting at the Kappa Alpha Theta house at UCLA. That night, more than half of the 60 girls present expressed a desire to receive Christ. In the course of the next few months, more than 250 students at UCLA, including the student body president, the newspaper editor and several top athletes, committed their lives to Christ.

What made the difference? Dr. Bright explains:

"This unprecedented demonstration of God's blessing was not an accident. God was responding to the prayers of many of His children.

"When God called this ministry into being, we immediately formed a 24-hour prayer chain, which we divided into 96 15-minute periods. Scores of Christians invested 15 minutes in prayer every day in behalf of our new ministry at the University of California at Los Angeles."

The surest way to build a movement that lasts is to build it God's way. And if we want to go God's way, we must begin a movement on a living foundation of prayer.

A. How to involve other students in prayer.

1. Begin by making prayer a personal priority in your own life. See Exhibit #6, "How to Spend Individual Time in Prayer."

2. Challenge other Christians with their responsibility as the leaders of tomorrow. To be wise leaders, they must spend time with God in prayer, seeking to know Him better and to know His will.

3. Emphasize their need to depend upon God for His direction.

4. Share answers to prayer with others. They will be motivated by the results you are seeing.

5. See Exhibit #9, "How to Lead Conversational Prayer," for information on group prayer.

B. How to establish a prayer ministry.

1. Choose a group of future leaders from those who indicate the greatest interest in prayer.

2. Choose a time to meet consistently together to pray.

3. Ask God to reveal His strategy for the campus as you pray.

4. Ask God to provide someone to coordinate the prayer ministry.

   a. Meet with him or her weekly for prayer and encouragement.

   b. Give the coordinator responsibility for implementing selected strategies (prayer chains, daily prayer groups).

C. How to organize prayer meetings.

1. Establish a daily or weekly time. Meet consistently.

2. Open with a five-minute devotional given by you or another leader (e.g., the prayer coordinator).

3. Allow at least five minutes for answered prayer.

4. Allow 20 minutes for prayer.

5. The meeting should last only 30 minutes. Longer prayer meetings often turn into talking meetings with little or no prayer.

6. Pray for personal needs, for the salvation of non-Christians, for Christian meetings and activities. Pray also for spiritual awakening in the nation and in the world.

7. Emphasize praise and thanksgiving as well as requests.

8. Pray for the needs of world missions listed in the "International Prayer Diary."

9. Choose someone to record the dates of prayer requests and the dates they are answered.

10. Emphasize to movement leaders the importance of attending these meetings. Our presence or lack of it communicates what is important to us.

D. How to conduct a prayer chain sign-up.

1. Plan a prayer night early in the semester to challenge Christians to pray and to invite them to participate in the prayer chain.

2. Clearly explain what is expected of each student.

3. Prepare a master schedule chart of available prayer times. Coordinate the chart with individual schedule cards.

4. Schedule prayer times to begin and end in accordance with class scheduling so that people can pray between classes.

5. Distribute cards at the beginning of the meeting.

6. Ask everyone to fill in three times he would be willing to pray.

7. Collect, sort and match the cards according to day, hour and partner. Record the names on the master schedule.

8. Announce to the students that their prayer times will be posted on the chart after the meeting and that they can begin that week.

9. Contact students individually in the event of conflicts in time.

10. See Exhibit #7, "Example of Prayer Schedule Card."

Chapter 7
What Do I Do First?

A. Step one.

Read and study the sections on Evangelism and Discipleship. Then go back and take notes on the parts you need for *this week*, especially the *exhibits*.

B. Step two.

1. Study Exhibit #8, "First 15 Weeks on Campus."
2. Make a "TO DO" list as you read the chart.
3. Start by *doing* what needs to be done today.
4. Pray through your "TO DO" list, committing each activity into God's hands for His glory.

C. Step three: Begin!

1. Remember that a dynamic movement begins with that first small step in faith. The World Trade Center had a humble beginning. Someone drove a little wooden stake in the ground to mark off the dimensions of the foundation.
2. See Exhibit #10, "How *Not* to Reach Your Campus."

D. First Fifteen Weeks on Campus

Exhibit #8 gives some specific guidelines for how to begin. It shows you where to begin, what steps to follow and in what order, and what you can expect to be doing several weeks from now. Keep the following points in mind as you study it:

1. Each campus is different!

2. If there are few Christians on your campus, you should devote most of your time in the beginning to evangelism to gather people. Therefore, you will start your Discovery Group later than this chart shows.

3. You may be on a campus with many Christians who can be gathered through the use of the Four-Question Survey (see Exhibit #12). Many of them will be ready for a Discovery Group right away. Some more mature Christians may be underchallenged and bored by the material. Emphasize that it will be good training for them in leading their own Discovery Groups.

E. Time Commitment.

Helping to lead a movement on your campus does involve a large investment of your time. The following are guidelines to show you the approximate amount of time you can expect to be devoting to reaching your campus for Christ. It costs to be involved in ministering in the lives of others, but it is worth it! Remember that you are not serving Campus Crusade for Christ: you are serving God!

Quiet Time	30 minutes a day
Readings	30 minutes a day
Evangelism	2 hours a week
Follow-up	1 hour a week
Discovery Group:	
Preparation	1 hour a week
Leading the meeting	1 hour a week
Meeting with group members	2 hours a week
Total	14 hours a week

PART II
EVANGELISM: THE CUTTING EDGE OF A MOVEMENT

How does God view the 4.7 billion people inhabiting the earth?

Sometimes we can become so involved in talking about reaching our world for Christ that people become numbers to us. It is God's will that we seek to help reach the campus—and the entire world—for Christ. But Christ died for the individual, and we must not neglect the individual in our attempt to help reach the world.

Probably the most accurate summary of God's vision and love for mankind was expressed by our Lord Jesus Christ in the Gospel of John: "For God so loved the world, that He gave His only begotten Son, that whoever believes in Him should not perish, but have eternal life" (John 3:16).

The preceding Part summarized an overall thinking process and strategy for helping to reach your campus and growing in your personal walk with the Lord. This Part will provide you with the reasons and methods for doing that which is closest to our Lord's heart: bringing men and women into an eternal, loving relationship with Himself.

Chapter 8
The Biblical Basis for Evangelism

The story of two roommates may motivate you to follow Jesus' example:

> A young man rushed back to his apartment after a Billy Graham meeting. He and his roommate had lived and worked together for several years. "I must tell you something," he said to his friend. "Tonight I invited Christ to be my Savior, and He has changed my life." His friend smiled and said, "Wonderful! I have been hoping you would do that. I have been living the Christian life for several years, all the time hoping that you would trust Christ as your Savior." Surprised, the new Christian said, "You lived such a perfect life that I kept trying to do it without Christ, since you seemed to be doing it without Christ. Tonight I invited Him to become my Lord and Savior because I failed to live the way you live. Why didn't you tell me how I could know Christ, too?"

If you asked the young man who was already a Christian why he didn't speak of Christ to his roommate, what are some reasons you think he might give? His answer probably would have been, "That pushy evangelism isn't for me. I just witness with my life. I didn't want to offend him and thought he wouldn't be interested."

Have you ever heard that attitude expressed? Have you ever had that attitude? It seems common in the Christian world today. And although this attitude—"just witnessing with my life"—sounds noble and good at first, it can be subtly twisted by Satan to neutralize our effectiveness for the Lord.

We all know that exemplary living is important, but normally it is not enough to reach people for Christ. People won't give Christ the credit for living a godly life unless you tell them about Him. Throughout the Old and New Testaments, we see both example of and exhortation for a more aggressive approach in evangelism. But here is the point at which Satan can mislead us: There is no choice between living a Christ-like life as a witness and verbally proclaiming the good news. It isn't an "either-or" proposition. Rather, it is a "both-and" situation. But we may easily be led to believe that it is an "either-or" choice, and therefore many of us may choose the path of least resistance (usually the path of least joy, fulfillment and fruit).

Many Christians have adopted the philosophy that tolerance should supersede truth: that it is narrow-minded and naive to "push" your beliefs onto others. As a result, many Christians don't share their faith.

However, in Mark 16:15 is a clear command by Jesus to take the gospel to the world: "And He said to them, 'Go into all the world and preach the gospel to all creation.'"

We need to understand the biblical basis for evangelism so we can answer the critics, as well as the questions in our own minds.

A. People are lost and separated from God.

1. People are lost without Christ (Matthew 9:36; Luke 19:10). Jesus' highest priority in coming to earth was to provide a way to bring men back to God. We should have an equally great burden to tell others how they can have a relationship with God.

2. People are unable to save themselves.

B. God has made a provision for salvation for those who will receive it (Romans 5:8; 10:13).

Christ alone has paid the penalty for man's sin. Christ was willing to die so that men might know God. Many people today know the facts of the crucifixion, but they do not understand its significance until it is explained to them.

C. God prepares people for salvation (2 Peter 3:9).

1. God convicts people of sin (John 16:8).

2. God initiates reconciliation and draws people with His love (1 John 4:10).

    a. He prepared the Ethiopian eunuch (Acts 8:26-35).

    b. He prepared Cornelius (Acts 10).

D. God commands us to be involved in evangelism (Romans 10:14,15).

1. People need to *hear* about Christ (Romans 10:14,15).

2. God has given us the *responsibility* to be *ambassadors* of Christ (2 Corinthians 5:20). In this verse we see that God has given us the work of reconciling men to Himself. We are His ambassadors. As ambassadors of Christ we have the privilege of bringing to others the saving knowledge of Christ.

3. God commands us to witness and to make disciples of every nation (Matthew 28:19,20).

4. Christ's love for me should motivate me to obey (2 Corinthians 5:14).

E. Case Study: Paul and the Philippian jailer (Acts 16:19-34).

You may feel a little better about aggressive evangelism when you see what it is *not* (and clear up some fuzzy thinking about it). *Aggressive evangelism is not high-pressure salesmanship.* Often when we think of aggressive evangelism, we picture a salesman who, once he gets his foot in the door, absolutely will not take "no" for an answer.

Unfortunately, some Christians have been insensitive, even obnoxious, in their zeal to witness to others. But while the Bible tells us that we are to be as wise as serpents, it also says that we should speak to others with gentleness. Jesus never criticized the disciples for their zeal. We should be eager to tell others about Christ, but we need to add wisdom to our zeal in order to make our witness more effective.

Our approach, our style and our methods should never be "high pressure." We should remember that some people will be offended by the message we carry—the gospel is not always popular and easily accepted. People may reject our message; we cannot help that. But we should expect that as we become wiser and gentler, we will see fewer and fewer people offended by our style of witness.

What, then, is aggressive evangelism? *Aggressive evangelism is simply taking the initiative to share Christ in the power of the Holy Spirit and leaving the results to God.* The key word is *initiative.* We are not to wait for others to come to us and ask about the Lord (although this happens occasionally). We are to take the initiative to talk to people about Him. In John 4:35, Jesus says, "Look on the fields, that they are white for harvest." When we take the initiative in evangelism, we are simply telling the Lord that we believe what He said is true. The harvest is ripe—men and women are ready to hear the gospel.

In summary, we have the most dynamic revolutionary message the world has heard or will ever hear—THE GOSPEL! Wherever it has gone, new life, new hope, and new purpose for living has resulted. God has commanded us to aggressively share this message with anyone who will listen. We are motivated by God's love for us and by our love for others who are lost without Christ. Although we use methods and techniques to better communicate to people, we depend on God and the simple gospel message to bring the results He desires to accomplish.

The filter process is a process the Holy Spirit uses in helping us identify people with the potential to disciple others.

This process involves broad proclamation of the gospel to a large population, and activities that allow Christians to demonstrate faithfulness and a desire to grow.

Before we get into the specifics of how we can use the filter process, let's first look at how Jesus used it. He is always our best example. There are three parts to the process.

First, He **evangelized** widely (Matthew 9:35). Everywhere Jesus went, He talked to people about spiritual matters and how they related to them.

Second, He **involved** interested followers (Mark 1:16-20). He took the *initiative* and He looked for particular qualities in people.

At this point in His ministry, Jesus had not yet chosen His 12 disciples. He was calling many to follow Him and to begin getting involved in the ministry. As He talked to people, whether individually or in large groups, He continually took the initiative to *involve* interested followers who had particular qualities. We will look at these qualities in the chapter on "How to Develop a Discipleship Group."

Third, He **selected** certain ones to be His key disciples (Mark 3:13,14), to have a special relationship with Him and with one another, and to have a *personal ministry*. We need to be careful to remember to *select* and not to settle on the first two or three Christians we find. Even though all Christians *should* desire to be discipled and to disciple others, not all do. Let's remember, we are involved in a *filter* process.

Jesus involved many in His ministry to help build them to a point of personal commitment to Him. Then came the time to *select and challenge certain* ones to be His key disciples and carry on His ministry.

In summary, remember three things.

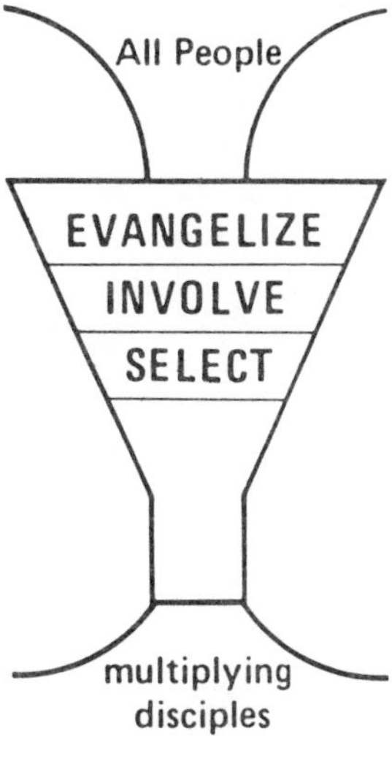

First, *the filter process helps us identify potential multiplying disciples for our ministries.* These disciples will ultimately help reach the entire world for Christ. Our responsibility is to take the initiative in faith relying on the Holy Spirit for guidance and wisdom. It is solely God's responsibility to produce the fruit.

Second, *the process involves sharing the gospel with people, involving interested ones in the ministry and challenging certain ones to discipleship.* We will discuss how to challenge people in following chapters.

Third, *this was the method Christ used. His plan was to speak God's truth to thousands, involve many and select and challenge a few who would go on to do the same thing.* The result is clear. Through Christ's plan and power, His purpose of reaching the world with the gospel will be accomplished.

Chapter 9
One-to-one Evangelism

Many Christians are afraid to tell others of their faith in Christ. They have difficulty getting started, or just do not know *how* to witness.

The tools and methods listed in this chapter have been designed to enable the Christian to be more effective in his witness for Christ. These techniques and materials were originally developed for the Campus Crusade for Christ staff, but are now available to anyone who wishes to use them. They are grounded in solid, biblical truth and have been used successfully by many people over the years to help lead many thousands into a relationship with Jesus Christ.

Remember, however, that people are not won to Christ through materials and methods, but through the ministry of the Holy Spirit, who uses men, methods and materials to draw others to the Savior for the glory of God.

The Four Spiritual Laws

"But you shall receive power when the Holy Spirit has come upon you; and you shall be My witnesses both in Jerusalem, and in all Judea and Samaria, and even to the remotest part of the earth" (Acts 1:8).

A. **The benefits of using the Four Spiritual Laws.**
See Exhibit #10, The Four Spiritual Laws.

1. It helps you begin a conversation.

   Simply ask the question, "Have you heard of the Four Spiritual Laws?"

2. It begins with a *positive* note: God loves you.

3. It presents the claims of Christ *clearly*.

4. It includes an *invitation* to receive Christ.

5. It offers suggestions for growth and emphasizes the importance of the church.

6. It helps you stay on the *subject*.

7. It enables you to be *brief*, prepared and confident.

8. It provides a transferable method for presenting Christ to others.

   Not only can you use the booklet to lead others to Christ, but because it is transferable, other Christians also can learn to use it.

9. It can be left with the individual.

10. It is an immediate follow-up tool.

    The new Christian can receive immediate follow-up from the Scriptures provided in the booklet.

B. Introducing the Four Spiritual Laws.

1. Initiating the conversation.

   Let's assume that the other person and you have been talking for a little while and are getting to know each other. In the course of the conversation, you can say something such as: "I've been sharing this booklet with some people and getting their opinions on it (or response to it). It explains how a person can have a personal relationship with God through Jesus Christ. Would you mind if I took a few minutes and shared it with you?"

   "Have you heard of the Four Spiritual Laws?"

   "I have been a Christian for years, but I have just recently found a way to express my faith that really makes sense. I would like to share it with you. Have you heard of the Four Spiritual Laws?"

C. Principles of presenting the Four Spiritual Laws booklet.

1. Personalize the presentation by using the person's name.

2. *Involve* the person by asking questions and by listening to him.

3. Give the person an *opportunity* to receive Christ.

4. Read through the *entire* booklet. By reading the entire booklet, you make sure he had assurance of salvation by asking the questions on page 11 and giving him a chance to respond.

5. Give the booklet to the person and *encourage* him to share it with someone else.

6. Always carry a Four Spiritual Laws booklet with you. Though the Four Spiritual Laws can be used effectively by simply reading the booklet to another person, you will eventually want to memorize the content so that it becomes very familiar and natural to you. Then you will always be prepared to communicate your faith whenever an opportunity arises.

D. Successful Witnessing.

The scriptural basis for successful witnessing (1 Corinthians 2:4,5) is simply taking the *initiative* to share Christ in the *power* of the Holy Spirit and leaving the results to God.

E. Essence of the Four Spiritual Laws.

1. God loves us.

2. We are separated from God by our sin.

3. Christ died on the cross to pay for our sins.
   —to show His payment was acceptable to God (Romans 3:25).
   —to provide for a person to have a new life in Christ (Romans 6:4).

4. Our response

"... and after he brought them out, he said, 'Sirs, what must I do to be saved?' And they said, 'Believe in the Lord Jesus, and you shall be saved, you and your household'" (Acts 16:30-31).

"For by grace you have been saved through faith; and that not of yourselves, it is the gift of God; not as a result of works, that no one should boast" (Ephesians 2:8,9).

The response one must make to the gospel is a definite, act of the will decision. This decision involves two things: first, repentance—turning to God from self, or wanting to go God's way; second, we must rely upon Christ and His sacrifice as the only way to pay for that sin that separates us from God and to put us in a right relationship with God. At this point we can begin to know God and the reality of His love. Many people with whom you speak will want to receive Christ into their lives if they understand who He is and how they can receive Him.

a. Revelation 3:20—Explains that opening the door of your heart and inviting Christ to come in is a helpful picture that clarifies the faith commitment one must make to become a Christian. It is a figurative expression of the choice one makes to depend or rely on Christ and His payment for sin.

b. Last Paragraph—Law 4

   Underline the key words as you read through "Receiving Christ Involves":

   1) Repentance.

   2) Trusting (another word for faith).

   3) An act of the will (emphasizes decision).

   4) Before moving on to the two circles ask, "Why would a person want to make this decision?" Those who do not put their faith in Christ will be faced with eternal separation from God, while those who accept Christ and His death on the cross have the promise of eternal life. (They are separated from God because of sin

and need to trust Christ and His payment for sin in order to spend eternity with God.)

This question will tell you if the person understands the gospel you have just presented. He will not be able to tell you what circle he is in if he doesn't understand the gospel. If he doesn't get it, quickly review the main ideas of laws 2, 3 and 4.

F. The Circle Diagrams.

The two circles represent two kinds of lives. The circle on the left represents the self-directed life. This is the person who has not made a decision for Christ. The circle on the right represents the Christ-controlled life. This person has made a willful decision to ask Christ into his life. Following the circles are two very important questions:

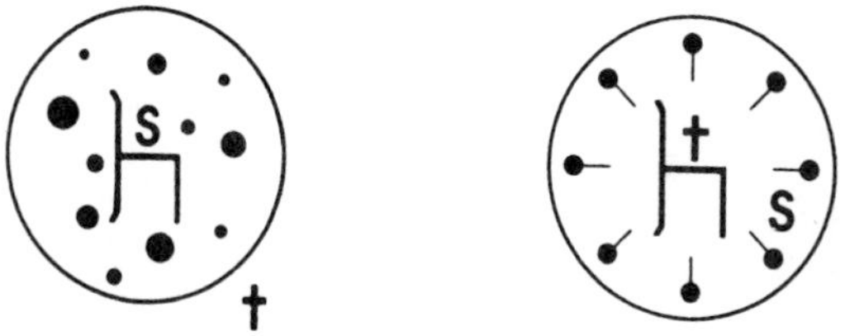

1. Which circle best represents your life?

2. Which circle would you like to have represent your life?

G. Purposes of the Circle Diagrams.

1. They further clarify *why* people need Christ.

2. They help a person *identify* his own relationship to God.

   However, it is important to remember that one of the objectives of the Four Spiritual Laws presentation is to show someone *how* to receive Christ, which is accomplished after the prayer is read. Don't allow the circle questions to stop you in your presentation, even if the person with whom you are sharing identifies with the circle on the right, the Christ-controlled life.

H. Responses to the two Circle Questions.

1. Which circle best represents your life? Now let's consider three possible responses to the first of the two circle questions. One response could be . . .

   a. If a person says his life is represented by the circle on the left, simply continue through the booklet by asking the next question.

   b. If a person says he is not sure which circle represents his life, or if he says he is inbetween, or if he remains silent, continue through the booklet by asking the next question.

   c. If a person says that his life is represented by the circle on the right, skip the second question and continue by saying, "Joe, it always interests me to find out how a person made that decision. When did you make that decision?"

2. Which circle would you like to have represent your life?

   a. If the person answers that he would like to have his life represented by the circle on the right, continue reading through the prayer.

   b. If he answers that he would like to remain in the circle on the left, maintain a positive and loving attitude. Continue the presentation by showing him how to pray and receive Christ if he should decide he wants to know Christ in the future. You might say, "Let me explain how you can invite Christ into your life when you decide to do so." Then continue reading through the prayer.

   c. If a person says he is not sure which circle he wants to have represent his life, continue reading through the prayer, showing him how to receive Christ should he want to do so in the future. Experience has shown that some people who may be antagonistic at first are open to receiving Christ when they hear the prayer. So keep reading whenever possible. If this is impossible, be kind and thank him for his time. Try to leave the booklet with him.

I. How to encourage a person to pray and receive Christ.

1. How to introduce the prayer.

   a. Read the prayer *aloud.*

   b. Ask, "Does this prayer express the desire of your heart?"

2. If the person says "yes."

   a. Ask, "What do you think would happen if you expressed this prayer to God?" There are individuals who, because of their religious background, will want to pray the prayer yet not really understand what it means to trust Jesus Christ as Lord and Savior. Their response to this question will help you to discern whether or not they have a clear understanding of their need for a Savior. If their answer indicates the need for more explanation, review the appropriate portion of the Four Spiritual Laws.

   b. Once you feel that the individual understands, ask, "Would you like to pray this prayer *now?*"

   c. If the person is ready, ask him to pray.

   Once a person expresses his desire to invite Christ into his life, explain that God is interested in the attitude of his heart, not the position of his body or even the exact words he uses. Let him know that he need not kneel or even bow his head to communicate with God. Tell him that he can initiate his relationship with Christ right where he sits. Suggest to him that he may pray in any of these ways:

   1) He can pray by himself *aloud.*

   2) He can repeat the prayer aloud, phrase by phrase, after you.

   3) He can pray *silently,* saying "amen" when he finishes.

d. If the prayer expresses the desire of his heart but he isn't ready to pray, do not become angry or upset. Always take the positive approach. At this point, share briefly how you came to know Christ. Let him know what your reasons were and the changes Christ has made in your life. Following your testimony, he may be ready to make his own commitment to Christ.

1) Be loving.

2) Be positive.

3) Share your *testimony.*

4) Give another *opportunity* to pray.

3. If the person says "no."

a. Make sure the person knows how to receive Christ. Ask him what he would do if at a later time he wanted to commit his life to Christ. Asking key questions such as this one is the most effective way to help you determine what the other person is thinking if he really understands the issue.

b. Explain what would happen if he received Christ (p. 13, Four Spiritual Laws).

c. Give him a *final opportunity* to receive Christ. As you continue to share things and ask questions, you may find that he wants to receive Christ. It is a good policy to give him further opportunities as you continue to share. However, always remember to be sensitive to him. Never become pushy.

If he still is not ready to pray, encourage him to continue to consider the issue.

4. If the person is not sure that the prayer expresses the desire of his heart, maintain a Christ-like attitude. Do not become upset or impatient. Continue to allow the Holy Spirit to direct your response.

The individual who is uncertain as to whether he wants to commit his life to Christ may be encouraged to do so through hearing your personal experience with Christ.

a. Be loving.

b. Be positive.

c. Share your testimony.

d. Give him another *opportunity* to receive Christ.

5. If the person states he has already prayed the prayer, sensitively discern if he has made a real commitment to Christ. Many people may tell you that they have prayed the prayer before; however, not all of those individuals will have genuinely trusted in Christ. To help determine whether or not a person has made that decision, ask him to share with you how he came to know Christ. However, be careful not to put him on the defensive.

   a. Be loving.

   b. Be positive.

   c. Ask him to share his *testimony.*

J. Key points in sharing the Four Spiritual Laws.

1. Be sure you are filled with the Holy Spirit.

   Through the Holy Spirit, we are given a supernatural love for others. As we allow Him to fill us, we will communicate this love to others.

2. Take a genuine *interest* in the person.

   a. Use his name.

   b. Watch your *attitude.* Calling the person by name from time to time will add to the warmth of your conversation and will help create a personal and friendly atmosphere.

   c. Be *sensitive* to his needs. As we allow God's Holy Spirit to shape our lives, His love for others will become our love for others. We share, not to earn God's favor, but rather because our love for Him and others compels us to do so.

d. Stop reading if necessary. You want to be sensitive in your presentation; there will be times when urgent needs or questions must be dealt with before going on. (Such interruptions are usually brief and happen infrequently.)

e. Be *gentle.*

f. Maintain eye contact. Maintaining occasional eye contact with the individual adds to the warmth and personal nature of the atmosphere.

3. Never *force* a person to listen.

Forcing an individual to listen to your presentation may cause him to develop an unfavorable impression of Christians. For example, he could easily conclude that we are pushy and insensitive or lack good manners.

4. Help him *understand.*

a. Hold the booklet so that the person can see it. Not allowing him to see the booklet creates the impression that you want to read the booklet to him rather than wanting to read it with him.

b. Read the booklet *aloud.*

c. Don't *speed* read the booklet.

Reading the booklet through at a very rapid pace may detract from his ability to focus on the message and understand it clearly.

5. Avoid *answering* questions until you have *finished reading the booklet.*

In many cases, a person's questions will be dealt with as you continue the presentation. As questions arise, say something like, "That's a good question. I think that it may be answered as we continue through the booklet. If not, let me know."

K. Basic Assurance.

1. Explain to him how to know that Christ is in his life.

   Turn to Page 11 in the Four Spiritual Laws booklet and begin to see how we can communicate some of these important facts to a new believer.

   a. Read the first question on page 11 of the Four Spiritual Laws. Allow the new believer to answer the question.

   b. Turn back to page 9 in the Four Spiritual Laws and ask the new believer to *read* Revelation 3:20. Then ask him the second question on page 11. There are additional questions to use if his answer is not a solid, "He is in my life."

   c. Ask the remaining two questions at the top of page 11. Let the new believer answer the last question. Use the answer in parentheses to support or clarify the one he gives.

   d. Listen to the person's response to each question to evaluate if he *understands* the scriptural principles involved. Do not proceed until you are sure he does.

2. The Bible promises eternal life to all who receive Christ (1 John 5:11-13). Read, or ask the new believer to read, this section aloud. Then ask these questions that require the person to evaluate his new relationship with Christ.

   a. What has God given us? Answer: *eternal life.*

   b. Where is the life found? Answer: in His *Son.*

   c. Do you have the Son? Answer: *yes.*

   d. If you have the Son, what else do you have? Answer: *life,* eternal life.

   e. When did eternal life begin for you? Answer: *when I received Christ.*

3. Encourage the new believer to thank God often that Christ is in his life (Hebrews 13:5b).

Now that the new believer knows that having Christ in his life assures him of eternal life, he must understand that he needs to invite Christ into his life only once.

a. What did He promise you in this verse? Answer: to *never leave* me.

b. How many times do you need to ask Him into your life? Answer: *once.*

c. Will he ever leave you? Answer: *NO.*

4. Caution him not to depend upon feelings.

Confidence that Christ will never leave him will grow as the new believer learns to live by faith, not by feelings.

a. Ask the new believer to describe the *train diagram* to you in his own words.

b. Read or ask the new believer to read the section entitled, "Do Not Depend Upon Feelings."

c. *Accept* his explanation, communicating positively any necessary corrections.

5. Read through the section "Now That You Have Received Christ."

A person may know Christ is in his life without understanding all the benefits of having Christ in his life. We've already discussed some of these benefits. Although you will want to read through all of them with a new believer, right now we will look at two in particular.

a. Read: Many things happened, including . . .

1) Your sins were forgiven.

a) What did God do with your sins (Colossians 1:14)? Answer: *forgave* them.

After reading point 2 in the Four Spiritual Laws booklet, look up Colossians 1:14. Ask the new believer, "What did God do with your sins?"

b) How many of your sins did He forgive (Colossians 2:13)? Answer: *all.*

If the new believer has trouble answering the second question, look up Colossians 2:13 and ask again, "How many of your sins did He forgive?"

2) You became a child of God (John 1:12). After reading point 3 in the Four Spiritual Laws, look up John 1:12 and ask these two questions:

a) What does this verse say you have become? Answer: a *child* of God.

b) If you and I are children of God, how are we related? Answer: We are *brothers* (or *sisters*).

b. Use the "thank You" prayer.

1) *Encourage* the person to pray a "thank You" prayer to God.

Say something like, "I'll pray first and then you can do the same, okay?" If he seems reluctant, then just pray for both of you.

2) Pray a "thank You" *prayer* yourself which leads the new believer to pray, too.

A suggested prayer is "Lord, thank You for coming into my life (specific number or "a few") years ago and forgiving all my sins. Now (*new believer's name*) wants to thank You, too."

L. Motivating new believers for follow-up.

It is important to remember that basic follow-up establishes the foundation upon which a new believer will grow.

1. Understand the definition of follow-up.

   Follow-up is the process through which we establish and *equip* new Christians with the basics of Christianity so that they can move on to *spiritual* maturity and become spiritual multipliers (Ephesians 4:12,13). See Chapter 22, How to Follow Up, for further information on follow-up.

2. Encourage the new believer to come to the first follow-up appointment.

   a. Seek to arrange an appointment with the new believer within 24 to 48 hours after he receives Christ (Mark 4:14,15).

      It is important to meet with the new Christian very soon after he receives Christ, because the moment a person trusts in Christ as his Savior and Lord, Satan goes to work. A baby Christian is especially vulnerable to Satan's attempts to bring doubt and confusion into his life. So it is important for you to be with the new believer in the early hours of his Christian experience.

   b. Make him aware of his need to grow in his relationship with God.

   c. Arrange a specific *time* and *place* to meet with the new believer.

      Point out to the new believer that being a Christian is having a relationship with God. As in any relationship, you have to spend time communicating with each other to see the friendship grow. Then tell him you would like to meet with him again to pass on some information that will help him learn how to grow in his friendship with God.

   d. Ask him to *review* the Four Spiritual Laws before you meet again and to *thank* Christ once more for coming into his life.

e. Give him the follow-up booklet, "Beginning Your New Life!"

If you have a copy of "Beginning Your New Life!" give it to the new believer. Encourage him to read John 1-3 and to start answering the questions in the booklet. If you don't have a booklet, plan to give it to him at the first appointment.

3. Help the new believer gain assurance of his salvation. Assume that a student named Joe has already received Christ and you want to help him be assured of his salvation.

You: "Joe, today you prayed and invited Christ into your life. You have now begun a personal relationship with Him. This is really only the beginning. We have just met each other today. In this sense, we have begun a personal friendship. But suppose that, after today, we never see or communicate with each other again. Will our friendship grow?"

Joe: "No."

You: "Why not, Joe?"

Joe: "Because a friendship depends on getting to know the other person and communicating with him."

You: "Well, Joe, it's the same way with Christ. Even though you began a relationship with Him today, if your friendship is going to grow, you need to get to know Him better. The better we know God, the more we will be able to trust Him. How do you think a friendship grows, Joe?"

Joe: "By spending time together, I guess. You know—talking with one another, doing things together."

You: "That's right. In other words, we need to learn how to communicate with Christ and allow Him to communicate with us. We need to learn how to spend time with Him so that our friendship with Him can grow. You know, Joe, I would like to get together with you and share how you can build your friendship with Christ. Would you be interested?"

Joe: "Sure."

You: "Are you free tomorrow about this time?"

Joe: "Yes."

You: "That's great! Why don't we meet right here at ______ o'clock tomorrow. Is that all right?

Joe: "Yes, that's fine."

You: "Joe, why don't you read through the Four Spiritual Laws on your own before you go to bed tonight. Then thank Christ that He has come into your life. By thanking God, you communicate faith, which pleases Him. There is a little booklet entitled "Beginning Your New Life!" that I would like to give you. It has a reprint of the Gospel of John in it. I want to encourage you to read the first three chapters because I found them very helpful to me after I received Christ. Also, if you have time, you might want to fill in the answers to some of the questions in the booklet."

Joe: "I'll do that."

You: "Great! It's been good talking with you, Joe, and having the chance to share these things. I'll look forward to meeting you tomorrow at ______ o'clock, right here. See you later."

Evangelistic Literature

Evangelistic literature (Rusty Wright's *Dynamic Sex: Beyond Technique and Experience; The New Testament—Can I Trust It?; A Funny Thing Happened on the Way to the End;* "Van Dusen letter"; *Athletes in Action* magazine; Josh McDowell's *More Than a Carpenter; Resurrection—Hoax or History;* "Jesus and the Intellectual") is designed exclusively to communicate the claims of Jesus Christ and the dynamics of knowing Him in a personal way to the non-Christian on the secular college and university campus. Because of the universal interest in collegiate life that exists in the hearts of both young and old, these articles or books have a wide, strong appeal to people of all ages from every walk of life.

Businessmen share them with their clients. Homemakers share them with their neighbors, and students distribute them among their fellow students. They are extremely effective evangelistic tools in sharing with non-Christians the wonderful discovery of knowing Christ personally. *They can be used as evangelistic tools in the following ways:*

A. **Give an article to someone you know.** Ask him to read either the entire publication or a particular article. Using the four simple questions below, move quickly and inoffensively into a personal presentation of the Four Spiritual Laws, giving the person an opportunity to pray and receive Christ.

Ask four questions:

1. "What did you think of the publication (or article)?"

2. "Did it make sense to you?"

3. "Have you made the wonderful discovery of knowing Christ personally?"

4. "You would like to, wouldn't you?"

Continue with the Four Spiritual Laws presentation giving the person an opportunity to pray and receive Christ. Leave copies with those who are especially interested.

B. **Approach individuals at random.** Ask them if they would take a few minutes to read an article, or part of one, and give you their opinion; or make an appointment for the next day.

C. **Use the books or magazines that contain the Four Spiritual Laws.** Ask a person to glance through the publication. Then turn specifically to the Four Spiritual Laws and ask if he has ever read through them.

D. **Use these publications in contacting individuals after evangelistic meetings and Campus Classics,** especially if the publication includes a feature article written by the speaker.

E. **Be familiar with the articles before you try to share the publication.**

F. **Use *Athletes in Action* magazine** to approach coaches, athletes and sports-minded people. Give them the magazine and set up an appointment on the next day to present the Four Spiritual Laws.

G. **Use the "Van Dusen letter."** This is a letter written by Dr. Bright to a prominent businessman (the name is fictitious). It may be left with students or mailed with a cover letter to friends, relatives, etc.

Evangelistic literature can open many doors for you to share Christ with others.

See Exhibit #10, "Evangelistic Literature."

See Exhibit #11, "Van Dusen Letter."

See Materials order blank at the end of the book.

Surveys

We live in a day when people are survey conscious. Surveys are regularly taken to determine the social and political thinking of people in our country and around the world. Religious surveys have frequently been taken, but not always with the specific intent of coupling them with an opportunity to share one's personal faith in Christ.

Our surveys have proved to be valuable tools:

—They help to determine the religious thinking of people in any particular community, campus, or segment of society.

—They provide numerous opportunities for students and laymen to share their faith and, therefore, become more effective in their witness.

—They have a flexibility that enables the Christian to make effective contacts with people in house-to-house visitation, in public places (beaches, parks, airports, bus stations), in churches, or on campus (student centers, living units, or at random).

—They gather valuable information about a person and his present spiritual condition in a very brief period of time.

—They develop a progression of thought that encourages the person to be honest about his own needs and, at the same time, to focus his attention on Jesus.

—They are helpful to those who are just learning to share their faith by providing them with an effective way to establish rapport with the one with whom they are talking.

For years, it has been appropriate and, in some cases, necessary to use the various kinds of surveys to help establish rapport prior to sharing the gospel through the use of the Four Spiritual Laws. In recent times, however, the Spirit of God has created such an unusual hunger for Christ in people's hearts that in day-to-day personal witnessing it *is easy to establish rapport without the use of a survey. The survey should primarily be used:*

1. As one of the means of helping those who are being trained to talk to others about their faith. *(However, it should be the goal*

of each person to learn to share the claims of Christ naturally as a way of life without the use of a survey). See the preceding section, "The Four Spiritual Laws," for examples of how to begin sharing the gospel with someone without the use of a survey.

2. *To filter a target group for evangelism* (see Chapter 20 on filtering target groups). For example, a survey would be helpful in situations where you are trying to systematically saturate a specific community, dorm, apartment, or other area with the gospel message.

A. Uses of the survey.

1. Dorm outreach.
2. Greek outreach.
3. Talking to friends.
4. Classroom outreach.
5. Talking to professors.
6. Neighborhood outreach.
7. Outreach at work.
8. Outreach to clubs.

B. Introducing the survey.

Copy this introduction at the top of your survey, so that you will know what to say as you begin the conversaion.

"Hello, my name is ________ This is (*your partner*). We are here to conduct a religious survey and to share some helpful information. Would you help us by giving your opinion in answer to a few questions?"

1. *State the reasons for the survey if the person questions you further on the purpose of the interview.* For example:

   a. "It helps us to know the trends in student thinking."

b. "It shows us the thinking of students on various campuses around the country."

c. "There are many people who are sincerely trying to find God. Others are looking for a purpose in life. We want to be available to those who want help."

d. "It helps us to know the trends in student thinking and to meet people who are interested in knowing how to establish a personal relationship with Christ."

C. Conducting the survey.

1. Ask questions.

2. Record answers.

3. Do not evaluate, argue with or question any responses given.

4. Do not allow the student to read the survey, or he will select the answer he wants. Say, "We want your spontaneous response."

5. If you do interact with the person to establish rapport, be sure that your comments are not argumentative or judgmental. Do not reflect negatively upon his answers to any of the questions.

D. Closing the survey.

1. Say, "This completes the first part of the survey. The second part involves getting your opinion of a little booklet called the Four Spiritual Laws. Have you ever seen it before?"

2. If the person says he has not heard of the booklet, ask him if you could go through it with him and get his opinion.

3. If the person has seen the booklet, find out what he thought about it. If he can't remember the content very well, offer to go through it with him and get his opinion.

4. Copy this transition at the bottom of your survey, so you will know how to lead into the Four Spiritual Laws.

E. Points to remember.

1. Be casual, relaxed and sensitive to the people you meet.

2. Use the introduction and closing exactly as outlined.

3. Conduct the survey in pairs. While one takes the survey, the other one should pray silently.

4. Alternate, so that each partner has an equal number of opportunities to use the survey.

5. Do not force a person to take the survey if he does not want to.

6. Remember that you are not to put your faith in techniques, but in the power of God. This realization will remove the pressure as you use the survey.

7. Move through the survey quickly, avoiding tangents. Don't answer for people and don't express disapproval or approval of the answers they give.

8. Maintain a neutral attitude during the survey.

9. Do not learn the person's name before taking the survey. Trying to get someone's name before taking the survey may cause him to be reluctant to participate. Ask for his name only if he shows a genuine interest or if he prays and receives Christ.

   Remember, if a person is not interested in hearing the Four Spiritual Laws or your personal testimony (though most people are), you need not share with him.

F. Surveying living units on campus.

The Great Commission cannot be fulfilled in this generation unless it is fulfilled in your academic community. Therefore, it is essential that each person on campus have an opportunity to hear the claims of Christ presented in a simple, meaningful way. Filtering a target group is the most systematic way of ensuring that this will happen.

1. Secure any authorization that may be necessary prior to surveying campus living units (dorms or apartments).

2. Prepare survey assignments carefully. Decide on a definite dorm or apartment that you wish to have surveyed. Assign specific floors or room numbers that are to be surveyed by you and your other callers.

3. Familiarize yourself with the survey form (Exhibits 21-30) and witnessing materials prior to taking the survey.

4. On the way to your survey assignment, *pray*. Pray while taking the survey.

5. During the survey, keep accurate records. (See Exhibits 20 and 21, "Survey Record" and "Survey Codes.")

   a. As you proceed through an assigned living unit area, record the results of every room number or apartment number, including those where the individual was not at home. Contact these unreached individuals in a follow-up survey.

   b. Copy the names and addresses of all who pray and indicate they received Christ. Follow up these people within the next 48 hours.

   c. Make a note of others who did not pray but who should be followed up because of their interest in the claims of Christ.

6. During the survey, be alert for other opportunities to witness—people you meet in the dorm hallways, etc. Make a note on your record sheet of any who should be followed up.

7. After the survey, thank God for what He has done. Be sure to follow up the new Christians within the next day or two.

8. Have those who participated in the survey share with each other the experiences and lessons they learned while taking surveys.

G. Making use of the results of the survey.

At one time, we tabulated the results of over 10,000 campus surveys. Sixty-six percent of the students expressed the desire for a more personal religious faith, but over 89 percent of them did not know how to become a Christian.

1. Have the members of a Discipleship Group tabulate the results of a survey they took in order to get a more accurate idea of the spiritual climate of their campus.

2. Following a dorm survey, secure permission to post the results on a dorm bulletin board.

3. Following a survey of a fraternity, sorority, or an entire Greek system, send a summary of the tabulations to each fraternity and sorority president, suggesting that the results be reported to the entire group.

4. Prior to a survey, arrange for the school newspaper to publish the results. Then you can tell those answering the survey that the results will be published in the paper.

H. Using the Four-Question Survey.

The *four-question survey is a very effective way to quickly filter a target group of people.* All of the principles applied to other surveys can also be applied here. However, there are some unique ways this survey can be used, which may vary in effectiveness according to the type of campus you are on. See Exhibit #12.

For example, on one campus, during the first week of classes, Christians surveyed 6,000 students as they went through the cafeteria lines. Others have had good responses by surveying the freshman class, or surveying students as they stood in registration lines at the beginning of the year. Still others created their own groups to survey by using such techniques as having a 50-foot banana split in the middle of a park frequented by students on a sunny spring day!

On commuter campuses, surveying nearby apartment complexes may be beneficial.

Think creatively—where is the largest number of students on your campus? If you put your mind to it, this survey can be used in a great variety of ways.

1. Cafeteria lines.

   a. Get permission from the cafeteria director to take the survey and explain that you won't hold up the lines.

b. Pick a good day—not Friday.

c. Pick a meal most people go to—lunch or dinner.

d. Have two people at each line to hand everyone a survey and pencil.

e. Say, "We're taking a four-question survey in all the cafeteria lines today. Would you take a minute to help us out?" (If the person wants more explanation, say, "Our purpose is to get a cross-section of the religious/spiritual thinking of students on our campus.")

f. Have each person check off answers and put the completed survey and pencil in a bucket. This method allows you to move quickly through the lines.

g. If anyone doesn't want to help out, smile and move on. Most people will help because "everyone is doing it."

2. Dorms.

a. Get permission from the dorm director to take the survey.

b. If possible, get the help of someone who lives in the dorm you are surveying.

c. Pick a time when most people are in—around 9 p.m.

d. Explain the survey as in the cafeteria line. Go door to door and leave it with everyone in each hall, telling him you will be back in 10 minutes to pick it up.

e. After you finish handing the surveys out, go back and collect them.

f. Have a time and room already picked out for a Discovery Group (Bible study) so that you can let those interested know about it as you pick up the surveys.

3. Registration lines (same as cafeteria).

4. Creative surveys.

a. Get proper permission from authorities to take the survey.

b. Have banana splits, etc.; before or while people are involved, pass out surveys.

c. Follow the same procedure as above.

5. Follow through. Always get back with anyone who shows an interest on the survey.

I. Setting up a Student Leadership Questionnaire.

1. Determine who the leaders are on campus.

2. Call for an appointment.

3. Use this sample conversation:

"Hello, ________, my name is ________. I am associated with a student group on campus called Campus Crusade for Christ. We're in the process of taking a leadership survey with leaders on campus. We find that leaders are most familiar with the thinking trends of students. Since you're a leader on campus, do you have 20 or 30 minutes when I could meet with you this week to get your opinion on these questions?"

(Make an appointment—day, time, location—and give him your name and telephone number in case something comes up.)

See exhibits:

a. Four-Question Survey—Exhibit #12.

b. Student Leadership Questionnaire—Exhibit #13.

c. National Collegiate Religious Survey—Exhibit #14.

d. Collegiate Religious Survey—Exhibit #15.

e. Black Student Survey—Exhibit #16.

f. Faculty Religious Survey—Exhibit #17.

g. Athletic Survey—Exhibit #18.

h. International Religious Survey—Exhibit #19.

Way of Life Evangelism

Planned witnessing is necessary and exciting! It motivates us to share our faith. We can train disciples through it. It's biblical (Jesus sent His disciples out two by two). It helps us have an organized method of reaching our campus.

Yet, is that the only thing God has called us to? No. Jesus stopped for water on a wearying trip north through Samaria. Disregarding His own needs, He spent time explaning to a seemingly disinterested woman her own need for the Messiah. He later told His disciples that people everywhere need Christ: The fields are white and ready for harvest (John 4:35). 2 Timothy 4:2 says, "Preach the Word, be ready in season and out of season."

Witnessing should be a natural part of our lives. It should become a habit to view each person we come in contact with (waitress, bag boy at a grocery store, salesman) as a divine appointment from God.

Even if we don't have time to go through the Four Spiritual Laws completely with a person, Isaiah 55:11 promises that the Word of God will not return to God void. Our part is to get the message to others—*to share Christ in the power of the Holy Spirit.* God's part is to take care of the outcome—we are to leave *results to God.*

How do I do it?

A. **Pray,** acknowledging the Holy Spirit as your source of power.

B. **Turn the conversation to Christ.** As you're talking casually with someone, use questions or a simple testimony. Say something like:

1. "Here is a book that has meant a lot to me. It talks about how to have a personal relationship with Christ. You will enjoy reading it when you get a break."

2. "Do you think about spiritual things very often?"

3. "Here's something that will answer some of your questions."

4. Share your personal three-minute testimony.

C. Always be prepared.

1. See everyone as an opportunity to talk about Jesus Christ.

2. Have evangelistic tools ready to leave with each person you initiate a conversation with.

    a. Four Spiritual Laws.

    b. Van Dusen Letter.

    c. *More Than a Carpenter* by Josh McDowell.

    d. "Jesus and the Intellectual."

    e. Evangelistic articles, such as "Resurrection—Hoax or History."

    *See Chapter 9 on Evangelistic Literature.

    See Exhibit #10, "Evangelistic Literature."

Our goal is to help the person understand the gospel and give him an opportunity to make a decision to trust Christ. Think creatively of ways to see that accomplished. The ideal is to sit down and share a complete and clear gospel message with the person. If you have only a minute, leave an evangelistic tool. *The Holy Spirit will work.* The more you sow, making the most of every opportunity, the more you will have the joy of reaping and seeing people come to know Christ.

Personal Testimonies

1 Peter 3:15,16 says that we are always to be ready to make a defense to everyone who asks us to give an account for the hope that is in us. One of the best ways that you can be able to explain to others the hope that is in you is through your personal testimony.

Although people can *try* and argue about the veracity of Christianity's claims, (e.g., the historicity of the resurrection, the reliability of the Bible), no one can argue with what Christ has done in your life. Often people are very interested in what the unchanging God of the universe is doing on a personal level. They want to know what Christ is doing in your life!

Examples of appropriate times to use your personal testimony are:

—When you have only a few minutes to talk with someone.

—When you want to give a personal illustration as part of an evangelistic presentation before a group of people.

—When you feel a need to clarify and personalize the Four Spiritual Laws.

A testimony is always more effective when it is organized and to the point. Let's look at four benefits of having a well-organized three-minute testimony.

A. Benefits of a well-organized three-minute testimony.

1. A *well-prepared* testimony can have a direct impact in nearly every witnessing situation. But no matter how well-organized your testimony is, in order for it to be effective, it needs to be given in the power of the Holy Spirit.

2. As one of the most critical tools in your ministry, it is equally *effective* in both large and small groups.

3. It is often more effective than a longer presentation. A well-organized testimony avoids extra material that could distract from the point of personal commitment. The three-minute time limit will force you to be very selective in what you include in your testimony, greatly improving the quality of your presentation.

4. It will help present Christ in such a clear, *attractive,* yet *simple* manner that many who hear it will want to know Him personally. *As you write your testimony, keep in mind that the emphasis should be on personal commitment to Christ and what this can mean in a person's life.*

B. How to write a testimony.

1. Ask the Lord to give you *wisdom* and guidance as you write.

2. Prepare your testimony in such a way that you can share it with *groups* as well as with individuals. Keep your testimony concise and emphasize a personal commitment to Christ.

3. Stay within the three-minute *time* limit.

4. Be *realistic.*

5. Consider your *typical* audience; write and speak to *communicate* to them.

6. Use a three-point outline containing the following. As you begin, choose something typical from your experience that relates well to the non-Christian, and build your testimony around that theme.

    a. What was your life like *before* you received Christ?

        1) What were your *attitudes,* needs and problems? Remember that examples will go a long way toward establishing you as a credible witness in the minds of non-Christians.

        2) Around what did your life *revolve?* What was most important to you? Give specific examples.

        3) What did you look to for *security,* peace of mind and happiness? In what ways did you find your activities not satisfying?

        Avoid a "religious" focus. Do not spend a great amount of time talking about your church activities before your life began to change.

    b. What led to your decision to *trust* Christ? Why did you decide to give Him complete *control* of your life, and how did you make this decision?

    This relates to the specific circumstances that surrounded your decision to ask Christ to come into your life. You could emphasize either the point at which you actually received Christ or the point at which you let Him begin to control your life.

        1) When did you first hear the *gospel?* How? Or, when were you first exposed to dynamic Christianity?

        Try to capsulize the gospel. For example: "That night as they spoke in my sorority it was the first time I can ever remember hearing that God loved me, that He sent His Son to die for my sin which kept me from knowing Him and that all I needed to do was commit my life to Him by asking Christ to come into my life."

2) What were your initial reactions to Jesus Christ?

3) When did you begin to have a *positive* attitude toward Christianity?

4) What was the turning point in your *attitude?*

5) What mental barriers did you experience?

An example of a mental barrier is, "Why should I want to let someone else run my life?" Your testimony should include how that mental barrier was removed.

6) How did you *receive* Christ?

c. What happened after you received Christ?

1) What *changes* did you see in your life—actions, attitudes and problems? (Use specific examples.)

This point relates to the changes you experienced after Christ came into your life or after you gave Him complete control. If you recieved Him at an early age, what happened after you yielded control of your life to Him as Lord?

If the changes you mention correspond to the problems that you expressed in the first part of the testimony, then you will have a constant theme and your testimony will be more effective.

2) How *long* did it take before you noticed changes?

3) What does Jesus Christ *mean* to you now?

As you think about this question, imagine that a non-Christian friend is asking you what Christ means to you. What would you say to describe how important Jesus is to you? Be as descriptive as you can.

C. Action Point.

1. See Exhibits 22 and 23, "Sample Testimony #1 and #2."
2. Ask your friends to take notes under each point of the outline as you informally tell *your* story.

D. Format.

1. Avoid the following terminology.
   a. Don't make statements that reflect *negatively* on churches, other organizations or other people.
   b. Avoid mentioning *denominations.*
   c. Don't use vague terms such as "joyful," "peaceful," "happy," or "changed" without *explaining* them.
   d. Avoid using biblical words such as *"saved," "born again," "converted,"* or *"sin"* without clarifying what you mean.
2. Learn the mechanics of writing a testimony.
   a. Begin with an *attention-getting* sentence or incident.

      Use only attention-getting phrases or rhetorical questions that are natural and won't make your audience tense.
   b. Be *positive* from start to finish.
   c. Be specific. Give enough *details* to arouse interest.
   d. Be *natural.*

      As you write, remember that most people write much more formally than they speak. Often a written, memorized testimony will be delivered in an artificial, stilted manner.

      As a general guideline, do your best to help people understand you and know you.
   e. Be *accurate.*

f. Include *relevant,* thought-provoking experiences.

g. Use one or two *Scripture* verses, but only when they relate directly to your experience and fit in naturally.

For example, you might relate Revelation 3:20 as someone shared it with you. But remember that most non-Christians don't know the difference between 1 Thessalonians and 2 Chronicles. You will distract from your presentation by forcing your favorite, precious verse to fit the context of your testimony.

h. Write a good closing to *complete* your testimony.

Avoid tacking a Scripture verse onto the end of your testimony. It's much better to refer to it in the main body of your testimony where it relates to your experience. Conclude with specific changes you've experienced.

i. Edit and *rewrite* as needed.

See Exhibit #24, "Testimony Worksheet."

The second worksheet is designed to help those who became Christians at an early age to communicate clearly with a non-Christian audience.

Beginning a testimony with statements such as, "I was raised in a Christian home," or "I became a Christian when I was 9," tend to alienate non-Christians. Instead, you should begin by establishing a common point of identity with non-Christians. Share experiences they can understand.

Later, perhaps in the section on how you first encountered dynamic Christianity or how you yielded your life to Christ, you can add a brief explanation of how you became a Christian.

E. Presenting your testimony.

Before you begin to present your testimony, here are some principles to remember so you can communicate effectively to a group.

1. Rehearse it until it becomes *natural.*

2. Share it with *enthusiasm* in the power of the Holy Spirit.

3. Smile often. Ask the Lord to give you a pleasant *expression.*

4. Speak *clearly,* but in a natural, relaxed tone. Speak loudly enough to be heard.

5. Do not talk on the way to or from your seat.

6. Avoid *nervous* mannerisms such as swaying, playing with a pencil or clearing your throat.

   Also, avoid such things as jingling coins in your pocket or using too many "you know's" and "ah's."

7. Avoid arguing or using high-pressure methods in your testimony to obtain decisions for Christ.

   According to the Bible, men and women are born of the Spirit, not through the persuasiveness or logic of others. Don't argue! Don't forget, a successful testimony is one that you give in the power of the Holy Spirit, leaving the results to God.

8. Avoid speaking in a "*preaching*" manner.

   Preaching won't communicate nearly as well as "sharing yourself" with the audience. Speak about personal experiences in your own life to which they can relate. Let the Holy Spirit do the convincing.

9. Action point.

   Practice your testimony with a friend.

   Memorize your testimony and present it to an individual or group, preferably non-Christians.

Chapter 10
Group Evangelism

Luke 4:14ff illustrates that Jesus began His public ministry with a public announcement. Throughout His ministry He spoke to people of all classes and all walks of life. He spoke to large crowds, and large crowds followed Him, hungry to be with Him and to hear His words. From these crowds came individuals needing special healing, and from the crowds came His disciples.

Why is group evangelism beneficial to you? One, like surveys, group evangelism acts as a filter for you to find out quickly who is interested in knowing more about Christ. Two, some people hear the gospel through group evangelism who may never hear it any other way. Three, group evangelism can be one of the most effective ways to build a positive image on campus and create a sense of momentum. Frequently, when a great talk is given in one fraternity, members of others will say, "Hey, did you hear about that speaker in the ________ house?" (However, it can work in reverse, so make sure your presentation is attractive!)

How to present Christ through evangelistic team meetings.

Team meetings have always been one of the important emphases of Campus Crusade for Christ. Thousands of students on hundreds of campuses have been introduced to Jesus Christ through team meetings. No Campus Crusade ministry is complete without a strong team emphasis in the various affinity groups (groups with a common purpose or living situation) on campus. These meetings consist of teams of students and staff informally sharing the reality of knowing Christ in a personal way, as Savior and Lord, in fraternities, sororities and dormitories.

A. Select a team.

1. Choose a team of three or four: an emcee, a speaker and one or two who will give testimonies.

2. Be selective. Consider these qualifications in selecting team members:

   a. Desire to see others come to Christ.

   b. Spiritual maturity.

   c. Teachable attitude.

   d. A good testimony.

   e. Ability to communicate to a group.

   f. Natural affinity with the groups to which the team will be speaking.

   g. Experience at follow-through, although this may not be true of those you are taking for training.

   h. Time to follow-through with those who respond.

3. Choose individuals who are well known, if they meet the above qualifications.

4. Consider using qualified professors and businessmen.

5. Do not, as a rule, have a student give his testimony in his own living group.

6. Realize that certain action groups will be a natural place from which to select a team.

7. Team members should be:

   a. Well-groomed.

   b. Well-trained in Campus Crusade methods.

   c. Spiritually attractive.

8. New Christians on campus may be used to make up teams as soon as they have proven faithful. One very new convert can provide an added punch to the message of any team.

B. Prepare for a team meeting.

1. Secure a list of Greek houses, dormitories, athletic teams and clubs. Include the president's or coach's name when possible. Greek houses and clubs are generally listed in the student activities office, dormitories in the housing office, and athletic teams in the athletic director's office.

2. Form several teams from qualifying students.

   a. Each team should have a team captain who is qualified to give a clincher. A Campus Crusade staff member or a staff-trained person is usually the team captain.

   b. Pray and discuss with the team concerning which groups you should contact first and in what order.

      Consider the influence of the group on your particular campus. Look for students involved in Campus Crusade for Christ who can establish contact within their own affinity group.

      Have each team, as more teams are formed, be responsible for a certain portion of the groups on campus.

3. Prepare and train the team well in advance of the meeting. (The preparation suggested below should not be so judiciously followed that it hinders the Spirit. However, an attractive meeting usually has much training and prayer behind it. You may choose to go through the material in training meetings with the team.)

   a. Help team members prepare a testimony.

      1) Go through how to prepare a testimony, in Chapter 9, with them.

      2) Most students need help in writing a good testimony. A staff member or trained student may find he has to devote most of two sessions, maybe three, to this task before the testimony is written well enough to begin memorizing.

3) A good way to begin is for the staff member to take down on paper the key thoughts as a student relates his experiences. Encourage him to talk until his best ideas begin to come. *Every* man who has found Christ has elements in his story which are genuinely interesting and appealing. Your job is to locate those points and then to capture them on paper so that they will not be lost.

4) As you are listening, when the student uses a particularly good phrase or an expression that catches the ear, jot it down immediately. The fact that the idea is his and not yours makes it doubly valuable. Be sure he remembers it and uses it. Do the same when he tells an unusually interesting experience. *Help him to find and to recognize his best thoughts.*

5) Team testimonies should not be over three minutes or, if really outstanding, not over five minutes.

b. Prepare a clincher.

1) A clincher should be thought out and written out carefully, with a sample clincher from the Campus Crusade director as a guide. (See Exhibit #25)

2) Thoughts should be chosen that would have appealed to you before you became a Christian or while you were in college.

3) Illustrations and examples should be used to make clear the gospel message.

4) The clincher should be memorized.

5) The clincher should be simple and include the following: humorous introduction tying into a serious thought; what is being done on other campuses; distinction between religion and relationship with Christ—always be positive; simple gospel in a winsome and attractive way; in conclusion, a challenge and an explanation of how one can become a Christian.

c. Train them in the material in Chapter 9 on how to make evanglistic contacts.

d. Study the yearbook with the team to get to know the names and faces of those in the house. Save newspaper clippings of the various athletes. Share them with the team and pray for them.

C. Secure a team meeting.

1. Line up as many meetings as possible immediately after the beginning of the semester. They are usually easiest to schedule at this time.

2. For the Greek houses and dorms, approach the president when he is least busy, usually before or after lunch or dinner. Do not call; just go to see him. (It is the usual practice to enter a fraternity house without ringing the doorbell. Check what is customary on your campus for entering sorority and fraternity houses.) On campuses with small fraternity houses, the president may not live in the house. Call him, in this case, and arrange an appointment on campus.

3. Take along a *Worldwide Challenge* and an *Athletes in Action* magazine to show the president or coach.

4. Call club presidents and make an on-campus appointment.

5. Contact coaches during their daytime office hours if possible.

    a. Emphasize the fact that Campus Crusade for Christ is an interdenominational student Christian movement and as such works with churches of all denominations around the world. Explain that you will present basic beliefs and not engage in controversial issues.

    b. Mention to the president anyone known to him who will be coming in with you for the meeting.

    c. Explain to the president the general format of the meeting.

    d. Ask the president when would be a good time to have the meeting, or suggest one or two dates. In a house, suggest a chapter meeting night as the best time, because everyone will be there.

e. Accept the invitation if you are invited for dinner. If you are not invited, you should politely explain that usually the team has dinner with the men or women because it gives an opportunity to get to know one another.

6. Encourage the president to schedule the meeting on his initiative. If the president insists on getting a final decision from all the members of his house, don't press the matter—trust the Lord and pray.

7. After the date is set, check with the members to be sure that they are available and will be present at the meeting. Check with the team members just prior to the date again to see that there are no "slip-ups," and set the time before the meeting to get together for prayer and review of the format.

8. Call the president no more than a day or two before the meeting to confirm the meeting. This serves as a reminder in case the president forgets to schedule your meeting.

D. Observe these principles for the pre-meeting situation in Greek houses.

1. Meet together for prayer and any last minute strategy before going to the meeting.

2. Arrive with the complete team 15 minutes before the meeting (or before dinner in some cases).

   a. Introduce yourself and the members of the team to the person who greets you at the door.

   b. Ask for the president of the house.

   c. Expect to be treated as guests.

   d. Extend yourself as a guest.

3. Be very warm, friendly and casual in your greetings and in talking with those you meet. Be interested in finding out about the other person.

4. Make an effort to remember names, especially those who express an interest in knowing more about Christ.

5. If the house has a housemother, stand when she enters the room. Approach her in a cordial manner. Compliment her about her friendliness or beauty, or something that is true of the house. Often she will introduce herself, or one of the house members will fulfill this obligation. Seldom will you have to take the initial step.

6. If you are there for dinner, enter the dining room first (after the housemother) with a host or hostess, if one has been assigned to you. Be alert for cues. Your conversation should not delay the entrance into the dining room.

7. Seat yourselves in various parts of the dining room so that the team can meet as many as possible. The speaker will usually be asked to sit at the head table beside the president.

8. Watch the host or hostess, the housemother or the president, or the person seated near you during dinner in order to avoid embarrassing mistakes.

9. Sit quietly and do not continue eating while house songs are being sung.

10. Do not center conversation at the table around Campus Crusade or its activities. When questions are asked, answer politely and tell enough to satisfy curiosity, but avoid discussion. Do not witness at the table.

11. Express appreciation for the dinner to the housemother, host, or hostess.

12. Announce the meeting at the dinner table if it is not a required meeting.

13. Allow the housemother to leave the dining room first.

14. Review with the president the procedure of the meeting. This should have been covered with him when the original arrangements were made. However, it is necessary to do it again, because he is not likely to have remembered everything.

15. Give the president a 3″x5″ card with the emcee's name and background on it so that he can give a proper introduction.

16. Ask the president about the team coming in later that night to have a question and answer session with those interested.

E. Observe these principles for the pre-meeting situation in dorms, and clubs and with athletic teams.

In each case, meet together for prayer and any last minute strategy before going to the meeting.

1. Try to schedule the dorm meeting during a mandatory floor meeting. In this case, meet the president before the meeting. Give him a 3″x5″ card with the emcee's name and background so he can make a proper introduction. If the floor meeting isn't possible, you will have to "search and hustle" to get an audience.

2. In clubs, meet the president before the club meeting. Give him the 3″x5″ card with the emcee's information on it. Spread out and sit next to club members. Get to know them before the meeting starts.

3. Athletic team meetings are usually held just before or after a team workout. It's best to watch the team work out several times before the meeting. You become a familiar face to them, and you can begin to recognize many of them; this helps in follow-through.

   a. Meet the coach just before the meeting and review what you want to do. Make any comments you can on recent team performance, etc.

   b. Ask him to introduce the emcee.

F. Present your prepared program.

1. Keep within the time limit. Be flexible. Adjust to unexpected circumstances that would shorten your time. Do not let interruptions disturb your meeting. Ignore them.

2. If you had dinner with the group, express the team's appreciation.

3. Include a *short* explanation of Campus Crusade for Christ, its origin and impact on campuses around the world.

4. Clear up misconceptions and put their minds at ease by stressing the fact that the team is not there to promote religion or to get them to join anything, but simply to present the reality and relevancy of a vital personal relationship with Christ.

5. Identify with those to whom you are talking. Do not talk down to them.

6. Introduce the team members. Comment on each team member's house (if you're in a fraternity or sorority), major in school, participation in athletics or dramatics, and some outstanding activity in which he is engaged.

7. Introduce the leader of the team to present the clincher of the meeting, or present the message yourself.

8. The expanded Four Laws should be used for the presentation.

9. Pass out comment cards.

   a. Have pencils available.

   b. Continue to make general comments while the cards are being completed. This helps you retain the attention of the audience.

   c. Repeat instructions on filling out the cards so that no one is in doubt about what to do.

10. In houses and dorms ask if anyone would be interested in getting together later that evening (e.g., 11:00 p.m.), if the team were to come back.

11. For athletic team meetings, bring one copy of the *AIA* magazine. While they're completing the cards offer to get a free copy to anyone writing "magazine" on the card. Get together with them later and find out their spiritual interest.

12. Secure appointments immediately after the meeting. See Chapter 9 on making evangelistic contacts.

13. Handle cynical or argumentative students through tact and prayer.

    a. Arrange to meet students privately. *Never argue.*

b. Pray silently that the person's heart be changed.

c. Know that most cynical or argumentative people are much closer to making a decision for Christ than many who are indifferent.

14. Thank the housemother, president, coach and any members who are around as you are leaving.

a. Remind them of College Life, discovery groups and other Campus Crusade meetings.

b. Avoid giving the impression that they must become members of Campus Crusade in order the accept Christ.

c. Leave together as a team. Do not leave the house meeting when in a fraternity or sorority.

G. Follow through with students from a team meeting.

1. Review the cards in a private location after the meeting.

a. Have prayer together and give thanks to the Lord for what He did and will do.

b. Evaluate the presentation. Encourage and counsel each other in order to develop a more effective presentation.

c. Pray individually for those who heard the message and responded positively.

d. Plan follow-through strategy while enthusiasm is high and memories of names and faces are clear.

2. Telephone those who are interested in getting together and arrange for an appointment. In telephoning, you could say:

a. "Hello, this is Joe Green with Campus Crusade. I'm contacting some of those who attended the meeting tonight and I'd like to get together with you to talk further about these things. Is there a time we could meet tomorrow?"

b. "Hello, Joe? This is Tom Brown. I'm bringing the material which I promised last night by the house when the men are there so they can have a chance to ask any questions individually. Do you have a break between classes when I can give it to you? What time is good for you?" How about getting together later today or sometime tomorrow?"

c. "Hello, Jane? This Sue Smith from Campus Crusade for Christ. When we were at your house last night, you indicated that you would like to meet to talk further. What time will be most convenient for you? How about getting together later today or sometime tomorrow?"

3. Meet with the group president. Keep a record of those met and of their response.

4. Take any materials to them which they indicated on their comment cards they would like to receive. Never charge for this initial material—ask other Christians to provide literature.

5. *Pray that God will raise up one or more in the living group who will want to see a discovery group get started there.* This group will conserve the fruits of the team meeting and draw others in. Special effort should be given to establishing one or more action groups in each house where the team speaks.

6. Inform living groups of your events.

7. With Greeks and clubs, write a thank you note within two days of the meeting. That's not usually necessary with coaches and dorm presidents (unless the dorm meeting was mandatory). Use note size stationary and make the note personal by writing it by hand.

8. Maintain a card file of houses, dormitories, clubs and teams and the results of any meeting. This aids you in future planning.

9. Forward all names and addresses of students who pray to receive Christ to Arrowhead Springs. They will receive a series of follow-up letters from Bill Bright designed to help them grow in their newfound faith.

H. Even though some will indicate on their comment cards a desire to get together, others will make appointments to talk further if approached properly.

Call on the telephone students who appeared to be interested but who failed to make an appointment. Ask them to meet you for a Coke or coffee. Explore their interest further, but avoid undue pressure.

College Life

A. Establish the format of College Life.

1. Examine the needs of the campus.
2. Consider the talent available: speakers, song leaders, emcees, pianist/guitarist.
3. Evaluate the basic nature of the facilities available.

B. Organize the College Life committee.

1. Plan College Life under the direct supervision of a staff member.
2. Place the Student Mobilization Leader at the head of the student committee for College Life.
3. Sub-committees needed are:
   a. Music (song leader, guitarist)
   b. Entertainment (screen questionable, poorly prepared entertainment)
   c. Skits and announcements
   d. Welcome
   e. Program (students and staff)

f. Refreshments

g. Thank you notes

h. Door prize

4. Chair committees with action group leaders or qualified students.

C. Select an emcee.

1. Spiritual sensitivity and commitment to Christ.

2. Desire to promote the College Life program.

3. Ability to communicate with students.

4. Effectiveness in uniting and directing a crowd.

a. Give an enthusiastic and genuine welcome.

b. Give a brief but well-thought-through explanation of Campus Crusade.

c. Write out a brief but complete introduction of the speaker. Include his name, educational background, present position, expression of confidence.

d. Include singing in your program (if you have a good guitarist and song leader).

D. Prepare and give a nugget talk.

1. The "nugget" is a one-point message answering a practical question about the Christian faith and explaining how to receive Christ. The speaker's purpose is to present clearly and logically how a person can become a Christian. The nugget talk should be informal but not careless in manner, content, or vocabulary. It's not a sermon, but a short talk that should not exceed 12 to 15 minutes.

a. Think in terms of making one point clearly.

b. Present Christ in a positive way.

c. Gauge your talk to your audience.

d. Choose an interesting title.

e. Be convinced of the truth you are presenting.

2. Close with a "pray with me" invitation. For example, say, "I close every meeting in the same way, without apology, because there are always some in a crowd this size who are not sure they have ever come to know Christ as we've talked about Him here tonight . . ." Law Four . . .

E. Arrange for refreshments.

1. Appoint a chairman.

2. Make arrangements in advance for punch bowls, paper cups, trays, napkins, etc.

G. Follow-through.

1. Arrange to meet students personally who have indicated interest.

2. Contact new people who signed the guest book. Phone them within 48 hours for an appointment.

3. Keep a record of all contacts.

Campus Classics

The purposes of a Campus Classic are: 1) to reach a large segment of the campus with the claims of Christ at one time; 2) to mobilize students; 3) to create a big image—i.e., to show that Campus Crusade for Christ is not a small, struggling group on one campus, but that it is a worldwide movement and has a message that all students need to hear.

The Classic is geared to very large audiences, is held infrequently and is a "pull-out-all-the-stops" event. The main attraction may be a speaker, a music group, etc. (See Exhibit #55, listing Campus Classics.) It should be scheduled strategically to contribute to momentum and should not conflict with other large campus events.

A. Evaluate the objective(s) of the Campus Classic.

1. Be sensitive to the needs of the campus. Make a list of the needs.

2. Meet with a group of student leaders to discuss what you want to accomplish with the Classic.

3. Pray that you will understand God's direction as to what He wants to do on the campus.

4. Project into the future to evaluate what the Classic will accomplish.

5. Determine how the Classic will relate to evangelism, follow-up and teaching (this is important).

6. Consider what has been achieved on other campuses through the Campus Classic.

B. Choose and secure a speaker for the Campus Classic.

1. Contact local staff members or the Campus Crusade for Christ Area Office to learn what speakers will be in your area and when they will be there.

2. Consider the attitude of the campus (intellectual, party, apathetic, etc.) to determine the type of speaker you should have. Compare the campus attitude with the speaker's background, personality and topics before inviting him to come.

3. If you have more than one Classic on a given campus in a year, vary the type of program.

C. Choose a date for the Classic.

1. Check the school calendar months in advance (in large schools, more than one year in advance) to avoid conflicts with other major campus activities.

2. Determine the date for the Classic based on the speaker's availability and openings as well as the school calendar.

3. Select a date when the students will be interested in attending (not during exam week, or late spring, especially May).

4. Contact both the university and the appropriate Campus Crusade ministry office for final confirmation when you arrive at a suitable date (see list of speakers, entertainers and their addresses at the end of this chapter). Register the date on all official campus and administration calendars, if possible. This will discourage other groups from arranging meetings on the same date.

Organizing a Classic

A. Mobilize student leadership.

1. Contact local Campus Crusade staff for supervision.

2. Have students, not staff members, give leadership to the Classic. Use the staff as a resource to give you overall direction and encouragement.

3. Mobilize students; this is the key to a successful Campus Classic.

4. See that the student leader and his appointees take the following preliminary steps:

    a. Make proper arrangements with the university administrative officials.

    b. Schedule the program.

    c. Organize student committees.

    d. Get the program on the school calendar.

e. Arrange for the place, housing for the performers, equipment, ushers and the emcee.

f. Print comment cards and tickets.

g. Order needed materials well in advance (consult staff members for the kind of materials and quantity).

h. Invite an interested faculty member to sponsor the Classic if Campus Crusade for Christ is not a recognized group on the campus.

i. Invite the president, vice president, dean of student affairs and other appropriate officials to be your guests at the Classic. Give them recognition when they attend.

B. Organize prayer for the Campus Classic.

1. Begin your planning with a prayer time; share prayer promises, requests and your personal concern for the Classic.

2. Have a prayer subcommittee as part of the Campus Classic committee.

   a. Ask for a volunteer or appoint someone to chair this committee.

   b. Make the Classic a priority in Discipleship Group prayer times.

   c. Have a noontime "prayer and share" meeting—sharing examples of God's leading in preparation for the Classic and sharing prayer requests.

   d. Write to churches, Sunday school classes, home Bible study groups, businessmen, fellowship groups, ladies' missionary societies, or other possible sources. Give them information on the Classic and request their prayer. Report results to them.

   e. Have the women's fellowship organize a prayer chain and involve members of interested churches in praying for the success of the meeting.

C. Raise finances for your operating budget.

1. Present the opportunity to local churches and concerned Christians. Ask if they would like to sponsor a Classic before you secure a speaker. Be confident of finances before you make further arrangements for the Classic.

2. Have the school or an organization at the school sponsor the Classic, or at least supply the facilities.

3. Keep expenses at a minimum. Assign a person to check three places for cost before entering into any contract commitments.

4. Set up an agreement with businesses to pay bills *after* contributions from lay people.

D. Publicize the Classic.

1. Remember, momentum is essential. Start slow, build up, and end big.

2. Personally invite students to come; word of mouth is most effective. Endeavor to get the students excited.

3. In addition to the standard means of publicity, use teasers as well as your own unique and original publicity.

4. Publicize the results and impact after the Classic.

5. To help spread the concept of the student-led ministry to other campuses, invite leaders from other schools to attend your Campus Classic.

E. Hold the Classic.

1. Supply a sharp and qualified emcee.

2. Disperse Christian students throughout the crowd for spontaneous and casual interaction during the meeting, and "divide and conquer" evangelism afterward.

3. Have a "trouble shooter" standing by for any possible last-minute jobs.

F. Follow up interested people.

1. Keep in mind that effective follow-up is necessary for maximum impact.

2. Make sure that students are well trained and organized in advance.

3. Use comment cards to find out audience response. Also, "divide and conquer"—have Christians spread out to share the Four Spiritual Laws, if appropriate, with individuals.

4. Have a back-stage group hand out preassembled packets to Discipleship Group members immediately after the performance, so that they can follow up personally those who respond.

5. Use report sheets to keep track of follow-up progress.

6. Mail out Van Dusen letters immediately.

7. Prepare a program of meetings for the new converts to attend. Use a mass follow-up exchange, a follow-up retreat, or a training class. Most important, channel new Christians into Discipleship Groups.

8. Make certain you have a sufficient supply of the following materials:

   a. Four Spiritual Laws booklets.

   b. Holy Spirit booklets.

   c. Tapes.

   d. Van Dusen letters.

   e. *Athletes in Action* magazines.

   f. Beginning Your New Life booklets.

   g. Discipleship Series booklets.

G. Evaluate the Classic.

1. Realize that proper evaluation means a better Campus Classic next time.
2. Keep records of all that is done.
3. Provide time after the event to evaluate.
4. Note mistakes and offer possible solutions for future use.
5. Get advice from staff members who have been involved with Campus Classics on other campuses.

Classics

Name	Type	Address/Phone
Josh McDowell	Traveling Lecturer	P.O. Box 5585 Richardson, TX 75080 (214) 234-0645
Rusty Wright	Traveling Lecturer, Classroom Lecturing	Campus Office 36-00 Arrowhead Springs San Bernardino, CA 9241 (714) 886-5224, ext. 5200
Tim Downs	Traveling Lecturer	Campus Office 36-00 Arrowhed Springs San Bernardino, CA 9241 (714) 886-5224, ext. 5200
Dick Purnell	Traveling Lecturer	Purnell Ministries International School of Theology 54-90 Arrowhead Springs San Bernardino, CA 9242
Ron Ralston	Traveling Lecturer	P.O. Box 5585 Richardson, TX 75080 (214) 234-0645
Craig Parton	Traveling Lecturer	3313 Arrowhead Ave. San Bernardino, CA 9240

Don Smedley	Traveling Lecturer	P.O. Box 5585 Richardson, TX 75080 (214) 234-0645
Lynn Overton	National Greek Representative	1626 Fordem Ave., Apt. 112E Madison, WI 53704
Crawford Loritts	Traveling Lecturer, Intercultural Ministry	227 Godby Rd., Suite 217 College Park, GA 30349 (404) 761-2936
Santa Fe	Contemporary music	Santa Fe c/o Mike Weist P.O. Box 50086 Indianapolis, IN 46250 (317) 842-1890
Prism	Contemporary music	Music Booking Office 37-00 Arrowhead Springs San Bernardino, CA 92414 (714) 886-5224, ext. 5540
Marajen Denman	Contemporary pop music Lecturer/team meetings	Music Booking Office 37-00 Arrowhead Springs San Bernardino, CA 92414 (714) 886-5224, ext. 5540
Paragon Productions	Evangelistic Multimedia Productions	Paragon Productions 86-00 Arrowhead Springs 86-00 San Bernardino, CA 92414 (714) 886-5224, ext. 1680
Athletes in Action	Basketball, soccer, wrestling, track, gymnastics	Athetes in Action 17102 New Hope St. Fountain Valley, CA 92708 (714) 957-1655
André Kole	Illusionist	Andre Kole Ministry 325 W. Southern Ave. Tempe, AZ 85282 (602) 968-8625

Drama Ministry	Evangeistic Drama	Master's Production Company c/o Jim Simmonds 3255 North Park Way San Diego, CA 92104 (619) 282-0050

Chapter 11
Applying What You Have Learned

A. Pre-evangelism.

Realize that there may be a few times when you can't go straight into the gospel. The person may not be open to listening, or perhaps he has rejected previous spiritual input. *Pre-evangelism is anything you do to prepare a person to hear and respond to the gospel.* It could be as simple as asking insightful questions to get to know a person better, or hosting a dorm party to set the stage for further evangelism, or spending informal time with an international student. Whatever the activity, your goal in pre-evangelism is to let the person know you are interested in him as a person and perhaps to open the door for further opportunity to share Christ with him.

See Exhibit #28 on Sample Evangelistic Socials.

B. Filtering a target group.

Now that you have looked at the different options for evangelism, keep in mind the filter process and how it applies to evangelism.

The first part of the filter process is evangelism. We need to share the gospel and reach people for Christ if we want to see many become multiplying disciples who will go on to help reach the entire world.

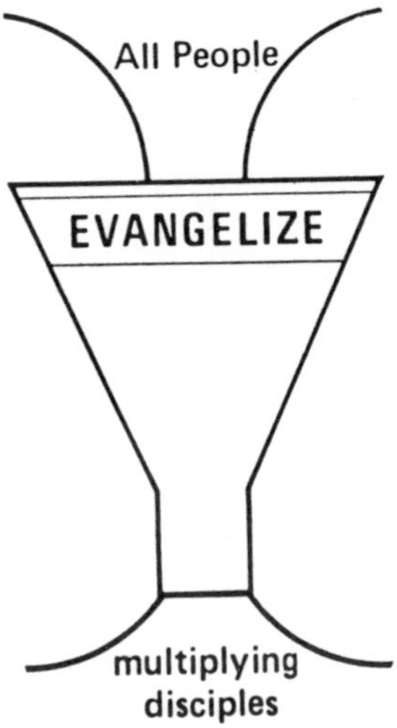

Using the filter process in evangelism, you must "think smart." Instead of randomly finding someone to share with each time—*think:*

"How can I filter through a group of people to find 1) people interested in knowing more about a personal relationship with Christ, or 2) Christians interested in being in a Discovery Group or becoming multiplying disciples?"

You could spend all semester randomly picking people with whom to share the gospel and find only a few who are interested—not really penetrating any area of campus thoroughly. However, through penetrating specific areas or groups (through surveys, group evangelism, etc.) and filtering out interested people, your witnessing time will be more effective. You will know ahead of time that the person you are talking with is interested.

The key to getting the full benefits of the filter process in evangelism is to determine which group would be the best to share the gospel with first. Our goal is to eventually reach everyone on the campus, but some groups have significant influence over other students, and by reaching them first you can reach the rest of the campus more quickly and effectively. So, before you begin to filter a group, decide on your TARGET GROUPS by answering the following questions:

1. What groups are most influential on your campus? Who are the opinion-setters (e.g., poitical leaders, Greeks, R.A.s) who, as they trust in Christ, will be more likely to influence others to do so?

2. Which of those groups are the most easily accessible?

3. What groups would be key in getting a movement going on your campus? Which ones could quickly reach others for Christ? (For example, the freshman class is significant, since these students will be there four years, they will assume leadership positions later, their time isn't monopolized yet, and they tend to be the most open to the gospel.)

C. Action points.

1. Make a list of people to whom you want to present the gospel (individuals or groups), how you plan to contact them, when you plan to contact them and what tools you should be prepared to use (see chart at end of chapter).

2. Be sure you have the right attitude and perspective.

   a. Be filled with the Spirit and allow Him to direct you in evangelism.

      1) Step out in faith and obedience to tell others about Jesus Christ (Acts 1:8; Matthew 28:19).

      2) Follow the Lord's specific leading to share your faith as a way of life (Acts 16:6-10).

      3) Pray that the Holy Spirit will give you sensitivity and tact (1 Peter 3:15; Galatians 5:22,23; 6:13,14).

   b. Pray and ask the Lord to work in the lives of those who hear (Romans 10:1).

   c. Trust the Holy Spirit to do His work (1 Corinthians 2:1-7).

   d. Clearly present Christ (Colossians 1:28). Make sure the issue is clear.

   e. Expect people to respond in different ways (Acts 17:11-13).

3. Study Acts 13 and 14 and answer these questions:

   a. What did God do to prepare the hearts of people?

   b. Who believed?

   c. What did Paul do to witness to them?

   d. What were some of the results?

   e. In what ways can you follow Paul's example?

Who (Target)	**How to Contact** (Filter)	**When**	**Tools**
1. Freshmen	As a group—using the surveys in their dorms.	First week of class, 10:00 p.m.	Four Question Survey, Four Spiritual Laws, Holy Spirit Booklet, Challenge to Discovery Group
2. Sorority or Fraternity President	Individually, using the Leadership Survey. Call and set up appointments.	Beginning of semester or just after elections.	Leadership Survey, Four Spiritual Laws, Holy Spirit Booklet, Challenge to Discovery Group

Chapter 12
The Basis for Follow-Up

Effective follow-up means having clear goals, a plan for accomplishing those goals, a relationship of love with the new believer and the quiet assurance that God is in control of causing the growth.

This chapter discusses the goals of follow-up, the interrelationship of differing components in follow-up, and general principles to remember as you begin to follow-up others.

A. Goals of follow-up.

1. To establish the new Christian's confidence in Scripture as the basis of his faith.

2. To help him understand scriptural principles of spiritual growth.

3. To begin building a friendship with him.

4. To introduce him to God's desire that all Christians communicate their faith with others.

5. To begin developing him into a disciple who can be trained to win people to Christ and build them in their faith.

B. Whose responsibility is follow-up?

1. *The work of God.*

    a. His sovereign plan: In His infinite wisdom God has

chosen, called and given new life to the believer (Ephesians 1:3,4; John 3; 2 Timothy 1:8,9). Yet His work in the new believer's life has only begun. God has a unique plan for his life and He will work to fulfill His purposes for him (Philippians 1:6). Follow-up helps the believer understand what kinds of things God wants to do in his life.

b. Growth: It is through God's Spirit that a person is reborn. God also takes responsibility for growth. "I planted the seed, Apollos watered it, but God made it grow. So neither he who plants nor he who waters is anything, but only God, who makes things grow" (1 Corinthians 3:6,7, NIV). Remember that it is God, and not yourself, who causes the growth. And He can do it!

2. *The work of the Word.*

A newborn needs two things in particular: loving, supportive care and nourishing food. The Word of God is the believer's food. It contains 100 percent of the nutrients we need to live. "Like newborn babes, long for the pure milk of the word, that by it you may grow up in respect to your salvation" (1 Peter 2:2).

3. *The work of the discipler.*

As the discipler, you have the privilege of providing care for the new believer. It is the impartation of your life as well as the growth principles, and it is the example of a Spirit-filled believer living supernaturally. "We were gentle among you, like a mother caring for her little children. We loved you so much that we were delighted to share with you not only the gospel of God but our lives as well, because you had become so dear to us" (1 Thessalonians 2:7,8, NIV). God makes us adequate for the task (1 Thessalonians 5:24; Philippians 4:13). We can trust Him to work through us. We don't want to overstate our role in follow-up because God ultimately does the work, yet we don't want to understate it because God *does* use people to help others grow.

4. *The work of the church.*

In Hebrews 10:25, the author tells us that we are not to forsake the assembling of ourselves together. He says that because Christians need each other. To maintain a healthy, maturing walk with God, we need the fellowship of other Christians in a local church and the in-depth biblical teaching it provides. See also Exhibit #30, "How to Achieve a Balance Between Evangelism and Discipleship."

5. *Spiritual battles.*

   In the parable of the soils (Mark 4:3-20), we are told that it is possible for the Word to be sown and Satan will come and snatch it away. The period immediately after a person receives Christ is a crucial time. Periods of doubts, questions, fears, temptations and misunderstandings can occur. Also, pressures from friends and family about his new faith can cause some wavering. You can be assured that Satan will be attacking him. In John 17:15, we see Jesus was aware of this fact and prayed for His disciples. We need to be aware of the spiritual battle which is taking place, and who the enemy is (Ephesians 6:12), so that we can be of help.

6. *The work of the new believer.*

   No two people grow in exactly the same manner. One may grow quickly while another may become fruitful in the future. People are affected by their environment: the attitude of others around them toward Christianity. They may be affected by their religious background: previous exposure to other Christians and the Scriptures. Yet the greatest determining factor will be the believer's own desire to grow. His desire to know God and obey Him needs to be encouraged to develop by you.

NOTE: God generally uses human instruments in both evangelism and discipleship. However, an overly-sensitive person may become so concerned over the spiritual growth, or lack of it, of those he introduces to Christ that he may begin to feel, "I don't dare lead anyone else to Christ because I just don't have the time to follow him up." Such an attitude is an insult to God. It fails to realize God's great burden for each person's eternal destiny and suggests that God is incapable of ministering to a person's needs apart from us!

Though person-to-person follow-up with those whom you introduce to Christ is desirable, it is also important to get the new Christian involved in some type of group follow-up, while you or another more mature Christian maintains contact.

As the Spirit of God continues to move in the people's hearts, you may be a part of campus- and community-wide efforts in which thousands will be introduced to Christ. Therefore, such follow-up will need to be carried out through small group sessions.

In summary, introduce as many as possible to our Lord Jesus Christ and then encourage them to get involved in groups where they can grow and develop in their commitment to Christ.

C. General principles of follow-up.

1. *Remember that God causes the growth* (1 Corinthians 3:6).

   Refer back to the introduction to this chapter if you still have any questions about this. Understanding this principle is critical to follow-up characterized by trusting God rather than becoming anxious.

2. *Build a relationship with the new believer.*

   Create an environment of love, encouragement and rapport. Become his friend: spend time together having fun. Share yourself with him and share how Christ relates to your life. Learn to be a listener.

3. *Create a desire within him to grow spiritually.*

   Make him aware of his need. Show him how Christ relates to that need by taking him to Scripture that has met a similar need in your life. Get him involved with other believers. Pray for him regularly.

4. *Meeting his need is more important than sticking to a schedule.*

   As you become involved in follow-up, it will soon become apparent to you that, while you may teach everyone the same material, each individual is unique and has different questions. Therefore, your follow-up of one individual will never be exactly like that of any other.

5. *The person is more important than the program.*

   Sometimes it may take three or four appointments to effectively communicate assurance of salvation, while at other times a person may grasp scriptural principles very quickly. Be sensitive to the person and his particular needs. Don't feel you have to fit everything into a rigid structure or schedule.

Chapter 13
How to Follow Up

There are many ways to follow up a new believer. One way to ensure that you are covering material essential to his growth is by using the "Beginning Your New Life" booklets. These booklets were designed to take the believer through five important concepts in a logical manner: assurance of salvation, God's forgiveness, the filling of the Holy Spirit, Bible study and prayer.

By using these booklets, you can be sure of covering enough material to teach the new Christian how to grow. Yet you will not give him so much material that he does not know where to begin.

We begin with the person who has just received Christ. Take him through initial assurance by going all the way through the Four Spiritual Laws booklet immediately after he has received Christ. Also, if you have one with you, give him a copy of the first follow-up booklet, "Beginning Your New Life!" Encourage him to read the first three chapters of the Gospel of John reprinted in the booklet. If you don't have the first booklet with you, plan to give it to him on the first follow-up appointment.

A. How to conduct a series of follow-up appointments.

1. *Appointment #1—Your New Life in Christ*

   After someone has received Christ, you should meet with him again within the next 24 to 48 hours.

   Ask him if he has had a chance to read John 1-3. If he did, ask him if he has any questions concerning what he read. Make sure that you have read these chapters several times and can answer questions he has about the passage.

If you are not able to complete the entire session in the first appointment, feel free to complete it during the second appointment. Our objective is not just to get through a booklet, but to help the new believer have assurance of his salvation and understand how to grow.

See the exhibit "Sample Conversation: First Follow-up Appointment"

NOTE: You will probably be able to answer most or all of his questions. However, if you cannot answer a particular question, don't bluff your way through it! Tell him that you are not able to answer his question adequately right now but that you will do some research and get back to him.

2. *Appointment #2—Your New Life in God's Love*

   The second session covers the basis of forgiveness and discusses how to experience God's love and forgiveness. At this point, you should be thinking ahead and acquainting the new Christian with the idea of sharing his faith.

   Begin to look for natural opportunities to talk about witnessing experiences you have had. Be enthusiastic and positive as you talk about how God has given you opportunities to tell others how they can have a relationship with Jesus Christ.

3. *Appointment #3—Your New Life in the Spirit*

   This session is an amplification of the Holy Spirit booklet and gives the new Christian an opportunity to pray and be filled with the Spirit. Following this appointment you should plan to take the new Christian witnessing.

   Continue to communicate enthusiasm as you invite him to go with you to tell others about Christ. If possible, it is best to set up an evangelistic appointment before you take him with you.

   Put the new Christian at ease by telling him that you want him only to watch you and pray for you as you witness to the other person. He doesn't have to say a thing.

After the sharing time, discuss what he observed and learned. Regardless of the outcome of the witnessing time, be positive about the fact that God is pleased with our obedience and emphasize that the results are in the Holy Spirit's control, not ours.

4. *Appointment #4—Growing in Your New Life*

   The fourth appointment begins to cover some of the principles of Christian growth. The new believer becomes acquainted with the importance of the Bible. This lesson also covers guidelines on how to study the Bible.

   Share with him how you study the Bible. Emphasize that he is studying the Scriptures to get to *know God*; he is not merely studying to learn *about God.*

B. Follow-up appointments for the more mature Christian.

1. *Initial meeting*

   a. Give him a copy of "Your New Life in Christ."

   b. Exchange names and phone numbers.

   c. Make an appointment within 48 hours.

   d. Explain that you'd like to get together and talk about some things that you feel he would appreciate knowing. Add that you would like to try and answer any questions he might have about his relationship with Christ.

2. *First appointment*

   a. Be friendly.

   b. Help him answer his own questions from the Bible.

   c. Discuss assurance of salvation. Many Christians simply do not know for sure that Christ is in their lives and that they have eternal life and will go to heaven.

   d. Close in prayer. If appropriate, suggest that each of you pray briefly.

3. *Continued appointments*

Depending upon his maturity level, challenge him to be in a discovery group or a discipleship group.

Advantages of placing him in a small group:

- Overcomes Satan's attempt to make him feel isolated.
- Demonstrates to him that there are other Christians on campus.
- Provides an informal, relaxed environment for growth.
- Exposes him to others who are applying Scripture to their lives.

C. Follow-up through specific activities.

Follow-up is best achieved through individual relationships and one-to-one appointments. However, there will be times when you are unable to follow up each person individually. When you have a major evangelistic event (a "classic"), there will be many people to follow up. The following means are available when it is not possible, because of time or manpower, to follow up each person individually.

All who receive Christ can be followed up through the following means: Bible studies, discovery groups (see the next section), College Life meetings, literature, tapes, church.

1. Invite them to a Campus Crusade meeting.

2. Introduce them to other Christians, especially those who live with them or who are in an affinity group with them (e.g., club or organization).

3. Tell them about a good church to attend and offer to take them whenever possible.

4. Begin to spend time with them personally, letting them see you in non-ministry situations. For example, eat a meal with them or go to a ballgame together.

5. Remember to listen. Sometimes people will be more honest about their Christian lives in circumstances outside of

appointment times. Let them talk about how they are doing, and make sure you have really listened before trying to give an answer to any problem they discuss.

6. Don't begin to discuss their spiritual struggles with other Christians who can't be involved in helping them.

D. How to follow up long-distance.

1. Correspond by letter.

2. Send the Christians' names to:

    Follow-up Dept. 70-00
    Campus Crusade for Christ
    Arrowhead Springs
    San Bernardino, CA 92414

    (They will receive a letter from Bill Bright.)

    If possible, have other Christians or a Campus Crusade for Christ staff member call on them.

3. Pray for them regularly.

Practical Helps in Follow-Up

Be a friend to the new Christian. Drop by his room. Don't always expect him to come to you.

Learn to ask questions to see if he is grasping the main truths. "Does this make sense?" "Do you have any questions about this?" Ask questions as you relate to them; avoid lecturing.

Never do the thinking for him if you can help it. You don't want him to become too dependent on you. As he learns to evaluate, think through information and draw conclusions on his own, he will grow in his understanding of scriptural truths.

Pray together if the believer is comfortable. Be sensitive.

You can initiate prayer by saying: "It's been good talking with you! Why don't we thank God for this time together before we leave. I'll say a few words (be brief!) and then you can feel free to add anything if you want to."

Approach follow-up as a time of sharing rather than of teaching (Philippians 2:3,4; 2 Timothy 2:24).

Cover only what he can digest in one session. We can't eat six meals all at once. Stick with one main idea each session.

Don't be afraid to admit you do not know all the answers.

Communicate a vision to him as to the significance of his personal abilities and his potential to be used of God, recognizing that Christ never called His men on the basis of what they *were* but rather what they could *become.*

Chapter 14
Using the Holy Spirit Booklet

Many Christians understand the truth of the gospel but do not understand the power of Christ in their lives.

Billy Graham once claimed that 90 percent of all Christians are carnal—that is, they're living defeated, unfruitful lives.

As Spirit-filled Christians, we have the responsibility of explaining to these believers how they can trust the Lord and experience victory in their Christian lives.

Since the Holy Spirit is the source of the powerful, victorious Christian life, it is imperative that we share His ministry with both new and older Christians as soon as we discover that they lack knowledge of this truth. If you haven't already, read Chapter 2, "The Holy Spirit: Our Power Source." It explains the ministry of the Holy Spirit in a way that has been helpful to many, many people.

This booklet explains the ministry of the Holy Spirit in a way that you can easily present to other Christians, just as you present the Four Spiritual Laws booklet.

A. Reasons to share the Holy Spirit Booklet.

1. To show Christians how to live consistent, victorious lives.

2. To make Christians aware that the Holy Spirit's ministry is to give power for living, to teach and to guide.

3. To offer a transferable method of explaining the ministry of the Holy Spirit.

B. When to use the Holy Spirit booklet.

1. *After reading the Four Spiritual Laws booklet.* If a person indicates that his life is represented by the circle with Christ on the throne and that he has received Christ into his life, say:

   "That's great! Tell me about how you received Christ."

   a. This will give you an opportunity to make sure that he understands what is involved in receiving Christ.

   b. If you are certain he does know Christ personally and has assurance of his salvation, proceed quickly through the remainder of the booklet. Then say:

      "There is another booklet that explains how to grow in your Christian life. It has been helpful to me in my own life. Can I explain it to you?"

      NOTE: If he is hesitant, make sure he understands that you aren't "booklet man" with a rainbow of colored booklets covering all problems in the Christian life.

2. *If you are talking with a friend you know is a Christian,* introduce the booklet by using one of these transitions:

   a. "Have you made the wonderful discovery of the Spirit-filled life?"

   b. "I have a booklet that explains how to live the abundant Christian life. I would like to share it with you."

   c. "I have found that every day can be an exciting adventure as a Christian."

   d. "I have discovered how to live the Christian life without feeling as though I'm on a spiritual roller coaster."

   e. "This booklet has helped me in my Christian life. Understanding and practicing these principles has helped me eliminate my emotional ups and downs and has given me peace."

After the person has agreed to listen, share the booklet in a way that will arouse his interest and keep his attention.

C. Using the Holy Spirit booklet.

1. *READ PAGES 2,3 TO THE BOTTOM OF PAGE 3.*
SAY: "This booklet explains how we can go from the life depicted by circle three to that of circle two."

2. *READ PAGES 4,5 TO THE BOTTOM OF PAGE 5*
SAY: "On whom is the spiritual man relying?" (the Lord)

3. *READ PAGES 6,7 TO THE BOTTOM OF PAGE 7*
SAY: "On whom is the carnal man relying?" (himself/his circumstances)

4. *TURN TO PAGES 2 AND 3. POINT TO THE CIRCLES.*
SAY: "Which circle best represents your life? Which circle would you like to have represent your life?"

5. *READ THE TRANSITION ON PAGE 7.*

6. *CONTINUE READING THROUGH EPHESIANS 5:18 ON PAGE 11*
SAY: "This verse contains an analogy in that it compares being controlled by the Spirit with being controlled by wine.

   "When one is drunk with wine, he is under the control of the wine and his behavior is altered. His speech can be slurred and his movements clumsy. When one is controlled by the Spirit, his behavior is also altered. He demonstrates love, joy, peace and all the other qualities that are produced by the Spirit."

7. *READ 1 JOHN 5:14,15. ASK HIM TO PARAPHRASE IT.*
SAY: "If someone tells you to do something, you know that what he has told you to do is his will. Therefore, we know that it is God's will for us to 'be filled,' since He commands it.

   "Although we receive Christ only once, we can be filled with the Holy Spirit many times."

8. *CONTINUE READING THROUGH PAGE 12. AFTER THE PRAYER, ASK IF IT EXPRESSES THE DESIRE OF HIS*

HEART. IF SO, ASK HIM TO PRAY, REPEATING THE PRAYER PHRASE BY PHRASE AFTER YOU.

9. *THEN, CONTINUE READING THROUGH THE BOOKLET TO THE END. READ THROUGH IT WHETHER OR NOT HE PRAYS THE PRAYER ON PAGE 12.*

10. *AS YOU READ THE LAST THREE PAGES, ASK QUESTIONS TO BE SURE THE PERSON UNDERSTANDS THE CONTENT.*
SAY: "Spiritual breathing at first will seem mechanical. But eventually it will become an automatic process to exhale and inhale. The important thing is for us to stay in a right relationship with Jesus Christ and to be empowered by the Holy Spirit."

11. *CONTINUE THROUGH THE BACK PAGE.*
SAY: "I have appreciated being able to explain this concept with you. I know it has been helpful to me. But there is a lot more to be learned as we walk with the Lord.

    "I have a Bible study booklet on the Spirit-filled life that I have found very helpful in understanding further what we have just discussed. Would you be interested in going through that study together?"

12. The Bible study is found in Ten Basic Steps Toward Christian Maturity, Step 3.

PART III
DISCIPLESHIP: STRENGTHENING A MOVEMENT

The most important element in discipleship is not a diagram. It's not a doctrine, a method or a training lesson. It is a person—the Holy Spirit.

The Holy Spirit is the source of growth because He is the source of power. When we neglect the Holy Spirit, we are robbed of power to change.

When the Christian fails to let the Holy Spirit control and empower his life, a cycle emerges. He looks at his life and sees little or no apparent fruit—neither the fruit of the spirit in Galatians 5:22,23 (love, joy, peace, etc.), nor the "fruit" of people coming to Christ. Therefore, he increases his self-effort in an attempt to manufacture fruit. But his attempts to be more Christ-like only make him more like his old self. Sin remains difficult to control, leading to guilt and frustration.

God is in the business of changing lives! He delights in taking the chronic worrier and making him joyful; He takes the hot-tempered man and makes him gentle. God wants to change our lives.

God also causes growth on His timetable. We can't produce a program for growth for our disciples or ourselves. Our growth in Christ is a lifetime process. Like all other growth, growth to Christ-likeness takes time. We are like oak trees, growing slowly but solidly throughout the years. As you read through Part III and think about changing lives, remember who changes them!

Chapter 15
A Biblical Pattern for Small Group Discipleship

In this chapter we will look at the objective of a discipleship group and observe some of the principles Jesus Christ used to accomplish that objective. We will conclude by examining some of the implications for us today.

A. The objective of a Discipleship Group.

1. The objective illustrated by the life of Christ.

   a. Jesus' life was ordered by His objective.

   Robert Coleman says in *Master Plan of Evangelism* that Jesus' life was ordered by His objective *to reach the world*: "Everything He did and said was a part of the whole pattern. It had significance because it contributed to the ultimate purpose of His life in redeeming the world for God. This was the motivating vision governing His behavior. His steps were ordered by it. Mark it well. Not for one moment did Jesus lose sight of His goal."* (See also John 17:4.)

   b. Men were His means of accomplishig that objective.

   Jesus' objective was to reach the world, but men were His means of accomplishing that objective. He knew that the men He chose would be responsible for carrying out the Great Commission after His own ministry on earth had ended. Since His whole plan hinged on these few men, He

*Robert Coleman, *Master Plan of Evangelism*, p. 18. ©Copyright 1964. Used by permission of Fleming H. Revell Company, Old Tappan, New Jersey.

was very careful when "He appointed twelve, that they might be with Him, and that He might send them out to preach" (Mark 3:14).

Discipling by small groups is not the only way that men and women become Spirit-filled and committed to helping reach the world. Although the Holy Spirit is not limited to using only small group discipleship, we will see that this was one of the primary elements of Jesus' discipleship ministry.

2. The objective defined:

The objective of a Discipleship Group is to develop a movement of Spirit-filled Christians who are obedient to God's Word and are actively involved in helping to fulfill the Great Commission in this generation.

B. Jesus' plan.

Let's briefly look at how Jesus developed some untrained men (called His disciples) into responsible, maturing men, capable of continuing this great task of taking the good news to people throughout the world.

1. *He selected a few potentially responsible men* (Mark 3:13,14).

Jesus realized that to accomplish the task of world evangelization, He needed to concentrate on a few men. Jesus devoted Himself primarily to a few men, rather than to the masses, in order that the masses be saved through multiplication. He desired to build into them a depth of maturity and conviction so that they would be able to carry on the task after He physically left the earth. Further, He chose men on the basis of what they would become, not on the basis of what they were (a great principle for us to remember).

NOTE: Jesus evangelized widely and involved many in the ministry before ever selecting His men. See the filter process, Chapter 8.

2. *He spent time with them* (John 15:27).

   Jesus gave high priority to his group of men, and His spending quality time with them was the crux of His training program. They ate, slept, fished and sailed together. Being together enabled the disciples to get to know Jesus and to see His heart for people (Matthew 24:37). The disciples witnessed firsthand Jesus' miracles and teaching. They learned how to pray and worship from His example. Such commitment required Jesus' constant attention and personal sacrifice, which He gladly gave.

3. *He required commitment from His disciples* (Matthew 16:24; Luke 14:25-35).

   If the message of reconciliation were to have any chance of continuing through time and space, it would take men who were willing to go to any length to see that the message was spread. No sacrifice would be too great. Jesus required commitment from His men, and He got it. Most of the disciples died martyr's deaths. In Matthew 16:24, He told them, "If any one wishes to come after Me, let him deny himself, and take up his cross, and follow Me." Jesus did not scatter His time among those who wanted to make their own terms of discipleship. Being a disciple of Christ involved the surrender of one's whole life to the Master.

4. *He taught them in the context of real life experiences* (Luke 5:17-26).

   Jesus' lectures were always accompanied by real life situations that illustrated and applied the principles He taught.

   For instance:

   —He used the calming of the storm on the Sea of Galilee to teach the disciples a lesson on faith (Mark 4:33-41).

   —He used His miracles to demonstrate that He was the Son of God (Mark 2:5-12).

   —He used their mistakes as an opportunity to teach them the correct way to think and act (Luke 9:46-48).

   —He turned His encounters with other people into teaching situations that His disciples could observe (Mark 9:25-29).

5. *He taught them by example* (John 13:15).

The disciples learned from the example Jesus set. He told them, "For I gave you an example that you also should do as I did to you" (John 13:15).

For instance:

—They learned what it meant to be a servant as they observed Him wash their feet (John 13).

—Jesus often let His disciples see Him conversing with the Father (Luke 11:1-13). He didn't force this lesson on them—He just prayed. His example caused the disciples to hunger to pray, and they asked Him to teach them how.

—Jesus demonstrated to the disciples a proper use and understanding of the Scriptures (Luke 24:32).

—The disciples saw His heart to win men and women to Himself (Luke 19:10). Watching Him, they learned how to do it.

6. *He gave them practical assignments* (Matthew 4:19).

Jesus *gave* them practical assignments to help them begin to follow His example. He delegated responsibility to them to witness, baptize, heal and cast out demons: "And He summoned the twelve and began to send them out in pairs . . ." (Mark 6:7). He also gave them administrative responsibilities such as getting food, arranging accommodations and handling money. Such delegation was important because the disciples needed to be able to take over when Jesus left. Also, as they carried out tasks that contributed to the cause, their commitment to the cause grew. Just as a mother eagle teaches her young to fly by pushing them out of the nest, so Jesus taught His men the skills they needed for discipleship by pushing them out into the world.

7. *He watched and supervised them* (Mark 8:17).

Yet, as He pushed, He watched and supervised. After returning from their assigned mission of evangelism and healing, "the apostles gathered together with Jesus; and they reported to Him all that they had done and taught" (Mark 6:30). He heard their reports and shared their joy. But after reports like these, He also explained the practical applications of their experiences to their lives. For example, in Mark 9:25-29, He responded to their futile efforts to heal an afflicted boy by gently rebuking their lack of prayer and belief in God. It is significant that our Lord rebuked His men for a lack of faith, never for a lack of innate ability.

8. *He commissioned them to carry on and finish that which He began* (Matthew 28:18-20, Acts 1:8).

   Jesus did more than simply build character and ministry skills into His men. He also commissioned His disciples to reproduce their lives into the lives of others, just as He had done with them. Therefore, although it would be enough for us to have only Jesus as an example, we also have clear models of the discipleship process in the ministries of the apostles. The book of Acts records how Jesus' disciples spiritually reproduced their lives into the lives of many. Their impact was so great that the non-believers in Thessalonica shouted in rage that these were the men who had upset the world (Acts 17:6).

C. Our involvement.

There was nothing haphazard in Jesus' plan for reaching the world—there was no wasted energy, never an idle word. His objective was clear, and He lived every moment of His life accordingly. Each of us needs to decide if he is going to be obedient to God by having the same objective and plan as Jesus did. It is obvious that the Great Commission of Matthew 28:18-20 is now the responsibility of the body of Christ—the church—in this generation.

"And Jesus came up and spoke to them, saying, "All authority has been given to Me in heaven and on earth. Go therefore and make disciples of all the nations, baptizing them in the name of the Father and the Son and the Holy Spirit, teaching them to observe all that I commanded you; and lo, I am with you always, even to the end of the age" (Matthew 28:18-20).

To fulfill this Great Commission, Jesus has given us a four-fold blueprint:

1. To fulfill Jesus' last command (Matthew 28:18-20) *we must build "multiplying disciples."* A "multiplying disciple" is one who is maturing in his own personal faith with a view to

reproducing his life in the lives of others. He is committed to sharing his faith with others and helping them grow to the place where they too can reproduce themselves spiritually. It is significant to note that Paul followed a similar approach in building multiplying disciples. He told Silas and Timothy to "entrust [his instructions] to faithful men, who will be able to teach others also" (2 Timothy 2:2).

2. To fulfill Jesus' last command (Matthew 28:18-20) we must have the *world* in view as we build multiplying disciples. It is not enough to reach one's own roommate, or dorm floor, or Greek house or athletic team. We must be committed to training others with a mindset (which we must first have) of making disciples for the rest of our lives, wherever we are, with a view to doing this in the whole world. Some may ultimately go to other places of the world. All can talk about the needs in the world, pray for the world, give of their resources so that the world will be reached.

3. To fulfill Jesus's last command to reach the world *we start with our own location and move out from there* (Acts 1:8).

   The disciples started in Jerusalem and then, guided by the Holy Spirit, moved out in wider concentric circles. Similarly, we can best be a part of reaching the world as students by starting in "our Jerusalem." That might first be our dorm floor. Then it might be expanded to our whole dorm, a Greek house or an athletic team. Finally, as the process continues, it could include our whole campus—and beyond!

4. To help fulfill Jesus' last command of building multiplying disciples, we have the *vehicle of a small group.*

   a. If Jesus approached the task of building multiplying disciples by developing a *small group of men*, it is logical to assume this same plan works in our day. Small group discipleship is still an effective plan for us today.

   b. It should be noted that discipling a small group of men is not the only means in which the gospel can be preached and men be built. Jesus did not exclude others from following Him. Nor did He refuse to meet with and minister to the masses. God can and does use a variety of ways to build disciples and perpetuate the news of the kingdom.

But, from observing the ministry of the Lord, it seems that developing a small group of men was a primary element of His ministry.

c. We in Campus Crusade for Christ have combined the biblical *command* to build multiplying disciples and the biblical *pattern* of using small groups into a strategy we call the Discipleship Group. The Discipleship Group concept will help you develop a significant personal ministry of evangelism and disciple building. It will allow you to have a vital role in reaching your campus and the world for Christ!

d. Please note that your total spiritual development does not take place in a Discipleship Group. In addition to the Discipleship Group, you need the influence of your personal study of the Word, earnest consistent prayer and the input and interaction of a local church in order to develop spiritually.

D. The three types of Discipleship Groups.

1. *The Discovery Group* (Vol. 1) will help give your potential disciples the biblical basis needed to find Christ, to live a victorious Christian life and to begin sharing their faith with others.

2. *The Discipleship Group* (Vol. 1) will help your disciples grow to a deeper level of spiritual maturity. They will develop more effective means of winning others to Christ and learn how to disciple those who become Christians.

3. *The Action Group* (Vol. 3) will help teach your disciples the biblical philosophy and methods for starting their own Discovery Group and Discipleship Groups.

NOTE: The Discipleship Series along with a Leaders Guide is available at your local Christian bookstore. You can also order it through Here's Life Publishers, Inc.

Conclusion:

The objective: "For the Son of Man has come to seek and to save that which was lost" (Luke 19:10).

Jesus' plan: "He appointed twelve, that they might be with Him, and that He might send them out to preach" (Mark 3:14).

Our involvement: "As the Father has sent Me, I also send you" (John 20:21b).

Chapter 16
Establishing a Discipleship Group

Selection of our disciples is one of the most crucial steps in the discipleship process. If we do not choose our disciples carefully, then the remaining principles of discipleship may frustrate us and the people we are trying to disciple. In this chapter we will examine Jesus' example of selection and how to go about gathering and challenging potential disciples to the group.

A. Jesus' example.

1. *He depended on God.*

   Looking again at Jesus' example, we see that the most important part of his selection process was His dependence on God.

   "I can do nothing on My own initiative. As I hear, I judge; and My judgment is just, because I do not seek My own will, but the will of Him who sent Me" (John 5:30).

   How much more essential it is for us to depend on the Father and the guidance of the Holy Spirit as we choose and disciple others! *God* is the only one who can give us success or produce fruit through our lives.

   "I am the vine, you are the branches; he who abides in Me, and I in him, he bears much fruit; for apart from Me you can do nothing" (John 15:5).

2. *He prayed.*

   Prayer was another important factor in Jesus' selection of His men.

   "And it was at this time that He went off to the mountain to pray, and He spent the whole night in prayer to God. And when day came, He called His disciples to Him; and chose twelve of them, whom He also named as apostles" (Luke 6:12,13).

   A clear demonstration of our dependence on God is to pray for disciples and expect results.

3. *He took the initiative*

   After Jesus prayed, He then took the initiative to call His disciples, challenging them to follow Him (Matthew 4:17-19). The Lord's initiative began in evangelism and continued to the point of involving and then challenging people to make disciples themselves.

   "Go therefore and make disciples of all the nations, baptizing them in the name of the Father and the Son and the Holy Spirit" (Matthew 28:19).

   After we have prayed for the disciples, we also need to take the initiative to *find, involve* and then *challenge* people to become disciples. This is sometimes a difficult step, but it is a necessary one. It is our active response to our Lord's command in Matthew 28:19.

B. Qualities to look for in potential disciples.

As Jesus chose His men, He looked for particular qualities in their lives. Two important ones were a *desire to know God* and *availability*. After Jesus called Simon and Andrew, they *immediately* left the net, and followed Him (Matthew 4:20). The fact that these men followed Him shows that they had a desire to know Him. The word *immediately* emphasizes their availability to the Lord.

Two other qualities Christ looked for in His disciples were *faithfulness* and *teachability*. Jesus often mentioned the value of faithfulness, as in the parable of the faithful servant (Matthew 25:21).

The disciples demonstrated their teachability by taking the initiative to go to Jesus to be taught (Matthew 5:1,2). We need to remember that a disciple is a *learner*. That's what the word means. Whether we are following or leading, we are *co-learners* in the discipleship process (Matthew 23:8-11). Ultimately it is the Holy Spirit who produçes disciples and disciplers. Discipleship is exciting because we're seeing God at work as we're obedient to Him.

We need to look for people who not only have these four qualities, but also have the potential ability to lead others. Our disciples need to have a potential ability to lead others. Our disciples need to have a potential for leadership that can be developed, even if it is not already evident. To discern if people have leadership abilities, observe their present involvement in leadership as well as their relationships with their peers.

Ask these questions about a prospective Discipleship Group member:

—Does the person have assurance of his salvation? (1 John 5:11-13)

—Does the person have a heart for God? (Matthew 4:20)

—Does the person demonstrate availability? (Matthew 4:20)

—Does the person demonstrate faithfulness? (Matthew 25:21)

—Does the person demonstrate teachability? (Matthew 5:1,2)

—Does the person demonstrate potential ability to lead others? (2 Timothy 2:2)

C. Potential pitfalls.

There are several *pitfalls* along the path of the *selection process*. Knowing what these pitfalls are can help you avoid them as you choose your key disciples.

1. *Loosing sight of our objective.* Our objective is not merely to have our own groups or build our own ministries; *it is to help reach the world for Christ.* Having this clear objective before us will keep us from settling for some other lesser objective that may be reached more quickly.

2. *Choosing people who are not "full of faith."* Acts 6:5a says, "The statement found approval with the whole congregation;

and they chose Stephen, a man full of faith and of the Holy Spirit." We are looking for people who demonstrate the kind of faith that moves them to action—the kind of action that results in a discipleship ministry. Unfortunately, we often spend far too much time trying to disciple someone who isn't responding to the leading of the Holy Spirit to become a man or woman "full of faith." The result is usually a frustrated leader, a follower who is unteachable and a breakdown in the spiritual multiplication process.

3. *Ignoring elements of maturity* that are crucial for a spiritual multiplier. One element is social maturity, the ability to relate well to others. Another is emotional maturity, the ability to follow through on commitments and responsibilities.

4. *Ignoring the potential disciple's ability to influence as well as his sphere of influence.*

   Everyone has some influence on others, and we should capitalize on that influence. However, we often avoid those who have the the greatest influence because we tend to relate to people who are on or below our social-cultural level. For maximum impact, however, we should try to reach and disciple those at the highest level of leadership on our campus. There are two reasons: First, leaders need and want to know God personally just as others do. Second, as leaders trust in Christ and begin to live for Him, they in turn can influence many others. As other students see the change in the leader's life, they will be more open to the gospel themselves. Leaders can reach certain people who may not listen to us. In light of this, we need to begin our ministries with people who can relate, or can learn to relate, to leaders.

5. *Imbalance in group affinity.* Too much affinity among group members can make the group become too in-grown and exclusive. Too little affinity could inhibit the development of friendships. Either extreme could seriously harm the relationships that are so crucial to quality discipleship.

6. *Not taking enough time to gather the right people.* Our objective is not just to start a group, but to trust God to raise up those disciples who have the right heart and attitude to help reach the world for Christ. Jesus did not randomly call twelve men to follow Him. He knew what was in their hearts. We

need to take the time to determine the true commitment and attitudes of those we choose to be disciples.

D. The filter process

Remember the filter process that Jesus used in His ministry (see Chapter 11).

Jesus *evangelized widely* before selecting His men. Jesus then took the initiative to gather or *involve many* interested followers in His ministry allowing them an opportunity to demonstrate faithfulness and a desire to grow. Only then did Jesus *select* and challenge certain ones to be His key disciples.

Like Jesus, we should not be too hasty in establishing our group by settling on the first few people that come our way. We need to keep in mind that discipleship is not the end but rather a means to the end of seeing the world reached for Christ. See Exhibit #44, "How to Achieve a Balance Between Evangelism and Discipleship."

Jesus said, "Go . . . and make disciples." As we enjoy being involved in a life-style of sharing our faith, we can trust God to lift up others who will want to come along with us to help reach the world for Him.

E. Some ways to go about gathering people.

1. Witness to non-Christians—evangelism.

    a. Use the surveys:

        1) Four Question Survey (Exhibit #12)

        2) National Collegiate Religious Survey (Exhibit #14)

        3) Student Leadership Questionnaire (Exhibit #13)

    b. Present the Four Spiritual Laws. (see Chapter 9)

    c. Have people read through the Van Dusen letter. (see Chapter 9 and Exhibit #13)

    d. Hold team meetings: (see Chapter 10)

        1) In dorms.

        2) In fraternities.

        3) In sororities.

    e. Speak at athletic meetings.

    f. Participate in classroom evangelism.

    g. Hold College Life meetings. (see Chapter 10)

    h. Have a campus-wide classic. (see Chapter 10)

2. Talk to Christians who need to get involved.

    a. Invite them to a movement-wide fellowship meeting.

    b. Explain the ministry of the Holy Spirit.

    c. Invite them to a conference.

    d. Follow up new Christians whom you helped lead to Christ.

e. Challenge them to a Bible study or to a Discipleship Group.

f. Invite them to a Leadership Training Class (LTC).

g. Give them a copy of *Collegiate Challenge.*

h. Invite them to a social.

F. Challenging students to a Discipleship Group.

Although discipleship groups may vary in the level of involvement, much of the material presented can be adapted to the needs of your particular situation. Use of a structured challenge will ensure consistency of content as it is transferred throughout the movement, even by third and fourth generation discipleship group members. In using this or any other structured challenge, keep in mind the following guidelines:

1. *Personalize* it by sharing your personal concern and burden for the world in general, and for your campus or community in particular.

2. Have the prospective discipleship group member look up the Scripture passages with you and ask him to read each one aloud.

3. Personally write in your goals. Goals could include reaching the freshman class by the end of the first semester, etc. Enthusiastically paint a verbal picture of what the ministry will look like when these goals are reached.

4. *Share the qualifications* of a discipleship group member in a positive and personal manner. Introduce them from the perspective that you, too, needed to meet these qualifications before you could be a discipleship group member.

5. As you share each qualificiation, ask the prospective discipleship group member what need that qualification fulfills. Review the scripture references if necessary.

   For example:

   a. *Teachable attitude*—one can never learn to be a teacher without being teachable.

b. *Heart for God*—one can never be happy serving Him without a desire to know Him better.

c. *Agrees with aggressive evangelism*—telling others about Christ fulfills Christ's command given in Matthew 28:18-20. Plus, we won't be joyful unless we are witnessing.

d. *Willing to become a Discipleship Group leader*—this fulfills the command to teach others to be teachers. It also fulfills our need to love others and be loved.

e. *Time to invest in the discipleship group meeting*—being in the meetings fulfills the need to be loved and to study the Word together.

f. *Time to invest in witnessing* (same as 3 above).

g. *Time to come to the weekly training or discipleship meetings*—participation in these activities fulfills the command to fellowship together (Hebrews 10:25), plus teaches us to be a leader-teacher (2 Timothy 2:2).

6. As you share the time involvements, explain that strong discipleship groups are impossible without a commitment of time. This requirement is a must.

7. Explain that as a discipleship group member he will receive training in establishing and evaluating goals for his overall personal development. Show him the "Personal Goals and Planning Sheet," Exhibit #3. Explain how this training has benefited you personally.

8. Conclude the challenge by saying something like:

   "So you see, Jim, the discipleship group strategy fulfills some of our deepest personal needs. Not only is our need to love and to be loved fulfilled, but also our joy is made full as we serve God and obey His commandments.

   "The choice is yours, Jim. Don't think that if you don't join the group you are unspiritual. I want you to do what God wants you to do, and only you can decide that. I know this strategy has really helped me, but you'll have to decide for yourself. What do you think you'd like to do?

"Would you like to be part of a discipleship group?"

9. If the prospective member *has a desire* to be involved in a strategy of multiplication but is unsure of how much time he has available, have him fill out a "Time Activities Analysis," Exhibit #4. This will reveal how many hours were unaccounted for in his past week (i.e., wasted) and how balanced his life is (usually quiet time and witnessing are neglected). You can then offer involvement in the discipleship group as a means of helping him balance his life.

10. Secure a definite decision from each person challenged.

    a. Give the person time to think and pray about it. Set up a convenient time to call him (within two to three days) to find out his final decision.

    b. If he responds positively, tell him what day and time the discipleship group meets and set up a time to go witnessing with him.

    c. If he responds negatively, assure him that he is still welcome to participate in the strategy at any time he considers himself ready. Encourage him to get involved in a Leadership Training Class, a discovery group, a retreat, a church program, etc.

    d. Do not pressure anyone; only God can bring the increase.

    e. From time to time, check back with those who chose not to be in a discipleship group initially. Perhaps their attitudes or circumstances have changed so they could now be in a group.

Chapter 17

Recognizing an Effective Discipleship Group

For a discipleship group to be actively involved in helping to reach the world for Christ, three characteristics should be evident in the group:

1. Its members need to exhibit a growing dependence upon and love for Christ.

2. They need to experience a growing love for one another and for other Christians within the body of Christ.

3. They need to have an increasing compassion and concern for a lost world.

In this chapter we will discuss these characteristics, their biblical basis and some problems that may occur.

A. A growing dependence upon and love for Christ.

The most important characteristic of discipleship group members is a complete love for and dependence upon Christ. This quality is foundational to the group's objective and supports the other two characteristics.

1. Scriptural example.

   A good example of this characteristic was the church at Thessalonica. Paul wrote these words to the believers there:

"Constantly bearing in mind your work of faith and labor of love and steadfastness of hope in our Lord Jesus Christ in the presence of our God and Father, . . . For the word of the Lord has sounded forth from you, not only in Macedonia and Achaia, but also in every place your faith toward God has gone forth, so that we have no need to say anything. For they themselves report about us what kind of reception we had with you, and how you turned to God from idols to serve a living and true God, and to wait for His Son from heaven, whom He raised from the dead, that is Jesus, who delivers us from the wrath to come" (1 Thessalonians 1:3,8-10).

The Thessalonians were having a tremendous impact on the world around them, but the foundation of their acitivity was their love for and faith in Jesus Christ. This characteristic is demonstrated in group members' lives by their desire to be conformed to the image of Christ and to serve God wholeheartedly.

A member's true dependence should be on Christ and His limitless resources, not upon the leader or other group members.

2. Problems.

   If group members fail to grow in their love for and dependence upon Christ, some problems will likely arise:

   a. *Introspection*: Members depend more on one another rather than on Christ.

   b. *Lack of power*: Members do not depend on God's Spirit to change their lives and problems.

   c. *Lack of loyalty*: The group shares no common objective.

3. Ways to point discipleship group members to Christ.

   Here are a few ways to direct the group members to focus on Christ, instead of on problems and circumstances.

   a. *Share biblical illustrations and promises*—as well as personal examples—of Christ's sufficiency. Encourage members to claim and personalize His promises for their own needs.

b. *Share examples of biblical characters* who faced problems or circumstances similar to theirs.

c. *Emphasize prayer*, praise and thanksgiving in dealing with difficult or negative circumstances in life.

4. Signs of growing love and dependence on Christ.

   a. Members have an *increased respect for God's Word* and its authority.

   b. They demonstrate *increased obedience* to God's Word.

   c. Each one has a *growing prayer life.*

   d. They demonstrate a *growing faith and confidence in Him.* They are focusing, not on their personal problems, but on Christ, who gives solutions.

B. Growing love and concern.

A growing *love for God* will ultimately result in a growing *love for group members and other Christians.*

1. Scriptural example.

   Centuries ago, during the Roman persecution, Christians met together in subterranean catacombs and attempted to protect their brothers and sisters at the risk of death. Under these circumstances, the early Christians not only persevered, but they also grew in number. This revolutionary growth in the first-century church was directly related to the love and concern the believers had for one another:

   "And they were continually devoting themselves to the apostles' teaching and to fellowship, to the breaking of bread and to prayer. And everyone kept feeling a sense of awe; and many wonders and signs were taking place through the apostles. And all those who had believed were together, and had all things in common; and they began selling their property and possessions, and were sharing them with all, as anyone might have need. And day by day continuing with one mind in the temple, and breaking bread from house to house, they were taking their meals together with gladness and sincerity of heart, praising God, and having favor with all the people. And the Lord was adding to their number day by day those who were being saved" (Acts 2:42-47).

2. Problems.

When members are not growing in love and concern for one another, the following may occur:

a. *The whole body of Christ will suffer* (1 Corinthians 12:26).

b. *A poor example is set* for both Christians and non-Christians (1 Thessalonians 1:6,7).

3. Ways to show love and concern for group members and other Christians.

a. Spend time together outside of group meetings.

b. Ask questions and *be a good listener.*

c. Share both the joys and hurts in one another's lives.

d. Help one another in areas of personal development.

e. Demonstrate love to one another in tangible ways.

C. Growing compassion and concern for a lost world.

As we grow in our love for Christ and for His people, we will also grow in our concern for those who don't know God. Christ's burden for others will become ours.

1. Scriptural example.

"And seeing the multitudes, He felt compassion for them, because they were distressed and downcast like sheep without a shepherd. Then He said to His disciples, 'The harvest is plentiful, but the workers are few. Therefore beseech the Lord of the harvest to send out workers into His harvest'" (Matthew 9:36-38).

2. Problems.

   Here are some problems that arise when this characteristic is not growing in the lives of the discipleship group members:

   a. They lack a vision for reaching the world for Christ.

   b. People die without Christ (2 Corinthians 2:15,16).

   c. They become introverted and focus on each other, not on Christ.

   d. The development of a movement of Spirit-filled Christians who are obedient to God's Word is thwarted.

3. Ways to encourage a growing compassion and concern for a lost world.

   a. *Pray* that each member will realize that people are *dying* without Christ. People need to hear how they can have eternal life in Christ.

   b. Take each member witnessing and demonstrate way-of-life witnessing when with them.

   c. Use the Bible to show them God's desire to see the world reached and saved (2 Peter 3:9).

Chapter 18
Leading the Group

This chapter explains your role as a leader, gives five essential principles of leading your discipleship group, and looks at your weekly schedule.

A. Your role as a leader.

As a leader of a discipleship group, you are to follow the model of Christ's ministry. As you study how He discipled His men, you will find three emphases:

He *taught* them how.
He *showed* them how.
And He *let them do it.*

It is not enough to give spiritual input, though that is a significant part of discipleship. It is not enough just to show your group how something is done. It is crucial that you let your disciples apply what they have seen in you and heard from you. One of the best things you can do for your disciples is to build an environment where they can be involved in *learning, observation* and *application.*

B. Principles of discipleship.

1. Defined objective.

The first principle that the group leader should always keep in mind is to have a clearly defined objective. Dr. Howard Hendricks, professor at Dallas Theological Seminary, once said,

"A leader is one who knows where he's going and is able to persuade others to go along with him."* As mentioned previously, the objective of a discipleship group is to develop a movement of Spirit-filled Christians who are obedient to God's Word and are actively involved in helping to fulfill the Great Commission in this generation. Keeping this objective in focus is crucial to preventing discipling others from becoming an end in itself.

*Dr. Howard Hendricks, "How to Lead I," in *The Ministry of Management,* Steven B. Douglass and Bruce E. Cook. ©Copyright 1972 Campus Crusade for Christ, Inc. Used by permission.

2. Biblical content.

   The second valuable principle is that the leader should provide biblical content. Reliance upon the authority of Scripture is the basic ingredient for discipling group members (Hebrews 4:12; 2 Timothy 2:15; 3:16,17; 2 Peter 1:21).

   We live in a culture that operates on the basis of feelings. We are besieged by man-made philosophies that are often quite subtle, steering us away from God's truths. There is constant pressure on us to conform to these ways of thinking.

   Like the psalmist, we need God's Word to direct our lives: "How can a young man keep his way pure? By keeping it according to Thy Word. With all my heart I have sought Thee; do not let me wander from Thy commandments. Thy Word I have treasured in my heart, that I may not sin against Thee" (Psalm 119:9-11).

   Because studying the Word tests our thoughts and helps us draw principles and conclusions for our lives, it is essential to use Scripture in discipling our group members.

3. Strategy and ministry tools.

   You can have a clearly defined objective, yet never reach it if you don't have a strategy and ministry tools. If a discipleship group leader inspires his disciples with a godly vision for reaching the world, but fails to give them the strategy or training to make that vision a reality, the group will become frustrated and confused.

The following diagram shows a simple strategy for discipling Christians. In this plan, biblical content has been arranged in a sequence of ministry tool lesson plans. These lesson plans ensure that we are discipling a person in the basics of the Christian life while we are accomplishing our objective.

This diagram shows how strategy and ministry tools are used in discipleship.

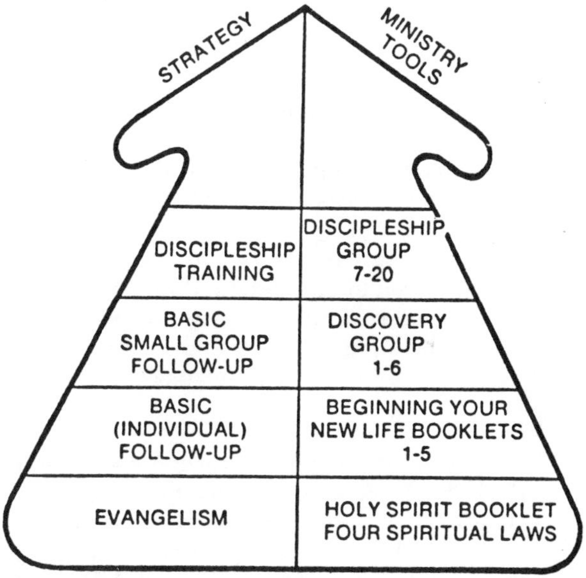

In the diagram we find that our basic tools in evangelism are the Four Spiritual Laws and the Holy Spirit booklets; our tools in individual follow-up are the "Beginning Your New Life" booklets 1-5; in small group follow-up we use the Discovery Group Lessons 1-6 and in discipleship training we use the Discipleship Group Lessons 7-20.

As you develop your strategy, remember to *think!* Ask yourself, why am I doing this? How is this going to help me accomplish my objectives?

Simply having a good strategy and good ministry tools, however, will not ensure discipleship. Another crucial element is the spiritual *environment* or *context* in which your disciples are being trained.

4. Spiritual environment.

   To provide a healthy spiritual environment where your disciples can flourish, you, as a leader, need to 1) give direction in personal growth and ministry, 2) be an example, 3) build relationships, and 4) impart a vision for evangelism.

   a. *Give direction.* A leader may know exactly where he is going, but unless he is able to give direction it will be difficult for his group members to follow.

   b. *Be an example.* "Modeling" means influencing the lives of your group members through the example of your own life and ministry. The apostle Paul said to the Philippian church, "The things you have learned and received and heard and seen in me, practice these things; and the God of peace shall be with you" (Philippians 4:9). Paul also refers to modeling in his letter to the church at Corinth: "Be imitators of me, just as I also am of Christ" (1 Corinthians 11:1).

      Most of us probably wouldn't want to say that to our disciples! This point shouldn't create guilt, however. None of us is perfect, and the Lord accepts us just as we are. But as group leaders, we are in positions of tremendous responsibility. Our disciples will imitate us—in the things we say, in our attitudes toward life, sometimes in our lifestyles and, occasionally, even in our manner of speech! Much more is "caught" than is formally "taught."

   c. *Build relationships.* We should seek to build friendships (1 Thessalonians 2:7-20) that include both encouragement and admonition. As we disciple others, we should be constantly encouraging them to live godly lives. Encouragement is discussed in the book of Hebrews: "And let us consider how to stimulate one another to love and good deeds, not forsaking our own assembling together, as is the habit of some, but encouraging one another" (Hebrews 10:24,25a).

Because we love those whom we are discipling, we may need to admonish them on occasion. The Bible gives us the guidelines for exhorting a brother or sister who is walking in sin. Galatians 6:1 states: "Brethren, even if a man is caught in any trespass, *you who are spiritual,* restore such a one in a spirit of gentleness; looking to yourselves, lest you too be tempted" (italics added).

d. *Impart a vision for evangelism.* The best way to impart to your group members a vision for evangelism is through your own example.

5. Right perspective on circumstances.

The last principle of the discipleship process is that the Lord uses our circumstances to mold us into what He wants us to be. He is the "Ultimate Discipler." He has His own discipleship curriculum, uniquely designed for each of our lives. Various circumstances—in the forms of trials, victories, failures or pressures—drive us to the Lord and result in our spiritual growth (James 1:2-4; Romans 8:28,29).

As disciplers, we will want to help our disciples realize that God desires to build our characters through circumstances (1 Peter 1:6,7).

C. Your weekly schedule.

There are certain things that you must plan into your weekly schedule in order to be an effective discipleship group leader.

1. First and foremost, *set aside quality time* to be alone with the Lord. Your walk with God needs to be your first priority. Unless we have fresh, consistent times with God, our ministries will soon become more of a burden than a joy.

2. *Meet on a regular basis* with your group, spending time with your disciples individually and taking them witnessing.

3. *Reserve adequate time for involvement and preparation* of your ministry.

NOTE: Involvement as a leader within a discipleship ministry requires time and commitment. Jesus never called His disciples to an extracurricular activity but to a life lived for His glory (Philippians 1:21; Luke 9:57-62).

An example: Specify weekly involvement/commitment of a discipleship group leader.

Weekly personal time with your Discipleship Group Leader sharing your faith (1-2 hrs./wk.)	Evangelism always precedes discipleship in building a movement; evangelism exposes potential disciples; ensures time to build a relationship with your leader; provides practical training in effectively communicating your faith through real life situations.
Weekly Discipleship Group meeting of which you are a member (1-2 hrs./wk.)	To study principles in Scripture; build relationships; encouragement; fellowship; vision; direction; to learn how to lead your own group.
Weekly movement-wide fellowship meeting (2 hrs./wk.)	Movement building; find potential disciples; for your own training, vision, encouragement, fellowship, unity; if you don't go your disciples won't go; movement directions and plans.
Leading your own Discipleship Group (1 hr./wk.)	Without it you won't multiply; builds momentum, leadership, knowledge of doctrine.
Weekly personal time with your Discipleship Group members sharing their faith (1 hr./wk./member; 3 hrs./wk. total)	People will receive Christ through your obedience; trains them to share their faith; creates discipline; helps develop way-of-life witnessing.
Any preparation for the above	Preparation aids learning; sets example for others.
Attendance at retreats, conferences, fellowships/socials, ministry prayer times and special events	Increases your own spiritual growth; provides valuable time spent with your Discipleship Group; provides time to get away with the Lord; brings people

	together to make major decisions; often causes accelerated growth in your disciples; contributes to the unity and momentum of the movement.
Local church involvement	Fulfills need to be committed to a local body of believers and Christ's command to do so (Campus Crusade for Christ is not meant to take the place of the church); gets you involved in what will probably be your major area of ministry after graduation.
Fun and recreation with your Discipleship Group members	Builds relationships; provides an opportunity for your disciples to learn from your example.
Availability to serve the movement (example: set up for Leadership Training Class, participate in prayer strategy, organize a fellowship, etc.)	Provides the environment that makes it possible to have such rapidly growing ministries; allows you to be more aware of your strategic part in having a great impact on the campus and the world.

(Total weekly time involvement when you are leading your own discipleship group of three people is between 8 and 12 hours.)

This is not a commitment to be taken lightly. Being a discipleship group leader requires a decision to incorporate the ministry of multiplication into your own lifestyle.

Chapter 19
Conducting the Group Meeting

Conducting your first discipleship group meeting can be an unnerving experience, but with God's power, it will be exciting and rewarding. In this chapter we will discuss the components of conducting a quality small group meeting.

A. Creating the atmosphere.

It's been said that in teaching a small group, the atmosphere you create is more important than the content you communicate. That is especially true in a Discipleship Group. The following list was given by a group of students at a recent Christmas Conference in answer to the question, "What are some characteristics of a quality small group meeting?"

1. An open atmosphere where it is easy to ask questions.
2. A friendly atmosphere, where people think they are special.
3. Warmth is expressed . . . you are accepted by the group.
4. Enthusiasm . . . people are positive and excited about learning.
5. Well planned . . . not just drifting along . . . has clear objectives.
6. Content hits "felt" needs—problems and concerns the group members are experiencing.
7. There is good rapport with the leader.
8. The people in the group have things in common.

Here are their responses to the question, "What does the leader need to do to help produce these characteristics?"

1. He gets together with individuals ahead of time to get to know them.

2. He accepts their answers and encourages good answers.
3. He shows interest in people personally and in what they have to sa
4. He is excited.
5. He states the objectives and summarizes at the end.
6. He knows the material well.
7. He asks good questions.
8. He is not threatened by questions he can't answer.
9. He helps individuals develop their personal walks with God.

B. Teaching the group.

Your role as a teacher is to help your group learn biblical principles in the areas of evangelism, discipleship and personal growth.

This responsibility will involve three steps:

1. Preparing.
2. Conducting the meeting.
3. Evaluating.

1. *Preparing.* Spend time in prayer. Pray that each person in the group will hear what God wants them to learn. Take time to define your goals for the meeting clearly by asking yourself the following questions:

    a. What do I want them to know? (Write it down.)
    b. What do I want them to feel?
    c. What do I want them to do?

2. *Conducting the meeting.* Think through ahead of time exactly how you are going to conduct the meeting. The format normally includes *sharing, Bible study, practical ministry* and *prayer* as a group. This format is designed to give you and your disciples an optimum environment for both spiritual growth and multiplication.

3. *Evaluating:* It's okay to make mistakes and it's inevitable that you will. But in order to be a good steward of your time and resources you need to evaluate each week. This will help you to improve your teaching. Use Exhibit #35, "How to Evaluate a Group Meeting."

NOTE: Included in this manual are some other resources for you to use as guidelines to help you be an effective leader.

Exhibit #34, "How to Lead a Sharing Time," discusses the purpose and benefits of a sharing time and how to conduct one.

C. Determining the content.

1. The content should vary according to the type of group. The lessons are contained in three books:

   The Discovery Group will help give your potential disciples the biblical basis needed to find Christ, to live a victorious Christian life and to begin sharing their faith with others.

   The Discipleship Group will help your disciples grow to a deeper level of spiritual maturity. They will develop more effective means of winning others to Christ and learn how to disciple those who become Christians.

   The Action Group will help teach your disciples the biblical philosophy and methods for starting their own Discovery Group and Discipleship Groups.

NOTE: The Discipleship Series along with a Leaders Guide is available at your local Christian bookstore. You can also order it through Here's Life Publishers, Inc.

D. Equipping the group.

Your role in equipping your members involves spending time with them in practical ministry training. This is an important part of your meeting. It will consist of explaining and role-playing all of the "how-to's" in this manual.

1. *Role-play* is an essential ingredient! Good role-play consists of actually sharing with someone in your group as if they were the person being talked to and then having the entire group evaluate the role play.

   Have them answer these questions:

   —What was good?
   —What needed improvement?
   —How can it be improved?

2. Exhibit #45, "Steps in Building a Disciple," gives you the specific items you will want to cover in training. For example, if most of the members in your group are unfamiliar with witnessing, you need to train and role-play the following:

—How to introduce the Four Spiritual Laws.
—How to present the Four Spiritual Laws.
—How to introduce and present the Holy Spirit booklet.
—How to motivate a new Christian for follow-up.

Chapter 20

Building Relationships With Group Members

At this point you may be wondering: "Where do relationships with people fit in?" "Am I just working with people to accomplish an overall task (i.e., that of reaching the campus)?"

This book is designed to give you a large amount of content in a very usable form. But content doesn't guarantee a great ministry. If you were to examine the lives of those who have successful ministries, one thing would override the content they present: Great disciplers love people and share their lives with others.

John, probably the disciple closest to Jesus, records of his Lord: "Having loved His own who were in the world, He loved them to the end" (John 13:1). Jesus didn't just give lectures on the kingdom of God; He lived with His men and continually showed His love for them. This same chapter of John describes how He washed their feet, giving a graphic demonstration of His loving servant's heart.

In Jesus' ministry, His love for His disciples came first; their development and ministry came next. Like Jesus, you should seek to love each individual; spend time with him, eat with him, get to know him well.

Most mistakes in discipleship occur when we try to present content without *seeing* and *loving* the person. People don't respond to programs. People respond to people who show love. Seek to love an individual as Christ loves him, allowing Jesus to love him through you. Spend about as much time talking about the person and his interests as you spend talking about Christ. Let your own love for Christ be reflected in your love for him.

Study the principles in this manual. They will prove invaluable in helping equip you for ministry and keeping your focus clear throughout all the dust storms of decisions that accompany any ministry. But don't neglect your love for people. Be real with them. It is a disastrous mistake in discipling to think that you should shield your weaknesses and faults from others, as if spirituality means being something other than human.

Share your trials with others. They will learn much more from how you respond to problems than they will from lectures on trusting God. And they will be refreshed to see that you still need a daily dependence on the Holy Spirit to make it through the day.

This chapter will give you some helpful suggestions on building relationships with your group members. We will also discuss how you can spend quality time with them one-to-one.

A. Helpful suggestions.

1. *Phone them frequently* to let them know they're on your mind and are important to you. Don't always call with a specific reason or request in mind. Phone just to say, "Hi!" This takes little time but shows much thoughtfulness.

2. *Relax with them.* Get together for dinner, spend an evening in the living room playing a game, watching a TV program, or discussing a current issue. Get to the kitchen and make popcorn or fudge together. Fix a meal together.

3. *Go places together.* Go sightseeing or camping. See a play or take in a sports event. Attend a Christian conference or meeting. Worship together at your church or theirs. Double and triple date.

4. *Have "special" time together.* Go camping on weekends. Organize a slumber party. Participate in one another's family events, as appropriate. Be at the places and activities that are important to the people in your group.

5. *Do "necessities" together.* Go shopping. Do the laundry. Run errands. Do chores (e.g., wash and wax the car, etc).

6. *Develop spiritually together.* Study the Word. Pray about one another's needs and concerns. Memorize Scripture. Go

together to talk to others about Christ. Work together in church responsibilities.

7. *Study together.* Drill on mutual class assignments. Work together on projects when possible.

8. *Exercise together.* Compete in sports. Play together on a local school, church, or intramural team.

9. *Show special kindnesses.* Visit a group member when he's sick, under pressure, studying or working hard. Drop by with some cookies or a soft drink. Don't stay long. Just let him know you care.

These are suggestions to help you know how to get to know (build a relationship with) your group members. It is not a checklist.

B. One-to-one time.

1. What is it?

Mary had one of her disciples over for dinner one evening. The dinner began to burn, and as Mary opened the oven door she exclaimed, "Oh Lord, thank you! Please show me how to salvage this dinner." Later Mary's disciple said, "You know, Mary, you've talked and talked to me about the Spirit-filled life, but tonight when I watched you handle that burned dinner situation, something clicked. I saw what you were talking about! I get it! The Spirit-filled life is moment by moment. He was right there with you and you depended on Him." Mary's disciple caught something from Mary's life. All that Mary had trained her in came alive right before her eyes.

a. One-to-one time is the time you spend with an individual in your group—talking, listening, building rapport, training through role-play, going witnessing together, doing follow-up together, setting up evangelistic meetings together, and just having fun!

b. It is crucial to the discipleship process because a discipler must get involved in the life of his disciple just as Jesus did! Don't just tell him to have a quiet time. Get together with him to have it! (See below.) Remember, people need to know you love them and care about them before you tell them all you know (content).

c. It is both structured and non-structured, but the primary focus should be on the relationship, not just on the content.

2. Structured one-to-one consists of:

a. *Having a quiet time with your disciple:* pray together; have your individual quiet times silently (different passage of Scripture or same passage); share with each other what you learned in your quiet time; share action points; close in prayer together.

b. *Memorizing Scripture together:* when you meet for your appointment, recite your memory verses for each other, check the accuracy of your group member's recitation; let him check yours (be a co-learner).

c. *Role-playing:* role-play "How to Introduce the Four Spiritual Laws," for example. See Exhibit #31, "Steps in Becoming a Disciple," for other items to role-play.

3. Unstructured one-to-one time consists of:

a. Talking about the Lord: Ask about his relationship with the Lord, what he's learning from the Word, how he's doing spiritually.

b. Talking about his ministry: Ask him about his progress in gathering men for his Discovery Group. How are his guys doing, what help does he need in working with his guys?

c. Talking about fun things: Ask how things are going with the boyfriend/girlfriend; talk about sports and other outside interests. It's important to talk about and do non-ministry things.

d. Sharing about yourself with him: tell him what you feel, think and believe God for.

PART IV
WAYS TO ACCELERATE A MOVEMENT

Chapter 21
Conferences

A student becoming involved in the ministry of Campus Crusade for Christ will soon learn of a host of conferences that are sponsored throughout the year. Conferences ranging from weekend fall retreats to regional five-day Christmas Conferences to week-long evangelistic outreaches at Daytona Beach to summer-long projects are uniquely designed to offer a student a tailored environment in which to grow in his or her relationship with the Lord.

As Campus Crusade for Christ continues to work toward the goal of helping to fulfill the Great Commission, conferences become an increasingly important medium for evangelism, training, fellowship, mutual inspiration and building greater unity and momentum into the total movement. They are essential to the process of *winning* men to Christ, *building* them in the faith and *sending* them into the world to help make disciples in all nations.

A. Benefits of conferences.

Considering the brevity of our time on earth and the mission that God has for us, keep in mind the benefits of a conference.

1. It enables students who do not know Christ to be in an environment where they can investigate the facts concerning His life and claims.

2. It gives students uninterrupted time to reevaluate their relationship with Christ and rededicate their lives to Him.

3. It exposes students to one another, to biblical truth, to training in ministry skills, and to the distinctive features of Campus Crusade.

4. It makes individuals aware of the value of being alone with God as well as the value of fellowship and the mutual encouragement available to all members of the body of Christ.

5. It exposes students to the momentum and excitement of being available to God, as they are given an opportunity to share their faith through the planned witnessing sessions.

6. It functions as a key tool in the ministry of multiplication. Those who attend a conference profit personally, and—as they go on to win and build others—hundreds of other people benefit indirectly.

7. In summary, a conference provides a place for students to draw away from their busy worlds (and busy lives) to meet God in a special way. The conference takes a person out of his immediate environment and places him in an atmosphere where accelerated growth can take place. Historically we see that setting apart a special time for spiritual nurture has been key to many of the great spiritual awakenings.

B. Conferences sponsored throughout the year.

1. *Fall Conference.*

   Usually a weekend conference, this is an excellent opportunity for one or more campuses to build unity and gain momentum in their movements. A fall retreat offers tremendous teaching from God's Word on a variety of themes or topics uniquely designed to meet the needs of those who attend.

2. *Christmas Conference.*

   These five-day regional conferences are held each year during the Christmas vacation break. Usually held in such major cities as Atlanta, Chicago, Dallas, Minneapolis and Philadelphia, each conference draws 1,000 to 1,500 students.

   Always a tremendously exciting time, the conference focuses around a theme designed to meet students' needs. Speakers vary from among some of the most well-known Christian leaders, seminary professors and speakers in the country.

   A wide variety of practical seminars are offered to help you be most effective in *living* and *sharing* the Christian life.

3. *Senior Panic.*

A weekend long conference, "Senior Panic" is designed for men and women who are confronted with the question: "What about the future?"

During this time, conferees give perhaps the most careful consideration they have ever given to their future, as college students and laymen meet to evaluate their life objectives and God's will. Thinking through the question, "How can I invest my life most significantly for the cause of Christ?", they have an opportunity to investigate various directions in which God might be leading.

4. *Operation Sonshine.*

"Operation Sonshine" is a week to be challenged and to share your faith.

Every year during Spring break, thousands of students flood into Daytona Beach, Florida, to find a moment in the sun they hope will last forever. Joining more than 1,000 other Christians from all over the country, you will be involved in helping to tell these hordes of students the life-changing message of Jesus Christ. You will be challenged each morning and evening through messages on various aspects of the Christian life. Afternoons offer opportunities to share Christ with students on the beach while having fun in the sun.

5. *Summer Projects.*

Few other environments can top a summer project in developing spiritual leadership and ministry skills that will equip you for an effective outreach on your college campus. Wherever the projects are—on the beach, in the city, on a ranch, at a national park, or overseas—they offer a nearly ideal environment in which to grow in your relationship with Christ, gain a better understanding of God's Word, increase your skills in evangelism and discipleship, and help influence a community for Christ.

Summer projects are not for everyone; a student must demonstrate many of the same characteristics that would enable him or her to lead a Discipleship Group on campus during the school year. Part of the application procedure also includes recommendations from a Campus Crusade staff member and the student's pastor.

a. *Stateside projects*—those within the United States—are held in beach and resort areas, camping environments, and major cities. These projects enable students to have full-time jobs (waitress, fast food cook, etc.) in the area as well as provide numerous opportunities for them to grow in leadership capabilities.

   Participation in discipleship groups will give you the chance to lead Bible studies as well as learn from Scripture the spiritual qualities of a leader. Campus Crusade staff members will also provide training on the practical application of biblical concepts. The ratio of staff working with students is approximately one to five. Half-way through the project the staff members leave and the students take over.

   What can you contribute to as well as gain from a project? PLENTY! Encouragement to others in faith stretching situations. Lasting friendships. Creative social interaction. A more personal walk with God.

   You will learn the importance of single-mindedness of approach—working with others toward a common goal. You will have the opportunity to see others commit their lives to Christ. At the same time, you will become bolder in your own commitment to Him.

b. *International summer projects* provide opportunities to take part in world missions firsthand as you work with people in Asia, the South Pacific, the Middle East, Europe and Africa. Working with our national and American Campus Crusade staff, you may:

   —enroll in a European university to study a language and minister to other students.

   —participate in classroom evangelism and discipleship.

   —have a ministry on a university campus.

   —work with pastors and churches in evangelism and follow-up.

—participate in large-scale showings of the "Jesus" film.

—join resource teams which canvass several countries (these projects include teaching Leadership Training Classes).

—help administrate an Institute of Biblical Studies or staff training in another country.

As a participant, you will be part of a team of qualified American youth and trained American Campus Crusade staff. The team members will work together to help meet physical and spiritual needs of the nationals in their assigned country.

As a full-time summer missionary, you will have the opportunity to develop a support team of concerned friends who will commit their prayers and financial investments to making the outreach a reality. You will raise approximately $3,000 for the project.

6. *Institute of Biblical Studies* (IBS).

The Institute of Biblical Studies is a three-summer program of graduate-level courses. The entire curriculum is centered on the Bible and has been developed to help equip Christians to be spiritual leaders in a world in crisis.

These courses, taught by highly-respected professors from leading seminaries, are equivalent to a first year seminary education. Credits can be applied toward a master's degree from the International School of Theology, affiliated with Campus Crusade for Christ.

C. Recruiting for conferences.

1. Suggestions to help your Discipleship Group members motivate other students to come to the conferences.

   a. Distribute conference brochures at least a month before the conference.

      1) Give supplies of these brochures to the discipleship groups on campus so that they can distribute them.

2) Give brochures to students on your campus who are interested but are not active in the program.

3) Obtain a mailing list of Campus Crusade student leaders on other non-staffed campuses and mail brochures to them.

4) Send brochures to students on campuses where Campus Crusade is not active.

5) Distribute brochures in collegiate groups at churches.

b. Make a list of all students, then divide the list among the Discipleship Groups to pray for each student.

c. Announce the conference at all get-togethers. Share benefits to motivate students to attend.

d. Have teams of students "hustle out" Christians from surrounding campuses where there is no ministry.

e. Publicize the conference with skits at College Life. Advertise in the campus newspaper.

f. Have students who have been to conferences give testimonies of what God did in their lives as a result of attending.

g. Show a slide show presentation of a previous conference.

h. Encourage students to personally invite others.

i. Organize a calling committee to call students at random—especially international students—and tell them about the conference.

j. Use direct mail to invite hundreds or even thousands of students—both those who have never come to any Campus Crusade for Christ meetings and those who have attended meetings.

k. Keep a file of publicity ideas.

2. Sample informal invitations to use to recruit other students.

2. Sample informal invitations to use to recruit other students.

   "Jeff, I've got something to tell you. In three weeks there's going to be a conference for college students who want to learn more about Christ and the Bible.

   "I'm going because these things have changed my life. There will be 150 students there from all over (name of state) from schools like (name other schools). It is so exciting to be there with so many other committed students.

   "I'd sure like you to come with me. I think you'd really like it. Can you come?"

   (At this point, he will probably ask you about cost, dates, speaker, location, etc. You can give him this information from the brochure. Then give him the brochure.)

   "Jeff, if you need a day or two to think about it, that's great. Tell you what—I'll call you the day after tomorrow to see if you can go. OK? I think you'd love it, and you'd meet some great people. I'll even drive you there if you'd like.

   "Talk to you in a couple of days."

3. Overcoming barriers in the recruiting process.

   Barriers, barriers and more barriers! As we invite people to come along with us to a conference, we can expect a number of them to express a personal barrier that is preventing them from coming.

   Our tendency in these situations is to use an overpowering argument to convince them that they should go. The problem with this type of recruiting is that even if they end up going, they go without their own convictions or they go out of guilt.

   Of course, it's not the process that's going to overcome the barriers, it's the Lord. But we can provide the best environment for God to work in an individual's life to cause him to make the right decisions. By prayerfully weighing all the factors, an individual can better determine whether or not going to a particular conference or project is God's best for him.

   In this section we will examine some principles of motivation and persuasion that can be applied to almost any recruiting situation. These will help you to be more effective in helping people to make the right decisions. On the following pages we will cover:

1. How not to recruit.
2. The key principle in recruiting.
3. A four-step process.
4. An example of this process applied to recruiting for summer projects.

4. How not to recruit.

a. A typical situation of trying to recruit to a summer project:

Our tendency is to try to convince a person by . . .

1) Listing all kinds of good reasons:

—He will learn more about the Bible.
—He will go witnessing.
—He will have fellowship with other Christian students.
—He will develop leadership, etc.

2) Listing Bible verses that will back up our position:

—Joshua 1:8.
—Mark 16:15.
—Hebrews 10:24,25, etc.

3) Attacking his other options:

—He won't be as effective for the Lord by working in a factory.
—He won't get any biblical input.
—He won't be able to do much evangelism.
—He won't develop as a leader, etc.

4) Attacking his reasons for not going on a summer project:

—If he needs to earn some money: "Money isn't eternal, souls are. You need to trust God for money."

5) Summary:

What we've done is to develop an over-powering argument in favor of our cause. What we've said may be true, logical, and biblical. In fact, we may have developed such a convincing, logical, biblical argument, that an individual will find it almost impossible to decide not to go on a summer project without feeling guilty.

b. What does this type of recruiting tend to produce?

1) It tends to produce people who don't know how to think for themselves. (They didn't have to think. We've given them all the answers.)

2) It produces people without personal convictions. (They've simply adopted our convictions, without developing their own.)

3) It generates extrinsic, rather than intrinsic, motivation. (They don't go because they want to, but because *we* want them to.)

4) It causes people to become defensive. (People don't like to be told to be convinced. As soon as they sense that we're trying to persuade them to do something, they'll put up their defenses. Our sinful human nature rebels against the law. If we try to lay down the law, if we try to tell them what to do, they may rebel even if they agree with us.)

5) It results in guilt motivation. (If a person doesn't necessarily want to do what we're trying to get him to do, and we present a logical, convincing, biblical argument for why he should do it, chances are that he's going to feel guilty.)

When people respond out of guilt, one of two things will usually happen:

a) They may agree to do what we want them to do, but in the long run, they will probably drop out. Why? Because people don't like to feel guilty.

They get tired of feeling guilty, and so they stay away from that which produces guilt.

b) They may rebel, in which case we'll probably never see them again.

HOW DO WE DO IT, THEN?

5. The key principle in recruiting.

We need to provide an environment that will nurture the development of an intrinsic motivation—a desire coming from within the individual so that it's something that he wants to do!

He needs to develop a personal conviction!

Our goal is not to convince the individual, but to have the individual convince himself!

(Go back over and contrast the two methods.)

(If an individual has developed personal convictions, if he is intrinsically motivated, if he has convinced himself that this is something that he wants to do, we won't be able to keep him from doing it!)

THAT'S THE PRINCIPLE; HOW DO WE DO IT?

6. A four-step process.

a. *Step I:* Arouse his interest.

1) Expose him to the conference continually from a variety of sources.

For example, when you recruit for summer projects, use the following:

a) Personal testimonies at weekly meetings—"How God used summer projects in my life."

b) People mentioning summer projects during sharing times.

c) Skits about summer projects at your weekly meeting.

d) Comments by the Discipleship Group leader during the Group meeting—"I learned how to do this at the summer project I was on . . ."

e) Summer project slide show at weekly meetings, etc.

2) Remember, you are not trying to force him to make a decision. You are simply attempting to arouse his interest and curiosity!

3) Share; don't preach.

b. *Step II:* Set up an appointment.

1) Make a list of people you want to recruit. Call each one and set up an appointment to get together with them personally.

(Tell him that you're not out to convince him to go, but that you'd like to explain to him what the summer project is all about and to ask him some questions to help him think it through.)

2) Have him come to you if possible!

c. *Step III:* Meet with him.

1) Build rapport and help him to relax, get information needed for close:

—hometown, major, reasons for coming to this college.
—future plans, career.
—family background.
—church background, how he became a Christian.
—options he considers better than going on a summer project.

2) Give him enough information so that he will be able to see how the summer project will meet his needs.

3) Ask questions that will . . .

a) Reveal his needs (both real needs and felt needs).

b) Show how the summer project will meet his needs. (Have him list these things on paper as you go along.)

4) In closing, ask the right questions!

a) Anticipate any objections he might have, and cause him to answer those objections himself.

b) Anticipate other options he might have, and cause him to convince himself that this option is best.

c) Cause him to convince you that he is the type of person that should go on a summer project.

d) Finally, bring him to a point of decision, at which point you get a firm commitment from him.

d. *Step IV:* Follow-up.

1) Warn him of doubts and suggest how to deal with them.

a) Have him read over the list that he made when doubts arise.

b) Explain the "train diagram" and caution him not to go by feelings.

2) Involve him with others who have made the same decision, so that it will be reinforced.

3) Have him share with others why he made that decision. (He needs to keep reminding himself that this is the best thing.)

7. Example: The four-step process applied to recruiting for summer projects.

Recruiting for Summer Projects: Appointment Format.

a. *Gather Information.*

Develop rapport. Ask about his background, family, his Christian life, future plans, etc.

Q. What options do you have for next summer, ______? Which one would you say is your best option?

b. *Provide information.*

—Go over the brochure and point out the different types of projects.

—Explain what a typical U.S. summer project is like.

—He will work at a full-time job, make money, save approximately $600.

—He will live with several other committed Christians; housing is arranged.

—The staff/student ratio is approximately one to five. He will be discipled by a staff member in a small group.

—He will receive teaching from God's Word; his personal walk with God will be emphasized.

—He will receive training in ministry skills by 1) teaching, 2) demonstration, and 3) experience.

—Half way through the project, the staff leave and the students take over.

c. *Answer any questions.*

d. *Benefits.*

Q. How do you think that going on a summer project would benefit you personally?
(Have him list these on a sheet of paper as he is telling you.)

(Below are some of the benefits that you want to make sure he lists. As he lists a particular benefit, *ask* him how the project would help him develop this particular quality.)

—Bible knowledge. (Q. How would a project help you learn more about the Bible?)

—Personal spiritual growth, and character development. (Q. What are some areas in which you want to see growth? What do you feel are some of your weaknesses? How would a project help you develop in each of these areas?)

—Learn and develop ministry skills. (Q. What are some ministry skills that you would like to develop? How would a project help you to develop them?)

—Stretch faith. (Q. In what areas would this stretch your faith?)

—Vision. (Q. How would this expand your vision?)

—Develop relationships. Learn how to relate to all kinds of people, work out problems, etc. (Q. How . . .?)

—Have a ministry in the lives of others. (Q. In what ways . . .?)

—Develop confidence, discipline, etc. (Q. How . . .?)

—Earn money to help pay for school.

—Travel, go to the beaches!

—etc . . .

e. *Close!*

(The purpose of this appointment is not to convince the individual that he should go on a project, but to have the student convince himself that it is something that he wants to do! Therefore, during the "benefits" section of the appointment, and during the "close," your job is simply to *ask the right questions.* Below are some suggested questions to use at this point in the appointment.)

Q. Considering your different options for the summer, how would a summer project be better than (name best option given during "gather information" section of the appointment)?

Q. If you were accepted on a project, your parents might not be real excited about the idea of your going away for the summer. How would you convince them that this would be the best thing for you to do this summer?

Q. Do you have a girlfriend (boyfriend)? He (she) might not be real excited about it either. How would you convince him (her)?

Q. You may not be accepted. Part of the application procedure is a recommendation from a staff member and one from a pastor. Why do you think you should be accepted on a project?

Optional Questions:*

Q. *Do you consider yourself a leader? Why? Are you willing to learn?

Q. *Do you feel you have a teachable attitude?

Q. *Are you the type of person who is willing to step out in faith to do what you know you ought to do, even when you don't feel like it?

Q. Well, ______, what do you think? Would this be the best thing for you to do this summer? Go ahead and fill this out, then. (At this point, hand him the brochure and have him fill it out. Help him select his top five project choices. If possible, collect the registration money right then and mail it in yourself.)

Chapter 22
Weekly Meetings

Weekly meetings provide an element to your movement that no small group can provide: momentum. Without this momentum, you will not have a movement. You will have only a number of small groups.

There are two types of weekly meetings to use in developing your movement: Prime Time and the Leadership Training Class.

Weekly meetings are similar to the time the apostles gathered together with the Lord in the Upper Room. They are designed to provide a place for Christians to gather and be encouraged through singing, teaching from the Word, and sharing what God is doing on campus.

A. Prime Time.

Its purpose is to be a gathering point for Christians where they can grow spiritually and find out what God is doing on campus.

1. *It provides a gathering place for Christians.*

   Attending a weekly meeting allows you to meet other Christians. On some campuses, the Campus Crusade for Christ weekly meetings draw several hundred students.

   You find people coming to the meetings and saying: "I am so glad to find out that I am not the only one on this campus who loves the Lord. Before I came here tonight, I wasn't sure if there were any other Christians on campus."

It is also exciting to see the attendance grow as more people receive Christ through the evangelistic impact of the movement. There is a continual stream of new Christians who are very enthusiastic about their new found faith and want to tell everyone about their Savior.

2. *It provides an environment for growth.*

   Hebrews 10:24,25 says that we are to meet together to encourage one another, "to spur one another on toward love and good deeds" (NIV). The weekly meeting can be a place of refreshment and growth for believers.

   Students are encouraged as they study the Scriptures together. Campus Crusade for Christ staff members are trained in how to speak on topics that will minister to students. They can work with you in determining the needs of the group. If they are not available to speak weekly, the staff can work with you on how to lead a meeting, how to give talks and how to find speakers.

   Students are encouraged to grow as they see the example of others. New believers come and hear how you and other leaders talk with a dormitory president and arranged to show an evangelistic film. A student shares how she has been able to start a Bible study in her sorority because people have heard her talking about Christ and want to know more.

3. *It provides an opportunity to communicate what God is doing on campus.*

   We all need vision. It is exciting to hear what God is doing in the lives of others. And at weekly meetings we can hear what God is doing on other campuses. One campus, for example, is working toward a goal of 1,000 attending their meetings each week.

4. *In acts as the "involvement stage" of the filter process.*

   Prime Time is open to all Christians who are interested in our movement. It shows them something of what we are all about: a movement to build multiplying disciples and to help make the gospel known on campus.

It also allows Christians at all levels of commitment to spend time together. New believers are learning from older believers about walking with the Lord and having a ministry.

5. *Sample Prime Time Format.*

Prime Time (Fellowship)

a. Emcee—introduces meeting sponsored by CCC (5 minutes)
—introduces songleader

b. Songleader—leads singing (10-12 minutes)

c. Emcee—makes necessary announcements (10-12 minutes)
—coordinates skits (if any)
—introduces speaker for the evening

d. Speaker—a 20-30 minute message (20-30 minutes)

e. Emcee—closes meeting (5 minutes) Total: 1 hour

B. Leadership Training Class

As your movement grows, there will be increasing numbers of Christian students who become involved in small groups, or who at least know people in small groups. You will find, however, that many of these Christians lack at least three important things: a knowledge of the Spirit-filled life; training in how to communicate their faith to others; and the ability to teach others through the process of spiritual multiplication. The Leadership Training Class (LTC) is specifically designed to help meet this need.

LTC is broken into three distinct levels: Basic, Intermediate and Advanced. The content of each level progressively moves students to higher levels of understanding and commitment.

1. *Why Leadership Training Class?*

More than two billion of the world's 4.5 billion people have never heard of Jesus Christ. The world needs trained Christians capable of teaching others to be involved with them in helping reach the world for Christ. LTC is a class to train leaders who desire to have a ministry for Christ on campus and want to help teach others the exciting principles they learn about Christian living.

This does not mean that everyone bears the title of "leader" as a result, but means that people act as leaders. A student who joins a church in a new city after graduating would not be recognized as a leader by the congregation, but he can lead others by teaching them how to live the Christ-controlled life and how to share their faith.

2. *What is taught in an LTC?*

Different content is communicated at each level.

a. Basic LTC (5 weeks)

The class presents the foundation for a successful Christian walk in the power of the Holy Spirit and gives training in how to share your faith. Topics include: "How to Experience God's Love and Forgiveness," "How to Share Christ," and "How to Help Fulfill the Great Commission."

b. Intermediate LTC (5 weeks)

These sessions focus on preparing your personal testimony and maturing in your walk with God. Topics include: "How to Have a Meaningful Quiet Time," "How to Prepare a Personal Testimony," and "How to Know God's Will for Your Life."

c. Advanced LTC (10 weeks)

These sessions are designed to help believers continue to grow in their relationship with Christ and learn how to follow up and disciple individuals through small groups. Topics include: "Your Identify in Christ," "The Theology Behind the Four Spiritual Laws," "How to Develop a Discipleship Ministry," and "Being Involved in a Spiritual Movement."

d. Sample LTC Format

1) Emcee—introduces meeting as sponsored by CCC (5 minutes)
—introduces songleader

2) Songleader—leads singing (10-12 minutes)

3) Emcee—makes necessary announcements
—coordinates skits (if any)
—announces LTC classes (Basic, Int., Adv.) and where they will be meeting

4) LTC Class meets (45 minutes)

5) Emcee closes (5 minutes) Total: 1½ hours

3. *How can I have an LTC on my campus?*

Included in the order blank at the back of this book are the LTC Leader's Guide and workbook. They are designed to make it easy for you to teach these classes even if it is your first teaching experience.

Before starting a LTC, talk with your Campus Crusade for Christ staff member. LTC can be a great asset to your movement in the proper stage of development. But it is meant for movements that already have a good core of leadership and a sizeable number of students who not only want to meet weekly, but who also want in-depth training in how to share their faith and how to have a ministry.

Chapter 23
Raising Financial Support

One of the more common barriers that hinders students from attending conferences or summer projects is finances. Students frequently say, "I'd really like to go, but . . . I'm broke," or "I need to save for school next year," etc.

Although these may be sincere statements, many of these students fail to realize that their heavenly Father promises to meet their needs as they trust Him. The apostle Paul states in Philippians 4:19, "And my God shall supply all your needs according to His riches in glory in Christ Jesus."

Barrier or Stepping Stone?

Finances then can either be viewed as a barrier that will keep you from attending a conference or as a stepping stone that will strengthen and enrich your faith. Raising financial support provides an excellent opportunity to trust God.

An opportunity to invest in something significant.

You are about to embark upon the exciting adventure of believing God to develop your finances for a ministry opportunity.

There are many ways you could view this task—as a necessary evil, a requirement, or a means to the end. However, none of these views can be substantiated from Scripture. These views give the impression that asking for money is a less than positive act. It is far from that.

Asking people to invest in you as you attend a Christmas Conference, Operation Sonshine, or an International Summer Project offers them a tremendous opportunity. You are allowing them to become involved with *reaching people for Christ* as you become better equipped to share the gospel and train other students to do the same. Investors become *partners* with you as you seek to see your dorm, fraternity, sorority, campus—even the world—changed as people come into a relationship with Christ.

As you ask people to invest in the cause of Christ, you need to realize that it is, in fact, a great opportunity for them to contribute to something of eternal significance. You will soon see that most people want to give more than you want to ask.

Think a minute about Charles Dickens' classic, *A Christmas Carol.* The three main characters are Bob Cratchet, Tiny Tim and, of course, Scrooge. Now, which of these characters would you consider abnormal? Scrooge, of course, because, at first, he doesn't have the *capacity* to give. Most people, however, want to be givers, and they would be involved with you if you would just simply ask.

Most people want to give, need to give and, in fact, must give. (Giving, by the way, is not limited to money, but also includes love, encouragement, etc.) You are offering people the exciting privilege of giving to a cause that is eternal.

Remember, Jesus said it is more blessed to give than it is to receive. So, be bold as you believe God and ask His people to be involved with you. Also, remember that He has given those He has chosen the desire to give.

A very effective method of raising a personal scholarship for a conference is through letters followed up with a personal phone call. Other methods for raising finances include speaking at your home church, at the church you attend in your college community and to other students on your campus.

On the following pages, we have outlined a way to ask people by letter to invest in your ministry activity. Included are a suggested outline for a special needs letter, things to avoid when writing, a sample letter and description of the letter. Following up each letter by phone or a personal visit is a very strategic step in this process.

We trust that these tools will be of benefit to you.

B. Raising financial support through letters.

1. Brief notes on letter writing.

   a. Use correct grammar, but write in an easy-flowing conversational manner.

   b. Keep type-written paragraphs to no more than six lines. Shorter paragraphs enhance the readability of the copy.

   c. If you have a second page, divide the sentence at the end of page one such that the reader will have to turn to page two to finish reading the sentence.

   d. Keep sentence structure simple. Guard against using incomplete sentences.

   e. Use correct spelling. When in doubt, look it up!

   f. Avoid beginning a sentence with "a," "an," or "the."

   g. Begin sentences with "action" words (such as gerunds) or good connecting words (such as propositions) to keep the interest of the reader and to enhance the flow from one thought to another.

   h. Avoid beginning a paragraph with "I."

   i. Vary paragraph beginnings.

   j. NEVER begin a paragraph with "a," "an," or "the."

2. Preliminary steps.

   a. Ask yourself the following questions:

      —What is your stated objective for writing?
      —When the reader is finished reading your letter, he should be able to take what action?
      —What will the reader learn from your letter?

   b. Then identify your need.

      —What is the reason for your letter?
      —How much is needed?

c. Determine the scope of your appeal.

—Who are you going to ask to meet this need?
—Who is your target audience?

C. Suggested outline for writing a letter.

Now you are ready to begin writing, using the following outline as a guide.

1. *Give your letter a specific date.*

2. *Address your letter to a person—not "Dear Friend"!*

3. *Acknowledge* your relationship with the reader. What can you say that helps the person identify with you? Refer to your last visit, your or his last note, business concerns, sports interests, known struggles, hobbies, etc., to help say, "I KNOW WHO YOU ARE!"

4. *Begin the education* process of your reader by demonstrating the challenge of your ministry—how God is dealing with you. Help the reader focus on the cause for which you serve by sharing your progress, new perspective, new environment, new responsibilities, as they relate to what God is teaching you.

5. In this context, share the new stretching opportunity—an opportunity to attend a Christmas Conference, summer project, etc. Show how this opportunity will cause spiritual growth in your life. Be sure your objective for writing is simply stated.

6. Then *involve your reader* by asking him for specific action, based on the needs that you shared. This can include challenging him to cover part or all of the cost of the conference or activity, stating the deadline you need the money, sharing benefits to you and to the reader as the need is met. *Specific action includes not only your request, but also your commitment to follow up by telephone.*

7. *Acknowledge* your relationship again with an emphasis on thanks, appreciation, gratitude, partnership and commitment. *This ties your opening acknowledgement to your request.*

8. Close the letter and sign.

9. Add a P.S. Commit yourself to specific action that you are taking. Example: "I'll be calling you April 22. I look forward to talking with you."

10. Underline key sentences and paragraphs, but do so sparingly.

D. Things to avoid when writing special needs letters.

When writing a letter for special needs, watch the following:

1. *Never apologize for writing or calling a person* whom you wish to involve in helping you meet a need.

   You are providing him with an opportunity to be involved in spiritual ministry through his resources. Remember, the giver needs to give far more than any person or cause needs to receive a gift. When you apologize, you end up appearing to be a beggar rather than a child of the King!

2. *Never ask for a general amount, with no time frame in which to take action.*

   You should challenge people to give a specific gift, or at least give them a specific range, such as $25 to $500.

3. *Never use "Campus Crusade slang"!*

   Use terms the reader can understand and relate to when you describe your ministry involvement.

4. *Never promise to call and then fail to.*

E. Sample special needs letter.

November 14, 1983

(A) Dear Mr. and Mrs. Johnson,

Continued reports of snow back your way have brought you to mind many times recently. It's always like that just before Thanksgiving. Will your whole family be together this year? I trust that it will be a good time of relaxing and fellowship for you.

(B) This has been a challenging term for me academically. I'm getting into my major more, now that I'm in my third year. Being in the accounting curriculum, I really have to stay on top of things. In most of my classes, we're starting to gear up for final exams. What a relief to have them before the winter break!

(C) Before I transferred to State, our church youth director told me about the Campus Crusade for Christ ministry here. He had acquired some practical ministry skills through Campus Crusade's training while involved in its ministry here. He encouraged me to look the organization up.

(D) Would you believe that I ran into some students involved in Campus Crusade right off! Two girls I met during registration invited me to go with them to Campus Crusade's Leadership Training Classes. I did, and began to learn some basic principles about the Christian life, including how to be sure I'm a Christian and how to effectively communicate the gospel to another person through using my personal testimony and the Four Spiritual Laws booklet.

(E) Putting this into practice, I used a copy of the Four Spiritual Laws to explain to another girl on my dorm floor how she could have a personal relationship with Christ. She was already a Christian and said she wanted to grow more in her faith, so we started meeting once a week for about an hour to study the Bible together.

(F) In October, I attended a weekend retreat sponsored by Campus Crusade, held at a nearby state park. A well-known, respected pastor from Birmingham gave a series of talks on Christian commitment. One of Campus Crusade's traveling speakers was also there, and he spoke on the life of David in the Old Testament. During our free time, I enjoyed getting acquainted with some of the Campus Crusade staff members and students from a neighboring college.

(G) It was such a joy and a privilege to meet and get to know other students who are committed to Jesus Christ! I returned to State Sunday evening refreshed and encouraged, strengthened in my walk with the Lord.

(H) Since attending the retreat, I've been praying about the possibility of attending a regional conference this Christmas in hopes of receiving some in-depth Bible teaching. Campus Crusade for

Christ sponsors about nine of these conferences in different areas of the United States and Canada annually. This will be the sixth annual conference held in Atlanta. I've included with this letter a brochure describing the upcoming conference.

(I) Right now, I'm in the process of putting the finances together. Rather than ask my parents to foot the bill for this, I've decided I'd like to trust God to use individuals He directs to help meet this need. To cover all expenses (registration, lodging, meals and travel), I'm seeking to develop $150.

(J) Presently, I'm writing to several people, asking them to be involved in meeting this need. The $150 needs to be confirmed in time to meet the registration deadline, December 9.

(K) Would you prayerfully consider whether it is God's will for you to help meet this need with a gift of $50. You have both been so encouraging and helpful to me as I have begun to learn to discern God's direction in my life. I am extremely grateful for you! I would
(L) like to call you in about a week to see what you have decided.

(M) Please pray for me, as this is quite a step of faith for me. I've never really trusted God with a specific financial need like this before. He has been so faithful to meet my needs for school. I'm confident that He will meet this need as well.

(N) Again, thank you for your love, concern and encouragement. You have really ministered to me, Mr. and Mrs. Johnson.

Sincerely in Christ,

Susan Stuart

(O) *P.S. I look forward to talking with you next Thursday or*
(P) *Friday.*

F. Description of the sample special needs letter.

Notice the structure of the preceding letter. Any good fund-appeal letter to a *cultivated* friend should follow the format of this letter:

(A) The letter begins with a reference to the relationship. This is ACKNOWLEDGING the past interest, communication or friendship with the person to whom you are writing. The single most overlooked part of an appeal letter to a friend is the OPENING ACKNOWLEDGEMENT. Without this, the letter becomes a cold, impersonal fund appeal.

(B,C,D,E,F,G,H)
These paragraphs lay a foundation and a justification for your writing. Here, you are EDUCATING the reader concerning the circumstances about which you are writing. Notice the natural progression of these paragraphs from the past experiences to the present opportunity.

(I) This paragraph introduces the need for the request that is yet to come.

(J) This paragraph demonstrates the defined scope of your plan.

(K) This paragraph is the specific appeal for the reader to be involved. A specific dollar amount is requested. You could also ask the reader to consider a range, such as $100 to $500.

(L) This paragraph promises a follow-up phone call.

(M) This paragraph focuses attention on the spiritual dimension of the challenge and the need.

(N) This paragraph again ACKNOWLEDGES your relationship to the reader. Gratitude and appreciation are expressed and the couple's name is repeated.

(O) The "P.S." commits you to specific action. This is often the first part of a letter that is read.

(P) The "P.S." has been italicized (or underlined) to draw attention.

Chapter 24

Working With the Administration and Other Groups

A. **How to maintain good relationships with other Christian groups.**

1. Initiate a relationship built on love and trust.

   View other groups as Jesus does and you will not become critical or judgmental. Never criticize them nor defend Campus Crusade. The Lord will take care of problems if we trust Him (1 Peter 5:7). Pray for those involved in other Christian organizations. Love and accept them as Christian brothers and sisters. We are all part of the body of Christ.

2. Share your objectives.

   a. Contact other Christian leaders and inform them of what you are doing. Present the goals, methods and materials to them if they are interested.

   b. Show them a Four Spiritual Laws booklet, explaining that this is what you use to show others clearly and simply how they can have a personal relationship with Jesus Christ.

   c. Never boast about Campus Crusade for Christ. Give to our Lord all the glory for any worthwhile achievements.

   d. Cooperate, but don't compromise on your goals. Unity without union is the philosophy of our ministry.

NOTE: Campus Crusade for Christ is a movement whose goal is the promotion of world evangelism and discipleship. In achieving that goal, we seek to serve the entire body of Christ. We feel that we should adhere to the basic foundational doctrinal issues that God has called us to emphasize: namely, those directly pertaining to the Great Commission, such as the person and work of Christ, and the believer's walk of faith.

For a statement describing the doctrinal beliefs of Campus Crusade for Christ, see Exhibit #38.

3. Understand their objectives.

   a. Accept the fact that there are differences in philosophy and program, and that other groups are accountable to the Lord as we are.

   b. Do not emphasize theological differences.

   c. Don't try to involve the leaders of other groups in our movement. Encourage them to be loyal to their own responsibilities. Pray for God to raise up leaders for our ministry.

4. Keep communication lines open.

   a. Leaders should do things together periodically—play racquetball, have dinner, pray and spend time in the Word.

   b. Seek to get all of the Christians together for a sharing time. Explain the vision of reaching the entire campus for Christ and that "many hands make work light." Find out what the other Christian groups are doing to avoid overlapping efforts.

   c. Go directly to the leader of the group if problems develop. Believe God for the answer. Admit that you were wrong in a situation if you were.

REMEMBER: Campus Crusade is only one part of the body of Christ, and we should *never* communicate that we are trying to reach the world—or even the campus—for Christ *on our own.* It is only as Christians from thousands of churches and organizations become involved in winning people to Christ and building them in their faith that the Great Commission will be fulfilled. Recognize that God has given each individual Christian, as well as each Christian organization, a special and necessary function within the body of Christ.

5. Implement the Trail West agreement.

   In 1971 the national leadership of the major interdenominational Christian organizations working on America's college and high school campuses met. The purpose for this gathering was to pray for the fulfillment of the Great Commission on our nation's campuses and to discuss how each organization could harmoniously interrelate while independently pursuing their common objective—reaching students for Christ. A copy of the agreement can be found in "Trail West Agreement" section.

B. How to interact with campus influencers.

1. How to relate to student government leaders.

   a. Arrange appointments with student leaders. Use the Student Leadership Questionnaire as listed in Exhibit #23. This will give you an opportunity to get to know the leaders, establish rapport with them, and explain the gospel to them at the end of the survey or at a later time.

   b. Have a student leader's banquet or a leadership prayer breakfast. Ask your staff member for ideas and help in putting this together.

   c. Encourage Christian students to run for a student government office.

   e. Become friends with those who are student leaders. Many times they face a lot of pressures and appreciate someone who is friendly and is willing to listen without seeking something for his own group.

2. How to work with your university's administration.

   Because you are a representative of Jesus Christ on your campus, your relationship with administrators is important. You can build a good relationship with them by showing love. Taking the initiative to establish and *maintain* rapport will build trust and understanding, and will result in new opportunities to spread the gospel (1 Corinthians 10:32,33).

a. Present a clear picture of Campus Crusade's purpose and philosophy to administrators.

b. Obtain a faculty adviser and keep him informed of the movement's activities on your campus.

c. Avoid possible misunderstandings by becoming familiar with campus regulations concerning student activities. Admit mistakes when they occur.

d. *Meet* administrators who are in charge of student affairs. Then contact them periodically to keep lines of communication open.

e. Students involved with the movement should seek academic excellence. Encourage them not to allow their ministry activities to jeopardize their studies.

Write to the National Campus Office for a package of brochures containing endorsements from different faculty, administrators and governmental leaders. Giving a brochure to an administrator or faculty member when you meet with him may help to increase your credibility.

3. How to interact with Greeks.

a. Begin by having Christian friends in sororities and fraternities acquaint you with the Greek system. Try to meet their friends and begin to be identified as someone they can talk with on a casual basis.

b. Begin to share your vision for the campus with Greeks who are Christians.

c. Try to expose Christian Greeks to staff members.

4. How to interact with the campus chaplain.

a. Introduce yourself to whomever coordinates student religious activities.

b. Keep him informed of what you are doing.

c. Sponsor a Campus Crusade for Christ speaker for Religious Emphasis Week.

5. How to work with local news media.

   a. Get to know the editor of the campus newspaper. Use a Student Leadership Questionnaire to establish contact and get to know his views.

   b. Encourage Christians to join the newspaper, radio or magazine staff.

   c. Have students submit articles that give a Christian perspective on relevant issues. Be on the lookout for newsworthy topics on which to write, and submit articles to the appropriate news medium. Be sure that your articles are well planned, well written and scripturally sound.

C. How to deal with those who are antagonistic

Most of those to whom we minister will appreciate our sincerity. But in the course of ministry, some may become antagonistic. This is often based upon misunderstandings, especially among Christian brothers and sisters.

1. Have an accepting attitude toward the person who is antagonistic toward you.

2. Meet him with an attitude of grace, trusting that the Spirit will give you wisdom in knowing what to say.

3. Meet *privately* with the person and explain that you would like to know his feelings and thoughts so that you can take steps to prevent this problem from recurring.

4. Listen to him attentively. He may have some valid criticism. Be willing to admit any wrongdoings and ask forgiveness if appropriate.

5. Explain what we are endeavoring to do and some of the results that have been achieved.

6. Do not defend Campus Crusade for Christ.

7. Don't drag out your appointment time with him.

8. Close the meeting in a way that communicates appreciation of his presence and his hurt. Communicate thankfulness that you could apologize and make some restitution.

REMEMBER: Seek reconciliation whenever you detect conflicts among Christians. But realize, too, that all conflicts may not be resolved.

Chapter 25
Campus Crusade Staff

A. Campus Crusade for Christ staff.

It is the privilege of each campus staff member to have as his full-time responsibility the task of helping to reach the campus for Christ through students who are multiplying disciples. Our staff are eager to help answer specific questions about your campus. They can also be of great encouragement to you personally and are available to disciple you as you disciple others.

Where to call:

Contact our International Headquarters:
Campus Crusade for Christ
Arrowhead Springs
San Bernardino, CA 92414
(714) 886-5224
Ask for the National Campus Office.

B. How to order materials.

We have included a list of materials for you to use in starting a movement. If you turn to the last pages of the manual, you will notice several pages describing the tools that are available. To help you get as many materials as possible, Here's Life Publishers has agreed to give you a 40% discount on your first order!

For materials not handled by Here's Life Publishers, we have included addresses and phone numbers of the appropriate distributors.

C. How to receive brochures for conferences.

Contact your staff member for brochures for the conferences listed in Part IV. Or contact the National Campus Office at our International Headquarters.

D. How to work with Christian faculty.

Christian faculty are a tremendous resource for your campus. They often know the overall thinking of the campus, can counsel Christians on career choices, and can provide a very credible witness to non-Christian students. Faculty usually remain on a campus more than the four-year term of most undergraduates. Their continuing presence on the campus can have a lasting effect for Christ.

Christian Leadership is a ministry of Campus Crusade for Christ that seeks to work with university educators—exposing non-Christian faculty to the gospel and helping Christian faculty members have dynamic impact for Christ in their spheres of influence.

Contact:
Christian Leadership
P.O. Box 20882
Dallas, TX 75220

E. How to apply for staff

Write to the Personnel Department 44-00, Arrowhead Springs, San Bernardino, CA 92414 requesting information and an application.

EXHIBITS

Exhibit 1
How to Enrich Your Time With God

The best way to increase the joy and freshness of your walk with God is by developing a habit of daily time with God.

Think back to those carefree days of childhood before you had to go to school. You played outside with friends in the summertime, coming into your house only long enough to eat a hot dog, slurp a cold drink, and grab more toys. Then you ran to meet your dad when he came home each day from work. Dad was greeted with several big hugs and stories of whom you had played with and what you had done all day.

Suppose that one day, after giving your dad his usual hug, you stepped back and exclaimed, "Daddy, I didn't get anything out of that hug! I don't think I'll give them to you anymore if I don't get presents in return."

Your father would have been stunned. He always thought that you enjoyed giving him hugs and talking to him because you wanted to show you loved him, not to get something in return.

Impossible? Yet we often treat our heavenly Father like this, refusing to have daily time with Him because we feel that we aren't "getting anything out of it."

A. The primary purpose for a quiet time is to fellowship with our Father.

1. To fellowship with God means:

   a. To concentrate on who God is as revealed in His Word; and

   b. To allow God to conform us to the image of Christ.

In our quiet time, it is important for us to concentrate on who God is rather than on what we're not. (It's also more encouraging!) And as we focus our attention on God, we will be conformed to the image of His Son. So it is crucial that we have an accurate view of God. This view can be obtained only through His Word.

B. A secondary purpose for time with God is to gain principles and perspectives for living.

1. We discover principles to direct our lives through His Word.

   As finite beings, we cannot know all the factors involved in any decision. But God knows them all and will guide us through His Word (Psalm 119:105).

2. Time with God helps us see life from God's point of view.

   Reality is seeing life from God's perspective. Anything other than His perspective is a distortion of reality.

   Consider Eve in the Garden of Eden. God's perspective was that it would be best for Adam and Eve to be obedient by not eating the forbidden fruit. Satan succeeded in giving Eve a false view of God (that He is overly strict and that He doesn't want them to become like Him). Satan made Eve doubt what God had said. Eve adopted a false view of reality, which led to ruin.

C. These practical suggestions will help you have a rich and rewarding time with God.

1. Set aside a regular time each day to spend with God.

   For many people, morning is best. The most important factor, though, is your alertness. Give God your best time, not your sleepy time.

2. Find a place where you can be alone, free from distractions (Mark 1:35; Psalm 119:18).

3. Have a notebook to record prayer requests and things God is teaching you from the Word.

4. Use variety in your quiet time.

   a. Occasionally have your quiet time in a special place (a "date" with God).

   b. Take a morning to memorize several verses and think about their implications for your life.

c. Listen to Christian music at the beginning of your time to help you think about the Lord.

5. Begin with praise and adoration.

   a. Praise and adore God through song (Psalm 28:7; 100:4).

   b. Praise and adore God through praying His Word back to Him (Psalm 103).

   Read passages of Scripture (Psalms, Old Testament prophets, the epistles, etc.) and pray them back to God, adapting them as worship, praise or requests.

   Listening to God is as important as speaking to God. Allow an unhurried time before God to listen with your heart and mind.

6. Ask God to search your heart (Psalm 139:23,24).

   a. Confess any sins the Holy Spirit reveals (Psalm 66:18; 1 John 1:9).

   As we experience the forgiveness of our sins, we are truly free to fellowship with God. Just think of the freedom that we experience through knowing God! The vast majority of people in the world are burdened with guilt over past mistakes and sins crushing down on them. When a person experiences God's love and forgiveness, that burden of guilt is lifted, and he's free and able to listen to the Lord.

   b. Make certain that you are walking in the Spirit (Ephesians 5:15,18,20).

7. Spend time in the Word.

   a. Have a plan for your daily reading.

   A plan makes your study systematic and keeps you from spending all of your time on a few favorite sections of the Bible. Discover some of the exciting things God has waiting for you elsewhere in His Word.

   b. Read a paragraph or chapter slowly and thoughtfully.

c. Ask yourself questions about how the passage applies to your life.

d. Try reading a passage aloud. (Scripture was written to be heard, not read, by its original audience.)

e. Personalize it by substituting your name in appropriate places and addressing the passage to God.

f. Underline parts of speech.

Notice all the verbs in a passage. Note how the different parts of a sentence work to convey meaning. This can help you concentrate on what you are reading.

NOTE: Remember that these ideas are simply suggestions to make your time in the Word more meaningful; they are not iron-clad rules that you must follow.

8. Spend time in prayer. See Exhibit #6 on how to spend individual time in prayer

D. To get you started . . .

1. I have set aside ______ as my regular time to meet with God.

2. I have picked ______ as my regular place to spend time alone with my heavenly Father.

3. I will begin my study of the Word by studying ____________

Exhibit 2
Personal Bible Study

Have you ever tried to participate in a sport you have never played before—like tennis or raquetball? You may have started to play the way you wanted, but before long you realized that you needed a few lessons on how to play effectively. Some simple "How to's" greatly increased your ability in and enjoyment of the sport. In a similar way, most Christians are interested in studying the Bible, but do not know how to go about doing it. When they learn *how* to be more effective in studying Scripture, they become better at understanding God's Word and can see its truth implemented in their lives.

As we begin to study the Bible for ourselves, it is very important to think through our view of its authorship. Is it actually God's Word and therefore true and eternally relevant? Or is it simply the thoughts and inspiration of men?

Ultimately our views of the authority of the Bible and of the incarnation of Christ are related. For instance, in John 10:34-36, Christ taught that the Old Testament was totally accurate. In Matthew 4:4-7,10, He quoted it as being authoritative. Furthermore, He taught His followers that He was speaking God's own words (John 3:34) and that His words would not pass away, but would be eternally authoritative (Matthew 24:35).

He even said that the Holy Spirit would bring to mind what He had said so that the disciples would preach and write accurately, not depending only upon memory and human understanding (John 16:12-15). Obviously, then, accurate views of the incarnation and of the inspiration of the Old and New Testaments are related.

Your view of inspiration should be related to your personal Bible study and meditation. Even though you believe in the Bible as a unique, written message from God, you would defeat the purpose of God if you failed to apply biblical truths to your life.

Consider some of the purposes for personal Bible study, as revealed in the following passages:

1. Name some practical results of a thorough study of the Word of God (2 Timothy 3:15-17).

2. In Acts 20:32, what does the apostle Paul say God's Word is able to do?

3. How does the truth in Psalm 119:127,128 relate to the relativistic philosophies many people follow today?

4. What should be the effect upon your own life of reading and internalizing the truth of the Bible (James 1:22-25)?

As you prepare to study the Bible, such as during your devotional time with God, it is important to set aside a definite time, find a definite place, and get your tools together. Some very helpful tools include a modern translation of the Bible, a notebook and pen, a dictionary, and possibly a concordance and a Bible dictionary. While these tools are helpful, however, remember that Bible study involves just that—studying the Bible. The other tools are merely to assist you in understanding the rich truths God has for you in His Word. They are not a substitute for reading the Bible.

One of the most helpful and readily applicable procedures to use in Bible study is the three-step approach involving skills of observation, interpretation, and application.

1. Observation: What does the passage say?

   Read it quickly for content.

   Read it again carefully, underlining key words and phrases.

   Ask: Who? What? When? Where? How?

2. Interpretation: What does the passage mean? What is the author saying to his audience?

   Ask God to give you understanding of the passage.

   Consult a dictionary or Bible dictionary for the precise meaning of words.

3. Application: What does the passage mean to me, and how can it be applied to my life?

   Make a list of:

   a. attitudes to change.

b. sins to confess and forsake.
c. actions to take/avoid.
d. examples to follow.
e. promises to claim.
f. other personal applications.

Other suggested Bible study methods:

1. Book Study: The Bible contains many books. Yet God's divine plan to redeem men in Jesus Christ runs throughout the entire Bible. Be careful to consider each book as a part of the whole. Read it through.

    a. Mark and underline key points as God speaks to you through His Word.

    b. Outline the book.

    c. List the principal characters—who they are and what their significance is.

    d. Select from each chapter key verses to memorize, and copy each on a card to carry with you.

    e. List teachings to obey and promises to claim.

    f. Consider the characteristics revealed of God the Father, God the Son and God the Holy Spirit.

    What book would you particularly like to study using this method? (It is best to start with one of the shorter ones.)

2. Chapter study: To get a grasp of the chapter, answer the following questions:

    a. What is the principal subject of the chapter?
    b. What is the leading lesson?
    c. What is the key verse? Memorize it.
    d. Who are the principal characters?
    e. What does it teach about God the Father? Jesus Christ? The Holy Spirit?

f. Is there any example for me to follow?

g. Is there an error for me to avoid?

h. Is there any duty for me to perform?

i. Is there any promise for me to claim?

j. Is there any prayer for me to echo?

Which chapter of which book would you prefer to study, using these questions?

3. Topical study: Take an important subject, such as grace, truth prayer, faith, assurance, justification, regeneration, peace, etc. Using a topical Bible and concordance, study the scope of the topic throughout the Bible. You will find it necessary to divide each topic into subtopics as you accumulate material; e.g., forms of prayer, prayer promises, examples of prayer in Scripture, Christ's teaching on prayer, Christ's ministry as we pray the ministry of the Holy Spirit in prayer, etc.

   What topic do you plan to study first?

   How much time have you scheduled for it?

4. Biographical study: There are 2,930 people mentioned in the Bible. The lives of many of these make extremely interesting biographical studies (1 Corinthians 10:1f; Romans 15:4). Using a concordance, topical Bible, or the proper name index in your Bible, look up every reference to the person in question. Answer the following questions:

   a. What was the social and political atmosphere in which he lived?

   b. How did that affect his life?

   c. What do we know of his family?

   d. What kind of training did he have in his youth?

   e. What did he accomplish during his life?

   f. Was there a great crisis in his life? If so, how did he face it?

   g. What were his outstanding character traits?

h. Who were his friends? What kind of people were they?

i. What influence did they have on him? What influence did he have on them?

j. Does his life show any development of character?

k. What was his experience with God? Notice his prayer life, his faith, his service to God, his knowledge of God's Word, his courage in witnessing, and his attitude toward the worship of God.

l. Were any particular faults evident in his life?

m. Was there any outstanding sin in his life? Under what circumstances did he commit this sin? What was its nature and its effect on his life?

n. What were his children like?

o. Was he a type or antitype of Christ?

p. Was there some lesson in this person's life that was outstanding to you?

Name the person you would like to study.

What is your reason for choosing that particular person?

You have probably been exposed to or used one or more of these methods already. But Bible study methods were meant to be used regularly, or else they soon become useless. There should be enough variety in these methods to allow you to keep yourself fresh in your intake of God's Word. Happy studying!

Action point:

Develop a two-week strategy for studying the Bible 30 minutes a day on at least two days per week.

Exhibit 3
Personal Goals and Planning Sheet

Introduction

A. Scripture gives the basis for planning and goal-setting.

1. Luke 2:52—"And Jesus kept increasing in wisdom [mental] and stature [physical], and in favor with God [spiritual] and men [social]."

2. 1 Corinthians 9:26—"Therefore I run in such a way, as not without aim."

3. Philippians 2:13—"For God is at work within you, helping you want to obey Him, and then helping you do what He wants" (Living Bible).

B. At the beginning of your planning time, pray and meditate on the past year of your life. List areas you feel God is impressing you to seek improvement in.

1. ______________________________
2. ______________________________
3. ______________________________
4. ______________________________
5. ______________________________
6. ______________________________
7. ______________________________

C. Below are questions designed to help you think through the following areas of your life: spiritual, mental, physical, social and personal ministry. Answer all the questions thoughtfully and prayerfully. Do not try to rush through. It may take as long as four hours.

D. Do not try to compare yourself with any other person. After Moses' death and Joshua's commissioning, it says, "Nor again has a prophet arisen in Israel equal to Moses" (Deuteronomy 34:10). Moses had one calling from God; Joshua had another. Joshua was not equal to Moses, but he was equal to the task to which he was called. "God has allotted to each a measure of faith" (Romans 12:3). What does God want *you* to trust Him for this year?

Personal Goals

A. Spiritual development.

1. Personal devotions.

   a. How much time do you plan to spend daily in personal devotions this year? ______________________

   b. When? ______________________

   c. What portions of the Bible do you plan to begin reading in your devotions?

   ____

   Why these portions? ______________________

   d. How much time spent in prayer? ______________________

2. Deeper study.

   a. Make plans for deeper Bible study. The Discipleship Series and the Ten Basic Steps Toward Christian Maturity will help you in this area. List the lessons here in the order in which you plan to work through them.

   ____

   b. Enter adequate time for this on the attached schedule.

   c. In addition to these materials, what methods will you use in your study?

   Book and chapter studies.

Which ones? ______________________________

Why? ______________________________

Character studies.

Who? ______________________________

Why? ______________________________

Word or topical studies.

Which ones? ______________________________

Why? ______________________________

Enter adequate time for this study on the attached schedule.

d. Which of the following standard study tools do you *not* own?

Concordance.

One-volume commentary (not just a handbook).

Bible dictionary.

Bible atlas.

Good, extensive English dictionary.

e. When do you plan to buy these tools? (day/month)

____

Where will you buy them? ______________________________

3. Faith.

List the areas of your life in which you have a difficult time trusting God. After each one, explain how you plan to deal with this problem when it arises (Philippians 4:13).

a. ______________________________

b. ______________________________

c. ______________________________

d. ______________________________

e. ______________________________

4. What passages of scripture do you plan to memorize and meditate on? List these in the order you plan to work on them.

   a. ______________________________

   b. ______________________________

   c. ______________________________

   When during the week do you plan to work on them?

   ____

   Enter the time on your schedule.

5. What particular promises from the Word are you claiming for this year?

   ____

6. Which commands has God particularly impressed you to obey this year?

   ____

7. What do you think is/are your spiritual gift(s)? Compare Romans 12:6-8; 1 Corinthians 12:4-11; Ephesians 4:11,12; 1 Peter 4:10,11.

   Do you believe these to be your gifts? Why?

   ____

   ____

How do you plan to develop and employ your gifts this year?

____

____

____

____

B. Mental development (scholastic achievement).

1. Considering your natural aptitude for certain subjects, your priorities and your desire to "do all to the glory of God," what grade do you feel God wants you to achieve in each of your classes this semester (if you are a student)?

   CLASS/GRADE-GOAL

   ________________/____   ________________/____

   ________________/____   ________________/____

   ________________/____   ________________/____

   How much overall study time per week will be required to achieve these grades? _____hrs. Enter into your schedule when you plan to do this studying.

2. Which books would you like to read this year? (Suggested: one per month.)

   ____________________   ____________________

   ____________________   ____________________

   ____________________   ____________________

   ____________________   ____________________

   ____________________   ____________________

3. What magazines (Christian and secular) do you plan to subscribe to?

____

C. Physical development.

1. Are there eating habits you feel the Lord wants you to change this year? Which ones?

____

____

____

What creative things would you like to try in this area?

____

____

____

2. How much sleep do you need each night to operate at peak efficiency? ____________________

When do you, without fail, plan to be in bed each night?

____

List below several obstacles to achieving your goal.

a. ____________________

b. ____________________

c. ____________________

3. The apostle Paul said that, "bodily exercise profits a little." What do you plan to do for physical exercise to increase your vigor and endurance?

____

When do you plan to do this?

Enter it on your schedule.

4. Our appearance is an important part of glorifying God, too. Are there any areas of personal grooming or wardrobe you need to work on? List them here, along with plans for improvement.

D. Social development.

1. Learning to love.

   a. List the specific ways in which you now feel comfortable in expressing love to other Christian brothers and sisters (i.e., what "love skills" have you developed thus far?).

   b. Note in Romans 12:9-21 that Paul instructs the Romans to learn to love others in very specific ways. What tangible ways of expressing your love to other Christians and non-Christians do you feel God wants you to develop? (Be specific.)

2. Fun and creativity.

   a. What kind of small group functions (cooking dinner, etc.) can you think of to invite a group of people to? When would you like to plan your first function?

   ____

   ____

   b. What hobbies and outside interests would you like to develop this year?

   ____

   ____

   c. What kind of fun outings would you like to go on (camping, athletic events, etc.)?

   ____

   ____

3. Neatness.

   Are you satisfied with your personal neatness around your room or apartment? If not, what do you plan to do in this area to improve?

   ____

   ____

E. Personal ministry.

1. Evangelistic ministry.

   a. Have you made plans to learn to share your faith with others? If not, when do you plan to learn?

   ____

   b. What is your "Jerusalem" (Acts 1:8)? That is, where would you like to concentrate your evangelistic ministry this year? List people with whom you would like to share Christ.

1) ____________________

2) ____________________

3) ____________________

4) ____________________

5) ____________________

c. Enter time for witnessing onto your weekly schedule.

d. What obstacles might hinder your achieving these goals? After each obstacle, list how you plan to deal with it.

e. What specific goals do you desire the Lord to achieve through you this year in the area of your personal ministry? (Be specific.) The key to motivation is vision, and the key to vision is being able to *see your objectives clearly*. Remember Proverbs 29:18: “Where there is no vision, the people are unrestrained” (i.e., unguided, without a goal, adrift).

2. Discipleship ministry.

“And the things which you have heard from me in the presence of many witnesses, these entrust to faithful men, who will be able to teach others also” (2 Timothy 2:2).

a. When do you plan to join a Discipleship Group or Discovery Group or other ministry to learn to disciple others in their faith?

____

b. What is your prayer goal for beginning your own Discipleship Group? When would you like to start it?

____

c. Whom can you think of as potential members of your Discipleship Group (new Christians, Christians from church, Christians on campus)?

1)	______________	6)	______________
2)	______________	7)	______________
3)	______________	8)	______________
4)	______________	9)	______________
5)	______________	10)	______________

3. Ministry skills.

Which areas do you need to improve in:

____ Presenting the Four Spiritual Laws (how to make the issue clear).

____ Sharing your personal testimony.

____ Allowing the Holy Spirit to control and empower your life (consistency, victory over wrong habits).

____ Using the Religious Surveys.

____ Using the *Collegiate Challenge* magazine and Van Dusen letter to secure appointments.

____ Conducting follow-up.

How do you plan to increase your confidence and ability in evangelism and discipleship?

____

____

____

____

"A GOAL MINUS A PLAN MINUS ACTION IS BUT A DREAM; A GOAL PLUS A PLAN PLUS ACTION IS A REALITY."

Keep these sheets and review them often.

Exhibit 4
Time and Activities Analysis

A. Beside each item, jot down the number of hours you spent in that activity in the last seven days.

Devotional Bible reading and prayer .... ______

Deeper Bible study and Scripture memory .... ______

Social activities, dates, outings .... ______

Reading (other than required for school) .... ______

Homework .... ______

In class time .... ______

Physical exercise .... ______

Sleep (other than class) .... ______

Eating .... ______

Personal hygiene .... ______

Travel and commuting time .... ______

Witnessing .... ______

Follow-up, teaching, ministering to Christians .... ______

Discipleship Group meeting, family action,
College Life, etc. .... ______

Personal errands (bank, store, etc.) .... ______

Work .... ______

Talking with friends .... ______

Other (itemize)

__________________________________ . . . . _______

__________________________________ . . . . _______

__________________________________ . . . . _______

__________________________________ . . . . _______

__________________________________ . . . . _______

B. Add up the total hours spent in all activities and subtract from 168 (total hours in seven days).

168 hours

—____ hours of activities

= total hours unaccounted for in seven days.

Exhibit 5
Weekly Schedule

SCHEDULE FOR WEEK OF:

	SUN	MON	TUE	WED	THU	FRI	SAT
6							
7							
8							
9							
10							
11							
12							
1							
2							
3							
4							
5							
6							
7							
8							
9							
10							
11							
12							
Add'l. Things To Do							

Exhibit 6

How to Spend Individual Time in Prayer

A. Part one: Preparation.

1. Begin your time with God early in the morning (Psalm 5:3).

    a. Find a place where you can be alone, free from distractions.

    b. Take your Bible, a hymnbook, and a notebook and pencil to record impressions from the Lord.

    c. "Enter into His gates with thanksgiving, and His courts with praise" (Psalm 100:4).

2. Ask God to search your heart (Psalm 139:23,24).

    a. Confess any sins the Holy Spirit reveals (Psalm 51; 52; 66:18; 1John 1:9).

    b. Make certain you are walking and praying in the Spirit (Ephesians 5:15-20).

3. Worship the Lord (Psalm 103; 104).

    a. Consider who God is.

    b. Praise Him for His attributes (Psalm 145).

    c. Rejoice in your fellowship with Him, as He delights in you (Proverbs 15:8).

    d. Read passages of Scripture and pray them back to God (Psalms 146-150).

    e. Sing to the Lord, using your hymnbook and meditating upon and praying from the lyrics.

4. Ask God to reveal the world to you from His point of view (Isaiah 55:8,9). Direct your thoughts away from material and physical needs toward eternal matters (2 Corinthians 4:16-18).

B. Part two: Intercession.

1. Pray your way around the world with unhurried, detailed intercession for others.

2. Begin with your non-Christian friends, relatives, neighbors, your pastor and church leadership, missionaries and other believers. Using your newspaper, continue on in prayer for your community, state and country.

3. Pray for those in authority (1 Timothy 2:1,2) and any others God may bring to mind. Ask specific requests for them.

4. Pray as Paul prayed for others in Philippians 1, Colossians 1 and Ephesians 1 and 3.

5. Ask for others what you ask for yourself. Desire for them what the Lord has shown you.

C. Part three: Personal petition.

1. Ask for understanding (Psalm 119:18).

2. Meditate on Scripture you have memorized or Scripture promises you know.

3. Read an entire book in the Bible (select one of appropriate length).

   a. Ask God to show you personal applications.

   b. Pray for yourself. See 1 Chronicles 4:10.

   c. Ask, "Lord, what do *You* think of my life?" Consider your activities: What are your life and ministry objectives? How do you spend your time? Is your time counting for eternity?

4. Record your thoughts.

5. Review or plan your use of time for God's greatest glory in various areas of your life: family, work, personal Bible study and devotions, church activities, etc.

6. Discuss with the Lord problems or decisions you may be facing. Record conclusions God brings to you mind. Look in the Scriptures for promises to claim and underline them.

Exhibit 7
Example of Campus Prayer Schedule Card

EXAMPLE OF CAMPUS PRAYER SCHEDULE CARD

	9:10 - 10:00	10:20 - 11:10	11:30 - 12:20	12:40 - 1:30
M				
TU				
W				
TH				
F				
SA				

Name ______________________ Phone ______________________

Partner Preference ______________________

Exhibit 8
First 15 Weeks on Campus

Week 1

The Movement:	Make a prayer list. Do personal evangelism. Do group evangelism. Four-question survey. Films or tapes. Popcorn parties.
Your Ministry:	Read Parts 2 and 3 in this manual. Follow-up survey, film, etc. List possible evangelistic contacts. Share vision for discipleship with Christians you met through surveys, meetings or one to one.
Your Growth:	Set aside 30 minutes for quiet time. Get with other Christians to pray for campus. Take one half day to set personal goals (see Exhibit #3).

Weeks 2-6

The Movement:	Continue evangelism. Continue follow-up from surveys, etc.
Your Ministry:	Continue evangelism and follow-up. Continue to share vision.
Your Growth:	Quiet time. Pray with others. Begin a reading program, one chapter a day in one of the following: *Disciples Are Made*—Henrichsen *Dedication and Leadership*—Hyde *Spiritual Leadership*—Sanders *Master Plan of Evangelism*—Coleman Read Transferable Concept #1. (WEEK 6)

Week 7

The Movement:	Continue evangelism. Continue follow-up from surveys.
Your Ministry:	Continue evangelism and follow-up. Prepare and teach lesson #1. Continue evangelism and follow-up. Continue to share vision. Challenge specific individuals to be in your Discovery Group, giving them a specific time to meet next week.
Your Growth:	Quiet time. Pray with others. Read a chapter each day in one of the above books. Read Transferable Concept #2.

Week 8

The Movement:	Continue evangelism. Continue follow-up.
Your Ministry:	Prepare for and teach Discovery Group #2. Vision: Mark 4:19, Acts 1:8. Take a group member witnessing. Begin one-to-one time with one or two group members.
Your Growth:	Quiet time, pray with others. Read a chapter each day in one of the above books. Read Tranferable Concept #3.

Week 9

The Movement:	Take Christians to a LTC at a nearby campus.
Your Ministry:	Prepare for and teach Discovery Group #2 Vision: Mark 4:19, Acts 1:8. Take a group member witnessing.
Your Growth:	Quiet time. Pray with others.

Read a chapter each day in one of the above books.
Read Transferable Concept #4.
Study Mark 4:19 and Acts 1:8.

Week 10

The Movement: Take Christians to a LTC.
Continue evangelism.
Continue follow-up.

Your Ministry: Prepare and teach Discovery Group #3.
Take group members witnessing.
Vision: John 17:4, Colossians 1:28-29.

Your Growth: Have a quiet time with one of your group members.
Read a chapter each day in one of the above books.
Pray with others.
Read Transferable Concept #5.

Week 11

The Movement: Take Christians to a LTC
Continue evangelism.
Continue follow-up.

Your Ministry: Prepare and teach Discovery Group #4.
Vision: 2 Chronicles 7:14, Psalms 127:1.

Your Growth: Quiet time.
Pray with others.
Read a chapter each day in one of the above books.
Read Transferable Concept #6.
Study 2 Chronicles 7:14, Psalm 127:1

Week 12

The Movement: Plan a weekend LTC and/or continue LTC at a nearby campus.
Continue evangelism.
Continue follow-up.

Your Ministry: Do something fun like having the group eat dinner together and share . . . then to a movie. Possibly have guys and girls together for this.

Your Growth:

Quiet time.
Pray with others.
Read a chapter each day in one of the above books.
Read Transferable Concept #7.
Study John 4.

Week 13

The Movement:

Continue to plan a weekend LTC.
Continue follow-up.
Continue evangelism.

Your Ministry:

Prepare and teach Discovery Group #5.
Vision: John 4.
Training: Benefits of the Four Spiritual Laws, in Chapter 12.

Your Growth:

Quiet time.
Pray with others.
Read Transferable Concept #8.
Study John 4.
Memorize two verses and review daily.

Week 14

The Movement:

Have a weekend LTC.
Continue LTC on a nearby campus.
Continue evangelism.
Continue follow-up.

Your Ministry:

Prepare and teach Discovery Group #6.
Vision: Acts 16:18.
Training: How to Use the Four Spiritual Laws, Chapter 12.

Your Growth:

Quiet time.
Read a chapter each day in one of the above books.
Read Transferable Concept #9.
Study Acts 16:18.
Spend a half day with the Lord to evaluate goals, pray and worship.

Week 15

The Movement:	Recruit for next Campus Crusade conference. Continue evangelism. Continue follow-up Continue LTC. See Campus Crusade staff for further direction and materials.
Your Ministry:	Prepare and teach Discovery Group #7. Vision: Mark 1:29-36. Training: Handling Responses in Four Spiritual Laws, see Chapter 12.
Your Growth:	Quiet time. Read a chapter per day in one of the above books. Study Mark 1:29-36. Pray for people to go to conferences.

Exhibit 9
How to Lead Conversational Prayer

A. Purpose.

Group prayer was one characteristic of the early Christians. We read in Acts 12:12 that Peter went to the house of Mary where many were gathered for prayer. Earlier in the book of Acts, we read that the disciples "went up to the upper room, where they were staying . . . . These all with one mind were continually devoting themselves to prayer, along with the women" (Acts 1:13,14). Old Testament characters also participated in group prayer. For example, 2 Chronicles 6:13-42 records Solomon praying as all Israel gathered around.

Remember that the purpose of your prayer time is to communicate with God. It should never be viewed as a ritual or as a time to "preach" to one another.

B. Conversational prayer.

During a time of conversational prayer the group members should talk to God as they would talk to a friend who is present in the room. Members should use contemporary conversational language and avoid "preaching" at others. Encourage the group (especially a group unfamiliar with group prayer) to feel free to pray sentence prayers, expressing only a brief thought in six words or so. They need not pray long, elaborate prayers. Everyone is free to pray, or not to pray, as the Spirit directs. Do not be concerned about silence. Allow God to speak to you and the other individuals in the group during times of silence.

C. Examples of leading conversational prayer.

1. Introduce prayer topics one at a time. Using this method, the leader introduces a topic which the group then prays about. When the group finishes praying for that topic, the leader introduces another. Both the number and types of topics introduced may vary. Below is an example:

    a. "Thank You" for one thing (e.g., the Lord Jesus, God's love, His forgiveness, the beautiful day, etc.).

b. "Thank You" for something that has happened in your life in the last 24 hours.

c. "Please help . . ." (yourself or someone else).

d. Ask for one thing for yourself.

e. Thank God for how He will meet those desires and requests.

2. Allow the group to share prayer requests.

a. As a prayer request is offered, you may wish to ask another member to be responsible to pray for that request during the prayer time. This ensures that each person's request will be prayed for by at least one other person during the prayer time.

b. You may wish to have group members record on a sheet of paper each request as it is offered. They could then refer to the list during the group prayer time as well as throughout the week as a reminder to continue to pray for one another.

c. You may allow group members to volunteer to pray for requests without assigning them or writing them down. The group would then rely on their memories during the prayer time.

d. You may wish to pray for each request as soon as it is given, before allowing the next request to be shared.

3. Pray through Scripture. This method allows the group to use one or more passages of Scripture as their prayer guide. You are free to choose passages from anywhere in the Old or New Testaments that you feel with be appropriate. The following is an example:

a. Choose a Psalm of praise (e.g., Psalm 103, Psalms 145-150).

b. Teach the group to pray using the following procedure:

1) The first person reads a phrase or an entire verse aloud, pausing to pray a simple prayer as inspired by the Scripture and led by the Lord.

2) Other members of the group join in audibly or silently agree.

3) The next person reads a different verse, pausing to pray aloud as he is impressed by the Lord.

4) Each continues in like fashion around the group.

4. Introduce the ACTS acrostic. (This can be developed at length with one or more studies on each word.) Guide the prayer time, praying silently or aloud. *Always* pray silently during personal confession.

a. Adoration.

Definition: Worshipping and praising God, exalting Him in your heart and your mind and with your lips.

1) Read Psalms such as 103 and 145 or choose praise portions from #8a of this outline.

2) Take time to adore God, praising Him for His attributes such as His lovingkindness, His holiness, His compassion, His majesty, etc.

b. Confession.

Definition: Agreeing with God concerning any sins He brings to mind in order to restore fellowship with Him.

1) Review 1 John 1:5-9.

2) As you spend time adoring God, He will bring to mind what you need to confess.

3) Allow time for confession (let God speak to each person about any unconfessed sin).

c. Thanksgiving.

Definition: Giving thanks to God for who He is, what He has done and what He will continue to do in your life; a prayer expressing gratitude.

1) Look at 1 Thessalonians 5:18, Ephesians 5:20, Psalm 108:3, Psalm 50:23.

2) Spend time in thanksgiving.

d. Supplication.

Definition: Imploring God by means of a petition or an entreaty.

1) Read Philippians 4:6,7; Psalm 116:1,2.

2) Lead the group in supplication, praying aloud.

5. Introduce the PRAY acrostic (may be developed in the same way as ACTS).

a. Praise.

b. Repent.

c. Ask for someone else.

d. Your own needs.

6. Pray for the fulfillment of the Great Commission, using Scripture.

a. Win men to Christ through prayer.

1) Pray that God will prepare individuals' hearts to understand and respond to the gospel (John 6:44).

2) Pray that God will raise up believers to share the gospel with the unbelievers (Matthew 9:37,38; Colossians 4:3).

3) Recognize that Satan has blinded and captivated the unbeliever, and acknowledge (claim) Christ's victory

over him (Ephesians 6:12; 2 Corinthians 4:3,4; 2 Timothy 2:25,26; 1 John 3:8).

4) Persist in these prayers (Daniel 10:12,13a; Luke 18:1-8).

b. Build men in Christ through prayer.

1) Thank God for them (Philippians 1:3).

2) Pray for deliverance from evil (unprincipled) companions (2 Thessalonians 3:2).

3) Pray that they will walk worthy of the Lord (Colossians 1:10).

4) Pray for wisdom and revelation in their knowledge of Christ (Ephesians 1:17).

5) Pray for them to be strengthened with might by His Spirit in the inner man (Ephesians 3:16).

6) Pray for their unity in the Spirit with other believers (John 17:23).

7) Pray that their love may abound and that they may approve the things that are excellent (Philippians 1:9,10).

8) Pray for boldness and opportunities to present the gospel to others (Colossians 4:3, Ephesians 6:19,20).

9) Pray that they may completely mature and be fully assured in all the will of God (Colossians 4:12).

10) Persist in these prayers (Ephesians 6:18).

c. Send men for Christ through prayer.

1) Recognize the problem of the labor shortage in the spiritual harvest (Matthew 9:37,38; Romans 10:13-15).

2) Make a list of candidates to be sent by the Lord (Isaiah 6:8; Matthew 9:37,38) and pray persistently for them.

3) Pray that laborers will be thrust forth into specific communities and countries.

4) Claim the fulfillment of the Great Commission in your area and the world, according to His command and promise (Matthew 28:18-20; 1 John 5:14,15).

5) Mobilize and teach others to pray for laborers (2 Timothy 2:2).

6) To help expand the group's world vision, pray for a specific country, overseas mission group, or overseas Christian workers. (Your group may want to "adopt" a country to pray for regularly.)

7) Sing a hymn prayerfully, and afterward, use the words of the hymn to guide the prayer time.

8) Select one or more attributes of God, and spend the time meditating on those attributes and praising Him for His attributes.

9) Share answers to prayer and spend the time thanking God for the answers and His faithfulness.

D. Motivating your group to pray.

1. Stimulate intercessory prayer.

a. Remind participants of men and women of faith in the past who saw God answer intercessory prayer in a mighty way.

1) When Abraham prayed, Lot was saved (Genesis 19:29).

2) When Hezekiah prayed, God turned back Sennacherib (2 Kings 19).

3) Jesus healed in response to intercession. A few examples:

a) Mark 2:3: Four friends brought the paralytic before Jesus.

b) Matthew 15:22: A Canaanite woman came to Jesus on behalf of her daughter.

c) Matthew 17:15: A man sought healing for his son.

4) An angel set Peter free in response to united prayer (Acts 12:1-17).

5) The early church flourished as Paul interceded for them: Romans 1:9; Ephesians 1:15-19, 3:14-19; Philippians 1:3-11; Colossians 1:9-12, etc.

6) The earnest prayer of a righteous man has great power and wonderful results. In James 5:17,18 we read, "Elijah was as completely human as we are, and yet when he prayed earnestly that no rain would fall, none fell for the next three and one half years! Then he prayed again, this time that it *would* rain, and down it poured and the grass turned green and the gardens began to grow again" (Living Bible).

b) Emphasize the priority God places on praying for those in authority (1 Timothy 2:1-4).

c. Encourage individuals to make note of the intercessory prayers of Jesus, Paul, Peter, etc., in their personal Bible study and to pattern their own prayers along similar lines.

d. Pray through Scripture portions to intercede for others, letting the Scripture guide your prayers and express your thoughts to God.

Examples:

1) Ephesians 1:16-19: pray for members of your family.

2) Ephesians 3:14-16: pray for your Sunday school teacher or superintendent.

3) Philippians 1:9-11: pray for a Christian friend.

4) Colossians 1:9-11: pray for your pastor.

2. Encourage praying in one accord.

    a. Instruct individuals to:

        1) Concentrate on what the other person is praying, agreeing in your heart.

        2) Trust the Holy Spirit to direct your thoughts and prayers when it is your turn.

        3) Do not be thinking ahead to what you will pray—you will miss the other person's prayer and neglect to pray in accord.

    b. Emphasize that the early church was accused of turning the world upside down when they practiced praying in one accord (Acts 4:24-31 and Acts 17:5-7).

    c. An earthquake opened prison doors for Paul and Silas when they prayed together (Acts 16:25,26).

    d. Remember that Jesus Christ Himself is actually present in the room. He promises in Matthew 18:19,20, "I also tell you this—if two of you agree down here on earth concerning anything you ask for, my Father in heaven will do it for you. For where two or three gather together because they are mine, I will be right there among them" (Living Bible).

3. Encourage individuals to pray continually.

    a. Remind them that God commands us to pray without ceasing (1 Thessalonians 5:17).

    b. Encourage them to recognize that God is present wherever they go and that He is always ready to answer prayer.

    c. Talk about how important it is to thank God for everything He allows to come into our lives (1 Thessalonians 5:18)—everything from a beautiful day to a flat tire. Thank Him that He is in control and that He causes all things to work together for good to those who love Him. (Your prayers can be a good example. Keep them simple, sincere, brief and reflective of your faith.)

d. Encourage them to talk to God when they feel a need—any time of the day or night.

e. Suggest that they use their time twice by developing a habit of praying as they go about daily activities that do not require total concentration; for example, while showering, driving, gardening, working with their hands.

4. Use other means to motivate your group to pray.

   a. Read short motivational verses or excerpts on prayer by Christian writers. Some suggested authors are Andrew Murray, E.M. Bounds, C.T. Studd, George Mueller, Hudson Taylore, Bill Bright, Charles Finney.

   b. Study some or all of the following motivational passages on the prayer life of Jesus.

      1) He prayed while being baptized by John (Luke 3:21).

      2) He fasted and prayed in the wilderness before being tempted (Matthew 4:2).

      3) He prayed in a lonely place after news of John the Baptist's death (Matthew 14:13).

      4) He prayed often in lonely places and in the wilderness (Luke 4:42; 5:16).

      5) He prayed in the early morning before going through Galilee (Mark 1:35).

      6) He prayed all night before calling the twelve apostles (Luke 6:12).

      7) He prayed alone after feeding the 5,000 (Matthew 14:23).

      8) He prayed before His transfiguration (Luke 9:28,29).

      9) He praised God aloud when the 70 returned (Luke 10:21).

      10) He prayed before teaching on prayer (Luke 11:1-4).

11) He prayed aloud before raising Lazarus from the dead (John 11:41-42).

12) He prayed for Peter (Luke 22:32).

13) He talked aloud with God during His last public discourse (John 12:28).

14) He prayed for the disciples after His farewell discourse (John 17).

15) He prayed in Gethsemane (Matthew 26:39-44; Mark 14:35-39).

16) He prayed on the cross (Luke 23:34-46).

17) He prayed at Emmaus after the resurrection (Luke 24:30).

c. Encourage your group members to prepare and use a personal prayer diary. The Great Commission Prayer Crusade's *Personal Prayer Diary* is a popular journal because of its easy-to-use format. It is organized by days of the week and includes praise portions, specific suggestions for prayer and plenty of blank space for personal requests. Its handy size makes it easy to use and carry.

d. Many additional suggestions may be found in the Great Commission Prayer Crusade's *Prayer Handbook* and *Strategy Manual.* Encourage your group to take time to read these practical guides to prayer. All of the suggestions in this appendix were adapted from the *Prayer Handbook.*

Exhibit 10
Evangelistic Literature

Rusty Wright

Rusty Wright has a B.S. degree in psychology from Duke University and an M.A. in religion from the International School of Theology. He is author of three books and speaks to thousands of students at major universities across the U.S. each year.

Dynamic Sex: Beyond Technique and Experience

A dynamic sex life. How can I have one? How can I get the most out of sex? Students are asking these questions around the nation. This article offers some practical principles dealing with those questions. It also includes the Four Spiritual Laws.

The New Testament: Can I Trust It?

"How can any well-educated person believe the New Testament? It was written so long after the events that we can't possibly trust it as historically reliable." This is a common question on the university campus and deserves the honest answers presented in this article. It also contains the Four Spiritual Laws.

A Funny Thing Happened on the Way to the End

Hundreds of cases have been recorded of people who returned from the brink of death to report on "the other side." This article considers whether these out-of-body experiences are really encounters with the afterlife . . . or something more deceptive. This also contains the Four Spiritual Laws.

Josh McDowell

Josh McDowell is a traveling representative of Campus Crusade for Christ. He is a graduate of Wheaton College and a magna cum laude graduate of Talbot Theological Seminary. In the last five years he has spoken to more than five million students on nearly 600 universities in 57 countries.

The Resurrection—Hoax of History?

This article is the essence of a message that Josh has presented for many years around the world. This article documents the historical evidence for the resurrection of Jesus Christ and shatters the most common theories that try to disprove He rose from the dead.

More Than a Carpenter

Men and women down through the ages have been divided over the question, "Who is Jesus?" This book is for people who are skeptical about Jesus' deity, His resurrection and his claims on their lives.

To order *More Than a Carpenter*, check your local Christian bookstore or write:
Living Books
Tyndale House Publishers, Inc.
Wheaton, Illinois

Dr. Bill Bright

Dr. Bright is the founder and president of Campus Crusade for Christ International, one of the largest nondenominational Christian organizations in the world. He is author of many articles and pamphlets and several books, which have helped millions find Christ and grow in their faith.

Van Dusen Letter

The Van Dusen letter was written by Dr. Bright to a prominent businessman who had requested information on how he could become a Christian. (The name, Dr. Van Dusen, is fictitious.) Millions of copies of this letter have been distributed around the world in most of the major languages. It is estimated that thousands have become Christians as a result of reading this letter. It is an expanded version of the Four Spiritual Laws.

"Jesus and the Intellectual"

People of any religion, if they know the facts, must acknowledge that Jesus Christ is the unique personality of all time. This booklet takes an intellectual look at the deity of Christ. It also contains the Four Spiritual Laws.

Athletes in Action magazine

A Campus Crusade for Christ quarterly publication with interesting articles about athletes who have placed their faith in Jesus Christ. Good to give to coaches and all athletes. It contains the Four Spiritual Laws.

To order any of the above materials (except *More Than a Carpenter*), see order blank at end of book.

Have You Heard of the

Four Spiritual Laws?

1

Just as there are physical laws that govern the physical universe, so are there spiritual laws which govern your relationship with God.

LAW ONE

GOD **LOVES** YOU, AND OFFERS A WONDERFUL **PLAN** FOR YOUR LIFE.

(References contained in this booklet should be read in context from the Bible wherever possible.)

God's Love

"For God so loved the world, that He gave His only begotten Son, that whoever believes in Him should not perish, but have eternal life" (John 3:16).

God's Plan

(Christ speaking) "I came that they might have life, and might have it abundantly" (that it might be full and meaningful) (John 10:10).

Why is it that most people are not experiencing the abundant life? Because . . .

2

LAW TWO

MAN IS **SINFUL** AND **SEPARATED** FROM GOD. THEREFORE, HE CANNOT KNOW AND EXPERIENCE GOD'S LOVE AND PLAN FOR HIS LIFE.

Man Is Sinful

"For all have sinned and fall short of the glory of God" (Romans 3:23).

Man was created to have fellowship with God; but, because of his stubborn self-will, he chose to go his own independent way and fellowship with God was broken. This self-will, characterized by an attitude of active rebellion or passive indifference, is evidence of what the Bible calls sin.

Man Is Separated

"For the wages of sin is death" (spiritual separation from God) (Romans 6:23).

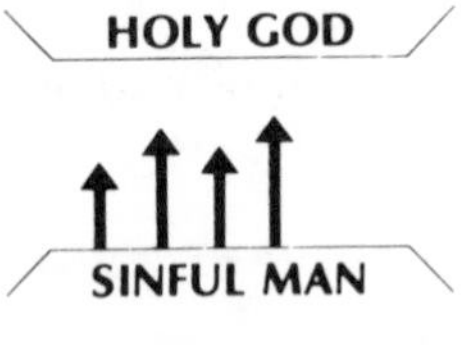

This diagram illustrates that God is holy and man is sinful. A great gulf separates the two. The arrows illustrate that man is continually trying to reach God and the abundant life through his own efforts, such as a good life, philosophy or religion.

The third law explains the only way to bridge this gulf . . .

LAW THREE

3

JESUS CHRIST IS GOD'S **ONLY** PROVISION FOR MAN'S SIN. THROUGH HIM YOU CAN KNOW AND EXPERIENCE GOD'S LOVE AND PLAN FOR YOUR LIFE.

He Died in Our Place

"But God demonstrates His own love toward us, in that while we were yet sinners, Christ died for us" (Romans 5:8).

He Rose from the Dead

"Christ died for our sins . . . He was buried . . . He was raised on the third day, according to the Scriptures . . . He appeared to Peter, then to the twelve. After that He appeared to more than five hundred . . ." (I Corinthians 15:3-6).

He Is the Only Way to God

"Jesus said to him, 'I am the way, and the truth, and the life; no one comes to the Father, but through Me' " (John 14:6).

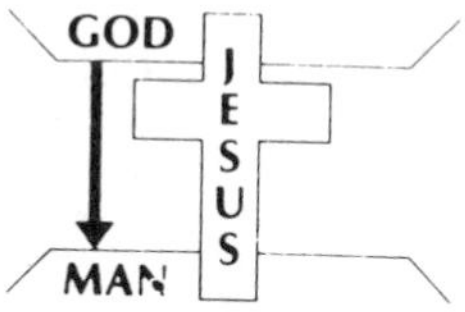

This diagram illustrates that God has bridged the gulf which separates us from Him by sending His Son, Jesus Christ, to die on the cross in our place to pay the penalty for our sins.

It is not enough just to know these three laws . . .

4 LAW FOUR

WE MUST INDIVIDUALLY **RECEIVE** JESUS CHRIST AS SAVIOR AND LORD; THEN WE CAN KNOW AND EXPERIENCE GOD'S LOVE AND PLAN FOR OUR LIVES.

We Must Receive Christ

"But as many as received Him, to them He gave the right to become children of God, even to those who believe in His name" (John 1:12).

We Receive Christ Through Faith

"For by grace you have been saved through faith; and that not of yourselves, it is the gift of God; not as a result of works, that no one should boast" (Ephesians 2:8,9).

When We Receive Christ, We Experience a New Birth.

(Read John 3:1-8.)

We Receive Christ by Personal Invitation

(Christ is speaking): "Behold, I stand at the door and knock; if any one hears My voice and opens the door, I will come in to him" (Revelation 3:20).

Receiving Christ involves turning to God from self (repentance) and trusting Christ to come into our lives to forgive our sins and to make us the kind of people He wants us to be. Just to agree intellectually that Jesus Christ is the Son of God and that He died on the cross for our sins is not enough. Nor is it enough to have an emotional experience. We receive Jesus Christ by faith, as an act of the will.

These two circles represent two kinds of lives:

SELF-DIRECTED LIFE

S — Self is on the throne

† — Christ is outside the life

• — Interests are directed by self, often resulting in discord and frustration

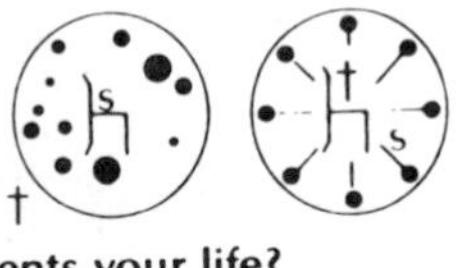

CHRIST-DIRECTED LIFE

† — Christ is in the life and on the throne

S — Self is yielding to Christ

• — Interests are directed by Christ, resulting in harmony with God's plan

Which circle best represents your life?

Which circle would you like to have represent your life?

The following explains how you can receive Christ:

YOU CAN RECEIVE CHRIST RIGHT NOW BY FAITH THROUGH PRAYER

(Prayer is talking with God)

God knows your heart and is not so concerned with your words as He is with the attitude of your heart. The following is a suggested prayer:

"Lord Jesus, I need You. Thank You for dying on the cross for my sins. I open the door of my life and receive You as my Savior and Lord. Thank You for forgiving my sins and giving me eternal life. Take control of the throne of my life. Make me the kind of person You want me to be."

Does this prayer express the desire of your heart?

If it does, pray this prayer right now, and Christ will come into your life, as He promised.

How to Know That Christ Is in Your Life

Did you receive Christ into your life? According to His promise in Revelation 3:20, where is Christ right now in relation to you? Christ said that He would come into your life. Would He mislead you? On what authority do you know that God has answered your prayer? (The trustworthiness of God Himself and His Word.)

The Bible Promises Eternal Life to All Who Receive Christ

"And the witness is this, that God has given us eternal life, and this life is in His Son. He who has the Son has the life; he who does not have the Son of God does not have the life. These things I have written to you who believe in the name of the Son of God, in order that you may know that you have eternal life" (I John 5:11-13).

Thank God often that Christ is in your life and that He will never leave you (Hebrews 13:5). You can know on the basis of His promise that Christ lives in you and that you have eternal life, from the very moment you invite Him in. He will not deceive you.

An important reminder . . .

DO NOT DEPEND UPON FEELINGS

The promise of God's Word, the Bible — not our feelings — is our authority. The Christian lives by faith (trust) in the trustworthiness of God Himself and His Word. This train diagram illustrates the relationship between **fact** (God and His Word), **faith** (our trust in God and His Word), and **feeling** (the result of our faith and obedience) (John 14:21).

The train will run with or without the caboose. However, it would be useless to attempt to pull the train by the caboose. In the same way, we, as Christians, do not depend on feelings or emotions, but we place our faith (trust) in the trustworthiness of God and the promises of His Word.

NOW THAT YOU HAVE RECEIVED CHRIST

The moment that you received Christ by faith, as an act of the will, many things happened, including the following:

1. Christ came into your life (Revelation 3:20 and Colossians 1:27).
2. Your sins were forgiven (Colossians 1:14).
3. You became a child of God (John 1:12).
4. You received eternal life (John 5:24).
5. You began the great adventure for which God created you (John 10:10; II Corinthians 5:17 and I Thessalonians 5:18).

Can you think of anything more wonderful that could happen to you than receiving Christ? Would you like to thank God in prayer right now for what He has done for you? By thanking God, you demonstrate your faith.

To enjoy your new life to the fullest . . .

SUGGESTIONS FOR CHRISTIAN GROWTH

Spiritual growth results from trusting Jesus Christ. "The righteous man shall live by faith" (Galatians 3:11). A life of faith will enable you to trust God increasingly with every detail of your life, and to practice the following:

G Go to God in prayer daily (John 15:7).

R Read God's Word daily (Acts 17:11)—begin with the Gospel of John.

O Obey God moment by moment (John 14:21).

W Witness for Christ by your life and words (Matthew 4:19; John 15:8).

T Trust God for every detail of your life (I Peter 5:7).

H Holy Spirit—allow Him to control and empower your daily life and witness (Galatians 5:16,17; Acts 1:8).

FELLOWSHIP IN A GOOD CHURCH

God's Word admonishes us not to forsake "the assembling of ourselves together. . ." (Hebrews 10:25). Several logs burn brightly together; but put one aside on the cold hearth and the fire goes out. So it is with your relationship to other Christians. If you do not belong to a church, do not wait to be invited. Take the initiative; call the pastor of a nearby church where Christ is honored and His Word is preached. Start this week, and make plans to attend regularly.

SPECIAL MATERIALS ARE AVAILABLE FOR CHRISTIAN GROWTH.

If you have come to know Christ personally through this presentation of the gospel, write for a free booklet especially written to assist you in your Christian growth.

A special Bible study series and an abundance of other helpful materials for Christian growth are also available. For additional information, please write Campus Crusade for Christ International, San Bernardino, CA 92414.

You will want to share this important discovery . . .

Want to share your discovery?

IF THIS BOOKLET HAS BEEN MEANINGFUL AND BENEFICIAL TO YOU, OR HAS HELPED YOU TO COME TO KNOW CHRIST PERSONALLY, PLEASE GIVE IT TO SOMEONE ELSE. For information concerning a special Bible study series and other helpful material for Christian growth, please write to Campus Crusade for Christ International, Arrowhead Springs, San Bernardino, CA 92404.

BILL BRIGHT, President

More than 25,000,000 copies of the Four Spiritual Laws have been distributed in most of the major languages of the world. Booklets are available at a nominal price for use by any and all interested individuals and organizations. Names of those who wish to distribute these booklets may be placed in the box provided below, if desired.

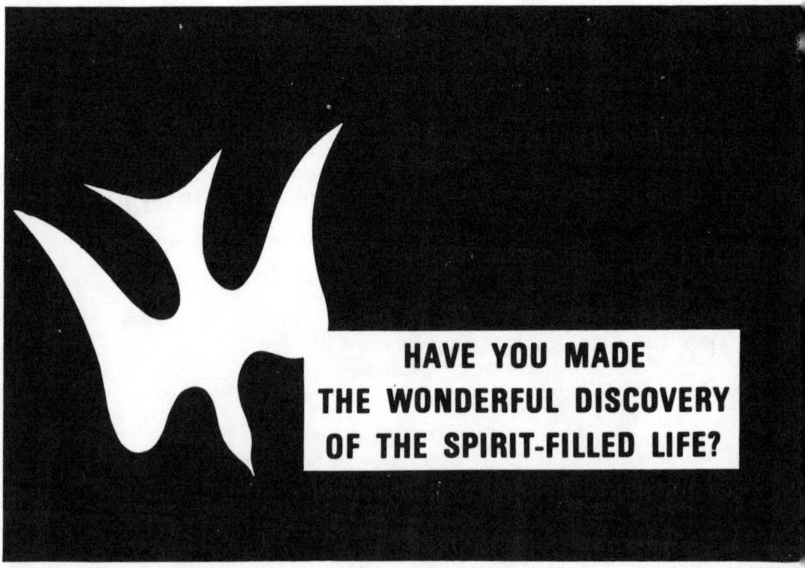

EVERY DAY CAN BE AN EXCITING ADVENTURE FOR THE CHRISTIAN who knows the reality of being filled with the Holy Spirit and who lives constantly, moment by moment, under His gracious direction.

The Bible tells us that there are three kinds of people.

1. NATURAL MAN

(One who has not received Christ)

"But a natural man does not accept the things of the Spirit of God; for they are foolishness to him, and he cannot understand them, because they are spiritually appraised" (I Corinthians 2:14).

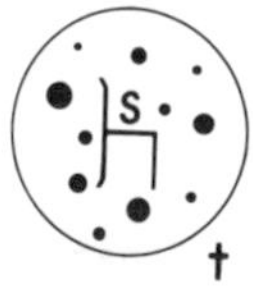

SELF-DIRECTED LIFE
S—Ego or finite self is on the throne
†—Christ is outside the life
•—Interests are directed by self, often resulting in discord and frustration

2. SPIRITUAL MAN

(One who is directed and empowered by the Holy Spirit)

"But he who is spiritual appraises all things . . ." (I Corinthians 2:15).

CHRIST-DIRECTED LIFE
†—Christ is in the life and on the throne
S—Self is yielding to Christ
•—Interests are directed by Christ, resulting in harmony with God's plan

3. CARNAL MAN

(One who has received Christ, but who lives in defeat because he trusts in his own efforts to live the Christian life)

SELF-DIRECTED LIFE
S—Self is on the throne
†—Christ dethroned and not allowed to direct the life
•—Interests are directed by self, often resulting in discord and frustration

"And I, brethren, could not speak to you as to spiritual men, but as to carnal men, as to babes in Christ. I gave you milk to drink, not solid food; for you were not yet able to receive it. Indeed, even now you are not yet able, for you are still carnal. For since there is jealousy and strife among you, are you not fleshly, and are you not walking like mere men?" (I Corinthians 3:1-3).

1. GOD HAS PROVIDED FOR US AN ABUNDANT AND FRUITFUL CHRISTIAN LIFE.

Jesus said, "I came that they might have life, and might have it abundantly" (John 10:10).

"I am the vine, you are the branches; he who abides in Me, and I in him, he bears much fruit; for apart from Me you can do nothing" (John 15:5).

"But the fruit of the Spirit is love, joy, peace, patience, kindness, goodness, faithfulness, gentleness, self-control; against such things there is no law" (Galatians 5:22, 23).

"But you shall receive power when the Holy Spirit has come upon you; and you shall be My witnesses both in Jerusalem, and in all Judea and Samaria, and even to the remotest part of the earth" (Acts 1:8).

THE SPIRITUAL MAN—Some personal traits which result from trusting God:

Christ-centered
Empowered by the Holy Spirit
Introduces others to Christ
Effective prayer life
Understands God's Word
Trusts God
Obeys God

Love
Joy
Peace
Patience
Kindness
Faithfulness
Goodness

The degree to which these traits are manifested in the life depends upon the extent to which the Christian trusts the Lord with every detail of his life, and upon his maturity in Christ. One who is only beginning to understand the ministry of the Holy Spirit should not be discouraged if he is not as fruitful as more mature Christians who have known and experienced this truth for a longer period.

Why is it that most Christians are not experiencing the abundant life?

2. CARNAL CHRISTIANS CANNOT EXPERIENCE THE ABUNDANT AND FRUITFUL CHRISTIAN LIFE.

The carnal man trusts in his own efforts to live the Christian life:

A. He is either uninformed about, or has forgotten, God's love, forgiveness, and power (Romans 5:8-10; Hebrews 10:1-25; I John 1;2:1-3; II Peter 1:9; Acts 1:8).

B. He has an up-and-down spiritual experience.

C. He cannot understand himself—he wants to do what is right, but cannot.

D. He fails to draw upon the power of the Holy Spirit to live the Christian life.

(I Corinthians 3:1-3; Romans 7:15-24; 8:7; Galatians 5:16-18)

THE CARNAL MAN—Some or all of the following traits may characterize the Christian who does not fully trust God:

Ignorance of his spiritual heritage
Unbelief
Disobedience
Loss of love for God and for others
Poor prayer life
No desire for Bible study

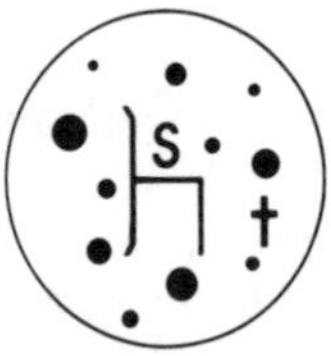

Legalistic attitude
Impure thoughts
Jealousy
Guilt
Worry
Discouragement
Critical spirit
Frustration
Aimlessness

(The individual who professes to be a Christian but who continues to practice sin should realize that he may not be a Christian at all, according to I John 2:3; 3:6, 9; Ephesians 5:5).

The third truth gives us the only solution to this problem . . .

3. JESUS PROMISED THE ABUNDANT AND FRUITFUL LIFE AS THE RESULT OF BEING FILLED (DIRECTED AND EMPOWERED) BY THE HOLY SPIRIT.

The Spirit-filled life is the Christ-directed life by which Christ lives His life in and through us in the power of the Holy Spirit (John 15).

A. One becomes a Christian through the ministry of the Holy Spirit, according to John 3:1-8. From the moment of spiritual birth, the Christian is indwelt by the Holy Spirit at all times (John 1:12; Colossians 2:9, 10; John 14:16, 17). **Though all Christians are indwelt by the Holy Spirit, not all Christians are filled (directed and empowered) by the Holy Spirit.**

B. The Holy Spirit is the source of the overflowing life (John 7:37-39).

C. The Holy Spirit came to glorify Christ (John 16:1-15). When one is filled with the Holy Spirit, he is a true disciple of Christ.

D. In His last command before His ascension, Christ promised the power of the Holy Spirit to enable us to be witnesses for Him (Acts 1:1-9).

How, then, can one be filled with the Holy Spirit?

4. WE ARE FILLED (DIRECTED AND EMPOWERED) BY THE HOLY SPIRIT BY FAITH; THEN WE CAN EXPERIENCE THE ABUNDANT AND FRUITFUL LIFE WHICH CHRIST PROMISED TO EACH CHRISTIAN.

You can appropriate the filling of the Holy Spirit **right now** if you:

A. Sincerely desire to be directed and empowered by the Holy Spirit (Matthew 5:6; John 7:37-39).

B. Confess your sins.

By **faith** thank God that He **has** forgiven all of your sins — past, present and future — because Christ died for you (Colossians 2:13-15; I John 1; 2:1-3; Hebrews 10:1-17).

C. Present every area of your life to God (Romans 12:1, 2).

D. By **faith** claim the fullness of the Holy Spirit, according to:

1. HIS COMMAND — Be filled with the Spirit.
"And do not get drunk with wine, for that is dissipation, but be filled with the Spirit" (Ephesians 5:18).

2. HIS PROMISE — He will always answer when we pray according to His will. "And this is the confidence which we have before Him, that, if we ask anything according to His will, He hears us. And if we know that He hears us in whatever we ask, we know that we have the requests which we have asked from Him" (I John 5:14, 15).

Faith can be expressed through prayer . . .

HOW TO PRAY IN FAITH TO BE FILLED WITH THE HOLY SPIRIT

We are filled with the Holy Spirit by **faith** alone. However, true prayer is one way of expressing your faith. The following is a suggested prayer:

"Dear Father, I need You. I acknowledge that I have been directing my own life and that, as a result, I have sinned against You. I thank You that You have forgiven my sins through Christ's death on the cross for me. I now invite Christ to again take His place on the throne of my life. Fill me with the Holy Spirit as You **commanded** me to be filled, and as You **promised** in Your Word that You would do if I asked in faith. I pray this in the name of Jesus. As an expression of my faith, I now thank You for directing my life and for filling me with the Holy Spirit."

Does this prayer express the desire of your heart? If so, bow in prayer and trust God to fill you with the Holy Spirit **right now.**

HOW TO KNOW THAT YOU ARE FILLED (DIRECTED AND EMPOWERED) BY THE HOLY SPIRIT

Did you ask God to fill you with the Holy Spirit? Do you know that you are now filled with the Holy Spirit? On what authority? (On the trustworthiness of God Himself and His Word: Hebrews 11:6; Romans 14:22, 23.)

Do not depend upon feelings. The promise of God's Word, not our feelings, is our authority. The Christian lives by faith (trust) in the trustworthiness of God Himself and His Word. This train diagram illustrates the relationship between **fact** (God and His Word), **faith** (our trust in God and His Word), and **feeling** (the result of our faith and obedience) (John 14:21).

The train will run with or without the caboose. However, it would be futile to attempt to pull the train by the caboose. In the same way, we, as Christians, do not depend upon feelings or emotions, but we place our faith (trust) in the trustworthiness of God and the promises of His Word.

HOW TO WALK IN THE SPIRIT

Faith (trust in God and in His promises) is the only means by which a Christian can live the Spirit-directed life. As you continue to trust Christ moment by moment:

A. Your life will demonstrate more and more of the fruit of the Spirit (Galatians 5:22, 23) and will be more and more conformed to the image of Christ (Romans 12:2; II Corinthians 3:18).
B. Your prayer life and study of God's Word will become more meaningful.
C. You will experience His power in witnessing (Acts 1:8).
D. You will be prepared for spiritual conflict against the world (I John 2:15-17); against the flesh (Galatians 5:16, 17); and against Satan (I Peter 5:7-9; Ephesians 6:10-13).
E. You will experience His power to resist temptation and sin (I Corinthians 10:13; Philippians 4:13; Ephesians 1:19-23; 6:10; II Timothy 1:7; Romans 6:1-16).

SPIRITUAL BREATHING

By faith you can continue to experience God's love and forgiveness.

If you become aware of an area of your life (an attitude or an action) that is displeasing to the Lord, even though you are walking with Him and sincerely desiring to serve Him, simply thank God that He has forgiven your sins — past, present and future — on the basis of Christ's death on the cross. Claim His love and forgiveness by faith and continue to have fellowship with Him.

If you retake the throne of your life through sin — a definite act of disobedience — breathe spiritually.

Spiritual breathing (exhaling the impure and inhaling the pure) is an exercise in faith that enables you to continue to experience God's love and forgiveness.

1. **Exhale** — confess your sin — agree with God concerning your sin and thank Him for His forgiveness of it, according to I John 1:9 and Hebrews 10:1-25. Confession involves repentance — a change in attitude and action.
2. **Inhale** — surrender the control of your life to Christ, and appropriate (receive) the fullness of the Holy Spirit by faith. Trust that He now directs and empowers you, according to the **command** of Ephesians 5:18, and the **promise** of I John 5:14, 15.

IF THIS BOOKLET HAS BEEN MEANINGFUL AND HELPFUL TO YOU, PLEASE GIVE OR READ IT TO SOMEONE ELSE.

Millions of copies of this booklet, "Have You Made the Wonderful Discovery of the Spirit-filled Life?" have been distributed in most major languages around the world. As a result, thousands of Christians have learned how to experience the power and control of the Holy Spirit, moment by moment. Through the abundant life which Christ promises, and which they are now experiencing, they have become more effective in sharing their faith in Christ with others. Experience has confirmed the validity of Christ's command to the disciples to wait until they were empowered by the Holy Spirit before going forth to the world to share the good news of His love and forgiveness. Most Christians, when they have learned this truth concerning the Holy Spirit, want to be actively involved in sharing Christ and in helping to fulfill the Great Commission in our generation.

WILLIAM R. BRIGHT, President, Campus Crusade for Christ International

A special Bible study series and other helpful materials for Christian growth and witness are available from Campus Crusade.

Exhibit 11

Van Dusen Letter

CAMPUS CRUSADE FOR CHRIST INTERNATIONAL

Arrowhead Springs, San Bernardino, CA 92404 · Telephone (714) 886-5224 · William R. Bright, Founder and President

This letter was written to a prominent business acquaintance who had requested information on how to become a Christian. The name, Dr. Van Dusen, is fictitious. In the last few years several million copies of this letter have been distributed around the world in most major languages.

Dr. Randolph Van Dusen
Groton Manor
Islip, Long Island, New York

Dear Dr. Van Dusen:

Cordial greetings from sunny California! Thank you for your recent kindnesses. The warm expression of your desire to know more about Jesus Christ, the Lord, encourages me to explain briefly the basic facts concerning the Christian life.

First, I would like to have you think of the Christian life as a great adventure, for Jesus said, "I am come that they might have life, and that they might have it more abundantly" (John 10:10).

Second, I want you to know that God loves us and has a wonderful, exciting plan for every life. We are not creatures of chance, brought into the world for a meaningless, miserable existence; but rather, we are creatures of destiny, created for lives of purpose and joyful service. Any student knows that there are definite laws in the physical realm that are inviolate; just so, there are definite spiritual laws that govern our spiritual lives.

Since man is the highest known form of life, and since there is a purpose for everything else, does it not make sense that there is a plan for us? If God created us for a purpose, does it not logically follow that that purpose somehow, somewhere has been revealed? Would this One who created us then leave us to shift for ourselves? All evidence would demonstrate the contrary. How, then, can man know God's plan?

There are eleven living religions, and most of them have their "sacred writings." Yet, when these are studied in an objective manner, it soon becomes very evident that the Old and New Testaments of the Bible differ vastly from the others. Though there is much good in the writings of these various religions, it soon becomes obvious that they in no way compare with the sacred Scriptures upon which Christianity is based.

While studying for three years in two of our country's leading seminaries under some of the world's greatest scholars, it was proven conclusively to me that, in a unique and special way, God has spoken to men through the writings in the Bible.

Every man is seeking happiness, but the Bible says that true happiness can be found only through God's way. Let me explain simply what this way is. The Bible says that God is holy and that man is sinful. There is a great chasm between them. Man is continually trying to find God (see Diagram 1). From the most ignorant savage to the most brilliant professor on the university campus, man is trying to find God and the abundant life through his own efforts. Through the various philosophies and religions of history, man has tried to cross this chasm to find God and a life of purpose and happiness. Man can no more bridge this chasm than he can jump across the Grand Canyon flatfooted, or climb to heaven on a six-foot ladder. The Bible explains that this is impossible because God is holy and righteous, and man is sinful. Man was created to have fellowship with God; but because of his own stubborn self-will and disobedience, man chose to go his own independent way and fellowship was broken. This is what the Bible calls sin.

Pull the plug of a floor lamp out of its wall socket; contact with the electrical current is broken and the light goes out. This is comparable to what happens to man when fellowship with God is broken. The Bible says, "For all have sinned and come short of the glory of God" (Romans 3:23); "For the wages of sin is death; but the gift of God is eternal life through Jesus Christ our Lord" (Romans 6:23).

You will observe that I am not saying that sin is a matter of getting drunk, committing murder, being immoral, etc. These are only the results of sin. You say, "What are the symptoms of a life separated from God?" In addition to some of the grosser sins, there are worry, irritability, lack of purpose in life, no goal, no power, no real interest in living, utter boredom, inferiority complex, frustration, desire to escape reality, and fear of death. These and many others are evidence that man is cut off from the only One who can give him the power to live the abundant life.

St. Augustine, one of the greatest philosophers of all time, said, "Thou hast made us for Thyself, O God, and our hearts are restless until they find their rest in Thee."

Pascal, the great physicist and philosopher, more recently said, as he described the longing in the human heart, "There is a God-shaped vacuum in the heart of each man, which cannot be satisfied by any created thing but only by God, the Creator, made known through Jesus Christ."

Now, if God has a plan for us, a plan which includes a full and abundant life, and all of man's efforts to find God are futile, we must turn to the Bible to see God's way.

The Bible tells us that "God so loved the world, that He gave His only begotten Son, that whosoever believeth in Him should not perish, but have everlasting life" (John 3:16). In other words, this great chasm between God and man cannot be bridged by man's effort, but only by God's effort through His Son, Jesus Christ. Let me call your attention to the fact that we cannot know God through good works. "For by grace are ye saved through faith; and that not of yourselves: it is the gift of God: not of works, lest any man should boast" (Ephesians 2:8-9). Good works will follow an acceptance of God's gift, as an expression of our gratitude.

Diagram 1

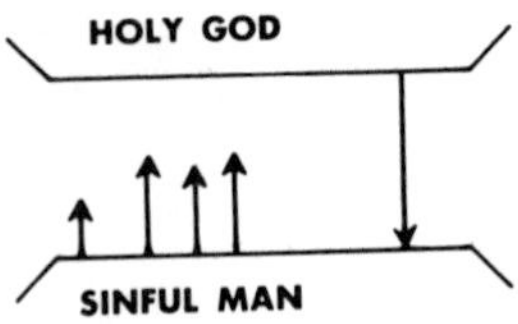

Diagram 2

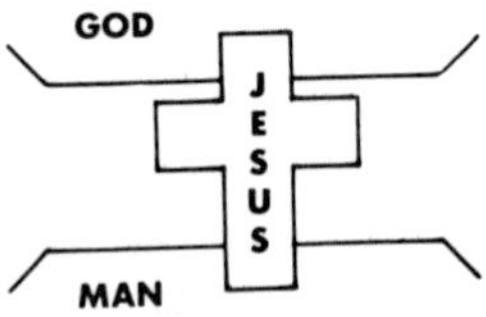

Religion and philosophy have been defined as man's best attempts to find God. Christianity has been defined as God's best effort to find man.

Now, who is this Person, Jesus Christ, that He, more than anyone who has ever lived, has the power to bridge this chasm between a Holy God and sinful man? (See Diagram 2.) By way of review, Jesus of Nazareth was conceived by the Holy Ghost and born of the Virgin Mary almost 2000 years ago. Hundreds of years before, great prophets of Israel foretold His coming. The Old Testament, which was written by many individuals over a period of 1500 years, contains over 300 references to His coming. At the age of thirty, He began His public ministry. Space will not allow for details except to say that, in the three years following, He gave men the formula for a full and abundant life, and for a life to come.

The life Jesus led, the miracles He performed, the words He spoke, His death on the cross, His resurrection, His ascent to heaven, all point to the fact that He was not mere man, but more than man. He himself claimed, "I and My Father are One" (John 10:30); and "he that hath seen Me hath seen the Father" (John 14:9).

Arnold Toynbee, eminent historian of our day, has given more space to Jesus of Nazareth than to any other six great men who have ever lived, including Mohammed, Buddha, Caesar, Napoleon, and George Washington.

The Encyclopedia Britannica gives 20,000 words to Jesus. Thinking men of all lands and religions, who have the opportunity to investigate the evidence, will agree that Jesus is the greatest personality the world has ever known.

It is important to consider that Jesus Christ claimed to be God. He claimed to be the author of a new way of life. Historically, we know that wherever His message has gone, new life, new hope and new purpose for living have resulted. Either Jesus of Nazareth was who He claimed to be, the Son of God, the Savior of mankind, or He was the greatest impostor the world has ever known. If His claims were false, more good has resulted from a lie than has ever been accomplished by the truth. Does it not make sense that this Person (whom most people knowing the facts consider the greatest teacher, the greatest example, the greatest leader the world has ever known) would be, as He himself claimed to be, and as the Bible tells us that He is, the one Person who could bridge the chasm between God and man?

You will remember Romans 6:23, to which I referred, "For the wages of sin is death; but the gift of God is eternal life through Jesus Christ our Lord." As you study the religions and philosophies of the world, you will find no provision for man's sin, apart from the cross of Jesus Christ. The Bible says that without the shedding of blood, there is no remission or forgiveness of sin (Hebrews 9:22). In Acts 4:12, we are told, "Neither is there salvation in any other: for there is none other name under heaven given among men, whereby we must be saved."

Jesus said, "I am the Way, the Truth, and the Life: no man cometh unto the Father, but by Me" (John 14:6). Let me quote to you what Jesus said to a man who came to Him for counsel. They talked, even as we have talked. Turn to the third chapter of John's Gospel and read the first eight verses. First, notice who Nicodemus was.

Nicodemus was a Pharisee, a ruler of the Jews, one of the great religious leaders of his day. We find that, so far as the law was concerned, he was above reproach. He was moral and ethical. He was so eager to please God that he prayed seven times a day. He went to the synagogue to worship God three times a day. Yet he saw in the life of Jesus something which he had never experienced himself; there was a different quality of life altogether. You will note that Nicodemus approached Jesus by saying, "'Rabbi, we know that thou art a teacher come from God; for no man can do these miracles that thou doest, except God be with him.' Jesus answered and said unto him, 'Verily, verily, I say unto thee, except a man be born again, he cannot see the kingdom of God.' Nicodemus saith unto Him, 'How can a man be born when he is old? Can he enter the second time into his mother's womb and be born?' Jesus answered, 'Verily, verily, I say unto thee, except a man be born of water and of the Spirit, he cannot enter the kingdom of God. That which is born of the flesh is flesh; and that which is born of the Spirit is spirit'" (John 3:2-6).

Consider, for example, a caterpillar crawling in the dust — an ugly, hairy worm. One day this worm weaves about its body a cocoon. From this cocoon there emerges a beautiful butterfly. We do not understand fully what has taken place. We realize only that where once a worm crawled in the dust, now a butterfly soars in the heavens. So it is in the lives of Christians. Where once we lived on the lowest level as sinful, egocentric individuals, we now dwell on the highest plane, experiencing full and abundant lives as children of God. An individual becomes a Christian through a spiritual birth. In other words, God is Spirit and we cannot communicate with Him until we become spiritual creatures. (This is what takes place when Jesus comes to live in our lives.) Without His indwelling presence, we cannot communicate with God; we know nothing of His plan for our lives; the Word of God is a dull, uninteresting Book. However, when Jesus comes into our lives, we become spirit-controlled; we love to be with Christians, we love to read the Word of God and we want our lives to count for Him. Just suppose, for the sake of illustration, that we are sitting in a room and we know that there are a number of television programs available to us. We are looking and listening, yet we cannot see the images or hear the voices. What is needed? An instrument — a television set. The moment that we move the television set into the room and turn the dial, we can hear a voice and see an image. So it is when Christ comes into our lives. He is our divine instrument, tuning us into God, making known God's will and love for our lives.

Basically, the only thing that separates an individual from God — and thus from His love and forgiveness — is his own self-will. (Please do not think me presumptuous. I do not wish to embarrass you by encouraging you to do anything that you are reluctant to do. However, because you expressed such genuine interest in knowing more about these matters when we talked face to face, I am taking the liberty, as one who sincerely cares, of encouraging you to enter into this relationship with Christ today — now!)

Well do I remember that night several years ago when, alone in my room, I knelt to surrender my will for the will of Christ. While in prayer, I invited Him to enter the "door" of my life, forgive my sin and take His rightful place on the throne. I must confess that there was no great emotional response, as some have — actually none at all — but, true to His promise, Christ came in; and gradually, like the blooming of a lovely rose, the beauty and fragrance of His presence became real to me. Though I had been perfectly happy and challenged with life, He gave me a new quality of life altogether — a promise of abundant life fulfilled in ways too numerous to mention.

God loves you so much that He gave His only begotten Son to die on the cross for your sins; and Jesus Christ, the Son of God, loved you enough to die on the cross for you. Here He is, the greatest leader, the greatest teacher, the greatest example the world has ever known. But more than this, He is the Son of God, your Savior. Can you think of anyone whom you would rather follow?

Perhaps you are asking, "Suppose I invite Christ into my life and nothing happens? Maybe the Lord will not hear me." May I assure you that you can trust Christ. He promised to come in. He does not lie. A chemist going into a laboratory to work an experiment knows that, by following the Table of Chemical Valence, he will get the desired results. The mathematician knows that the multiplication table is tried and dependable, and that the law of gravity is inviolate. Just so, the laws of the spiritual realm are definite and true, and when God, who created all things and established the laws that govern all things, says that He will enter and change your life, you may accept this promise without question.

However, a word of caution is in order. Do not put undue emphasis on feelings. There must be a balanced emphasis on fact (intellect), faith (trust, involving the will), and feeling (involving the emotions). Meditate on the following verses:

Jesus said, "Behold, I stand at the door, and knock: if any man hear My voice and open the door, I will come in to him, and will sup with him, and he with Me" (Revelation 3:20). "I am come that they might have life, and that they might have it more abundantly" (John 10:10). He has come to forgive your sins. He has come to bring peace and purpose to life.

Our lives are filled with many activities, such as business, travel, finances, social life and home life, with no real purpose or meaning. Jesus knocks at the heart's door, seeking entrance. He will not force himself. Jesus wants to come into your life and make harmony out of discord — to create meaning and purpose where now there is something lacking. He wants to forgive your sin and bridge the gulf between you and God. He does not want to enter your life as a guest, but He wants to control your life as Lord and Master.

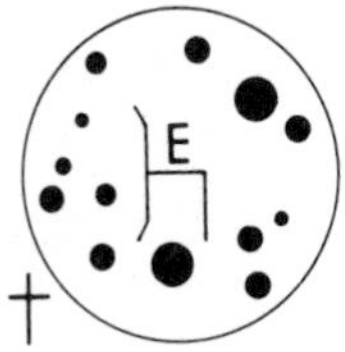

E—Ego or self on the throne
●—the various interests and activities under control of finite self, resulting in discord and frustration

There is a throne in each heart. All of these years, your ego has been on the throne. Now Christ waits for you to invite Him to be on the throne. You must step down and relinquish the authority of your life to Him.

You can see from this simple diagram how, when Christ becomes Lord of your life, He becomes Lord of every activity, which, as you can see, makes for a harmonious life. Is it not better to be controlled by the infinite, loving God who created you and suffered for you than to continue under the control of finite self?

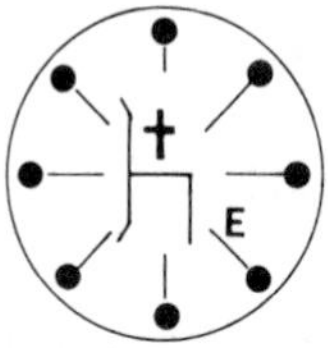

t—Jesus Christ on the throne

●—the various interests and activities under control of God, resulting in harmony and in purpose

The great difference Christ makes may be seen in the realm of marriage. Notice that, according to Harvard University's famous sociologist, Dr. Pitirim Sorokin, two of every five marriages in recent years in the United States ended in divorce. However, in Christian marriages, where the family practice of Bible study and prayer is daily observed, there is only one divorce in every 1,015 marriages. Why the difference? This is simple. The ego of the husband reacts against the ego of the wife, or vice versa. Friction and discord result. Yet when Christ is on the throne of each life, there can be no discord, only harmony, as He does not war against himself.

In John 1:12, we are told, "But as many as received Him, to them gave He power to become the sons of God, even to them that believe on His name." "And this is the record, that God hath given to us eternal life, and this life is in His Son. He that hath the Son hath life; and he that hath not the Son of God hath not life" (I John 5:11-12). (Speaking of life, few people give serious thought to the fact that we must one day die. The Scripture reminds us that "it is appointed unto men once to die, and after this the judgment" [Hebrews 9:27]. Christ prepares men for death as well as for life, and a man is not ready to live until he is ready to die.)

"Therefore if any man be in Christ, he is a new creature: old things are passed away; behold, all things are become new" (II Corinthians 5:17).

Will you not sincerely invite the Lord Jesus into your heart, and surrender your will completely to Him, right now? We can talk with God through prayer. Why not find a quiet place where you can kneel or bow reverently in God's presence and ask Christ to come into your heart. In your prayer, you can say something like this:

"Lord Jesus, I invite You to come into my life, forgive my sins, and become my Lord and Master." Pray in your own words. God knows your heart and is not concerned with your words, but rather with the attitude of your heart.

To invite Christ into your life is absolutely the most important decision that you will ever make; and when you do so, several wonderful things will happen:

1. Christ will actually come to live in your heart.
2. Your sins will be forgiven.
3. You will truly become a child of God.
4. You are assured of heaven.
5. Your life becomes a great adventure, as God reveals His plan and purpose.

Did you ask Christ into your heart? Were you sincere? Where is He right now? In the event that you are disappointed because there may have been no great emotional experience — though some may indeed know this immediate joy — I want to remind you again that a Christian must place his faith in the Word of God, not in feelings; for emotions come and go, but the Word of God is trustworthy and true. Christ promised to enter when you opened the door. He does not lie. Meditate again on the truth of Revelation 3:20; John 1:12; I John 5:11-13; II Corinthians 5:17. Take time right now to thank God for what has happened to you as you have prayed.

Since you have never been satisfied with mediocrity in your business, you will certainly not want to be an ordinary Christian. It costs us nothing to become Christians, although it cost God His own dear Son to give us this privilege. But it will cost us both time and effort to be the kind of Christians which God would have us be. For obvious reasons, a Christian should be a better businessman, father, husband, mother, student, or whatever.

Here is a suggestion that will enable you to grow quickly in the Christian life, illustrated by a simple little word . . . GROW: Go to God in prayer daily; Read God's Word daily; Obey God moment by moment; Witness for Christ daily through your life and words.

In Hebrews 10:25, we are admonished to "forsake not the assembling of ourselves together . . . " Several logs burn brightly together; put one aside on the cold hearth and the fire goes out. So it is with you and your relationship to other Christians. If you do not belong to a church, do not wait to be invited. Take the initiative; call the pastor of a nearby church where Christ is honored and the Bible is preached. Make plans to start next Sunday and to attend each week.

Be assured of my love and prayers as you make this all important decision. We shall be looking forward to hearing from you soon.

Sincerely yours,

William R. Bright, President

WRB:br

If, after reading this letter you have prayed to invite Christ to come into your life, a special series of informative and practical letters to assist you in your Christian growth and to aid you in your study of the Bible is available simply by asking that your name be added to the Bible study correspondence course. You may also request information regarding the **Ten Basic Steps Toward Christian Maturity,** a series of booklets designed for individual or group study.

Exhibit 12
Four-Question Survey

Example #1: For a "Religious Campus"

1. Do you think the spiritual area is important to most college students?

   Yes No Maybe

2. Is the spiritual area important to you?

   Yes No Maybe

3. Would you be interested in a small group Bible Study?

   Yes No Maybe

4. Would you be interested in talking with someone about your relationship with God?

   Name________________________________
   Address ______________________________
   Phone # ______________________________

Example #2: "Typical Campus"

1. Year in School

   Fresh ____ Soph ____ Jr ____ Sr ____

2. Religious Background

   Protestant ____ Catholic ____ Jewish ____ Other ____

3. Who, in your opinion is Jesus Christ?

   ____

4. Would you be interested in investigating what the Bible has to say about a personal relationship with God through Jesus Christ?

   Yes ____ No ____ Maybe ____

   If so, which format would interest you most?

   Discussion with another individual _______?

   Small Group Discussion _______?

   Name________________________________
   Address ______________________________
   Phone # ______________________________

Exhibit 13

Student Leadership Questionnaire

1. What qualities do you think make a man or a woman a leader?

2. In your opinion, what are the major problems confronting students today?

3. What major problems are confronting people of the world today?

4. It has been said that a leader is someone who knows where he is going and can motivate others to follow him. Do you feel confident that you know where you are going?

5. As a leader, what do you hope to accomplish in your lifetime?

6. People often follow the example set by others.

   a. Is there someone who has served as a model leader for you? (Why or why not?)

   b. Are you satisfied with the model you project to others? (Why or why not?)

7. Most people who have had the opportunity to investigate the evidence agree that Jesus Christ is the most outstanding leader of history. In your opinion, what qualities of leadership did He demonstrate?

8. Jesus Christ can be known in a personal way. Have you ever had the opportunity to begin a relationship with Him?

Exhibit 14
National Collegiate Religious Survey

National Collegiate Religious Survey

INSTRUCTIONS

DO NOT USE PEN OR BALL POINT. A standard number two (No. 2) lead pencil should be used. Make broad, dark marks that completely fill the area between the pairs of lines. Do not mark beyond the ends of the lines. Completely erase any marks you wish to delete.

1. SEX
:::::MALE :::::FEMALE

2. UNIVERSITY OR SCHOOL ______________________

3. CLASS
:::::FRESHMAN :::::SOPHOMORE :::::JUNIOR :::::SENIOR :::::GRADUATE

4. WHAT IS YOUR MAJOR?
:::::LIBERAL ARTS :::::BUSINESS :::::MEDICINE :::::NURSING :::::SCIENCE :::::EDUCATION :::::ENGINEERING
:::::UNDECIDED :::::FINE ARTS :::::LAW :::::AGRICULTURE :::::OTHER

5. ARE YOU A MEMBER OF ANY RELIGIOUS GROUP?
:::::YES :::::NO :::::USED TO BE :::::IN PROCESS OF JOINING

6. WOULD YOU CARE TO GIVE THE NAME OF THIS GROUP?
:::::NOT A MEMBER :::::ASSEMBLY OF GOD :::::BAPTIST :::::BUDDHIST :::::CHRISTIAN :::::CHRISTIAN SCIENCE :::::CHURCH OF CHRIST :::::CONGREGATIONAL :::::EPISCOPAL
:::::HINDU :::::INDEPENDENT CHRISTIAN :::::ISLAM :::::JEWISH :::::LUTHERAN :::::LDS-MORMON :::::METHODIST :::::NAZARENE :::::PRESBYTERIAN
:::::REFORMED :::::ROMAN CATHOLIC :::::SEVENTH DAY ADVENTIST :::::OTHER

7. AT WHAT AGE DID YOU BECOME A MEMBER? :::::NOT A MEMBER
:::::0-2 :::::3-5 :::::6-10 :::::11-15 :::::16-18 :::::19-21 :::::22-25 :::::26-30 :::::31-40 :::::41 AND UP :::::NOT SURE

8. AT PRESENT, HOW OFTEN DO YOU ATTEND SERVICES?
:::::MORE THAN ONCE EACH WEEK :::::ONCE A WEEK :::::ONCE A MONTH :::::TWICE A MONTH :::::SELDOM :::::NEVER

9. ARE YOU ACTIVE IN ANY CAMPUS RELIGIOUS GROUP? WHICH ONE?
:::::NO :::::EPISCOPAL :::::BAPTIST :::::LDS-MORMON :::::JEWISH :::::PRESBYTERIAN :::::LUTHERAN :::::OTHER
:::::ROMAN CATHOLIC :::::CHURCH OF CHRIST :::::CHRISTIAN SCIENCE :::::METHODIST :::::CAMPUS CRUSADE :::::UNITED PROTESTANT CENTER :::::IVCF

10. ABOUT WHICH RELIGIOUS FOUNDER DO YOU KNOW THE MOST?
:::::MOHAMMED :::::BUDDHA :::::MOSES :::::JESUS CHRIST :::::OTHER :::::NONE

11. WHO IS JESUS CHRIST ACCORDING TO YOUR UNDERSTANDING?
:::::SECOND PERSON OF TRINITY; SAVIOUR; GOD-MAN :::::MAN, LEADER :::::FOUNDER OF CHURCH :::::CREATOR; SUPREME BEING; RULER OF WORLD
:::::PROPHET :::::I DO NOT KNOW :::::NOT SURE :::::OTHER

12. FROM WHAT SOURCE DID YOU GAIN THIS UNDERSTANDING?
:::::BIBLE :::::BOOKS :::::CATECHISM :::::CHURCH MINISTER :::::SUNDAY SCHOOL :::::CHURCH SCHOOL :::::PROFESSORS :::::FRIENDS, STUDENTS :::::OTHER

13. IN YOUR OPINION, HOW DOES ONE BECOME A CHRISTIAN?
:::::BELIEVE IN CHRIST AS PERSONAL SAVIOUR :::::LIVE A GOOD LIFE :::::BELIEVE THE BIBLE :::::UNDERSTAND AND FOLLOW TEACHINGS OF CHRIST
:::::HOLD PERSONAL CONVICTIONS :::::BAPTISM :::::JOIN CHURCH OR SEE MINISTER :::::REARED TO BE OR BORN :::::DON'T KNOW

14. ACCORDING TO EARLIER RESULTS OF THIS SURVEY, THE MAJORITY OF COLLEGE STUDENTS TODAY FEEL THE NEED FOR A MORE PERSONAL RELIGIOUS FAITH. WHY DO YOU THINK THEY HAVE THIS NEED?
:::::I DO NOT KNOW :::::NEED TO BELIEVE IN SOMETHING :::::COMPLEX WORLD PROBLEMS :::::INSECURITY :::::AWAY FROM HOME AND FAMILY
:::::NEED ADDITIONAL STRENGTH :::::NEED GUIDANCE :::::CONFLICTING MORAL STANDARDS :::::OTHER

15. DO YOU FEEL THE NEED FOR A MORE PERSONAL RELIGIOUS FAITH?
:::::YES :::::NO :::::I DON'T KNOW

:::::RC :::::N :::::AC :::::WP :::::NO :::::HS :::::FP :::::FL :::::FC :::::FT

Exhibit 15
Collegiate Religious Survey

1. Sex
   ____Male ____Female

   University or School ____________

2. Class
   ____Freshman ____Sophmore ____Junior ____Senior
   ____Graduate

3. What is your Major?
   ____Liberal Arts ____Business ____Medicine ____Nursing
   ____Education ____Engineering ____Fine Arts ____Science
   ____Law ____Agriculture ____Math ____Social Science
   ____Other ____Undecided

4. Are you now, or have you ever been, a member of any religious group or church?
   ____Yes ____No ____Used to be ____In process of joining

5. Would you care to give the name of this group, denomination or church?
   ____Not a member ____Assembly of God ____Baptist ____Buddhist
   ____Christian ____Christian Science ____Church of Christ
   ____Congregational ____Episcopal ____Hindu
   ____Independent Christian ____Islam ____Jewish ____Lutheran
   ____LDS ____Mormon ____Methodist ____Nazarene
   ____Presbyterian ____Reformed ____Roman Catholic
   ____Seventh Day Adventist ____Other

6. If asked to explain your philosophy of life, would your answer be:
   ____Definite ____Vague ____None

7. To what extent could you honestly say you live according to your philosophy of life?
   ____All of the time ____Most of the time
   ____Half of the time ____Seldom

8. What, in your opinion is the basic problem of man (humanity)?
   ____Intolerance ____Racism ____Poverty ____War
   ____Lack of education ____Religion ____Environment
   ____Self-centeredness ____Politics ____Economics
   ____Sin ____Other ____None

9. Does your philosophy of life include a solution for the basic problem of man (humanity)?
_____Yes _____No solution

10. Do you believe in a God who is both infinite and personal?
_____Yes _____No

11. Have you ever seriously read through the New Testament?
_____Yes _____No _____More than half _____Less than half

12. Who, in your opinion, is Jesus Christ?
_____Teacher _____Philosopher _____Prophet
_____Founder of church _____Myth _____Son of God, God-Man
_____Other _____Not sure _____Don't know _____Philosophical Ideal

13. How have you come to this understanding?
_____Religious education _____Secular education _____Pastor
_____Bible _____Friends _____Books _____Personal study

14. In your opinion, how does one become a Christian?
_____Believe in Christ as personal savior _____Live a good life
_____Believe the Bible _____Understand and follow teachings of Christ
_____Hold personal convictions _____Baptism _____Join church or see minister
_____Reared or be born one _____Don't know

15. If you could know God personally, would you be interested?
_____Yes _____No _____Unsure

This ends the survey. We would, however, like your opinion on four more points. Do you have some more time?

Exhibit 16

Black Student Religious Survey

1. University or school: ______________________________

2. Sex: ____male____ female

3. Class in High School: ____________________
   College: Fr_____ So _____ Jr _____ Sr _____ Grad _____

4. Major ______________________________

5. About which black religious leader do you know the most? (Martin Luther King, Malcom X, Jesse Jackson, Elijah Mohammed, etc.)

   ____

6. About which religious founder do you know the most? (Mohammed, Buddha, Jesus Christ, other)

   ____

7. Are you a member of any religious group or church?
   Yes ________ No ________

8. At what age did you become a member? ____________

9. At present how often do you attend services or meetings?

   ____

10. Is your church or group all black? _____%

11. What influence has religion played in your life? __________

    ____

12. What influence has Jesus Christ played in your life? ________

    ____

13. Who is Jesus Christ according to your understanding? ________

    ____

14. From what source(s) did you gain this understanding? ________

    ____

15. In your opinion, what is a Christian?____________________

____

16. In your opinion, how does one become a Christian?__________

____

Exhibit 17
Faculty Religious Survey

FACULTY RELIGIOUS SURVEY

INSTRUCTIONS
DO NOT USE PEN OR BALL POINT. A standard number two (No. 2) lead pencil should be used. Make broad, dark marks that completely fill the area between the pairs of lines. Do not mark beyond the ends of the lines. Completely erase any marks you wish to delete.

1. SEX
MALE FEMALE

2. UNIVERSITY OR SCHOOL ______

3. WHAT IS YOUR POSITION?
INSTRUCTOR ASST. PROF. ASSOC. PROF. PROF. ADMIN. OTHER

4. WHAT IS YOUR FIELD?
FINE ARTS BIOLOGICAL SCIENCES HUMANITIES MATHEMATICS BUSINESS
PHYSICAL SCIENCES SOCIAL/BEHAVIORAL SCIENCES AGRICULTURE (vet. med.)
HOME ECONOMICS EDUCATION ENGINEERING MEDICINE DENTISTRY LAW
PHARMACY ADMINISTRATION OTHER

5. ARE YOU A MEMBER OF ANY RELIGIOUS GROUP?
YES NO USED TO BE IN PROCESS OF JOINING

6. WOULD YOU CARE TO GIVE THE NAME OF THIS GROUP?
NOT A MEMBER ASSEMBLY OF GOD BAPTIST BUDDHIST CHRISTIAN CHRISTIAN SCIENCE CHURCH OF CHRIST
CONGREGATIONAL EPISCOPAL HINDU INDEPENDENT CHRISTIAN MUSLIM JEWISH LUTHERAN LDS-MORMON
METHODIST NAZARENE PRESBYTERIAN REFORMED ROMAN CATHOLIC SEVENTH DAY ADVENTIST OTHER

7. AT WHAT AGE DID YOU BECOME A MEMBER? NOT A MEMBER
0-2 3-5 6-10 11-15 16-18 19-21 22-25 26-30 31-40 41 AND UP NOT SURE

8. AT PRESENT, HOW OFTEN DO YOU ATTEND SERVICES?
MORE THAN ONCE EACH WEEK ONCE A WEEK ONCE A MONTH TWICE A MONTH SELDOM NEVER

9. ARE YOU ACTIVE IN OR A SPONSOR FOR ANY CAMPUS RELIGIOUS GROUP? WHICH ONE?
NO EPISCOPAL BAPTIST LDS MORMON JEWISH PRESBYTERIAN LUTHERAN OTHER
ROMAN CATHOLIC CHURCH OF CHRIST CHRISTIAN SCIENCE METHODIST CAMPUS CRUSADE UNITED PROTESTANT CENTER IVCF

10. ABOUT WHICH RELIGIOUS FOUNDER DO YOU KNOW THE MOST?
MOHAMMED BUDDHA MOSES JESUS CHRIST OTHER NONE

11. WHO IS JESUS CHRIST ACCORDING TO YOUR UNDERSTANDING?
SECOND PERSON OF TRINITY; SAVIOR ; GOD-MAN MAN, LEADER FOUNDER OF CHURCH CREATOR; SUPREME BEING; RULER OF WORLD
PROPHET I DO NOT KNOW NOT SURE OTHER

12. FROM WHAT SOURCE DID YOU GAIN THIS UNDERSTANDING?
BIBLE BOOKS CATECHISM CHURCH MINISTER SUNDAY SCHOOL CHURCH SCHOOL PROFESSORS
FRIENDS, STUDENTS OTHER

13. IN YOUR OPINION, HOW DOES ONE BECOME A CHRISTIAN?
BELIEVE IN CHRIST AS PERSONAL SAVIOR LIVE A GOOD LIFE BELIEVE THE BIBLE UNDERSTAND AND FOLLOW TEACHINGS OF CHRIST
HOLD PERSONAL CONVICTIONS BAPTISM JOIN CHURCH OR SEE MINISTER REARED TO BE OR BORN DON'T KNOW

14. ACCORDING TO EARLIER RESULTS OF THIS SURVEY, THE MAJORITY OF THOSE ON THE CAMPUS TODAY FEEL THE NEED FOR A MORE PERSONAL RELIGIOUS FAITH. WHY DO YOU THINK THEY HAVE THIS NEED?
I DO NOT KNOW NEED TO BELIEVE IN SOMETHING COMPLEX WORLD PROBLEMS INSECURITY AWAY FROM HOME AND FAMILY
NEED ADDITIONAL STRENGTH NEED GUIDANCE CONFLICTING MORAL STANDARDS OTHER

15. DO YOU FEEL THE NEED FOR A MORE PERSONAL RELIGIOUS FAITH?
YES NO I DON'T KNOW

RC N AC WP NO HS FP FL FC FT.

FOLLOWING IS A KEY TO THE CODE USED: RC-RECEIVED CHRIST, N-NO DECISION, AC-ALREADY CHRISTIAN, WP-WILL PRAY, NO-NO OPPORTUNITY, HS-APPROPRIATED FILLING OF HOLY SPIRIT, FP-FOLLOW-THROUGH PERSONALLY, FL-FOLLOW-THROUGH BY LETTER, FC-FOLLOW-THROUGH BY CHURCH, FT-FOLLOW-THROUGH BY TEN BASIC STEPS.

INTERVIEWER______ DATE______

Exhibit 18
Athletic Survey

1. What goals do you have in athletics?

2. What is the most difficult aspect of athletics you face?

3. Every athlete experiences defeat at times. How do you keep going when you lose?

4. In your opinion, how important is motivation to an athlete's success?

   _____ absolutely the most important ingredient
   _____ very important
   _____ average importance
   _____ not an important ingredient

5. What motivates you personally to compete?

6. Do you ever lose your motivation? Why or why not?

   How do you regain it once it is lost?

7. When are you motivated the most? (at games, practice, off-season)

8. What personal character qualities are necessary to succeed in your sport?

9. Do you have a way of developing these qualities? How?

10. Many of the character qualities of a successful athlete are demonstrated in the person of Jesus Christ. Do you believe a personal relationship with God could help you develop the qualities you need to succeed in your sport?

    _____ yes _____ no _____ not sure

11. If you could know God personally, would you be interested?

    _____ yes _____ no _____ not sure

12. In your opinion, how does one begin a personal relationship with God?

Exhibit 19
International Student Survey

1. What is your home country and city?
2. What is your major field of study?

   What is your year in school?
3. What degree do you desire to obtain?

   What do you hope to do after you have this degree?
4. What high schools and colleges did you attend in your home country?
5. How long have you been in the United States?
6. What do you wish to do in this country before returning again to your home country?
7. What has been the most pleasant experience you have had since coming to this country?
8. What has been the most difficult experience you have had since coming to this country?
9. What, in your opinion, is the basic problem of man today?

10 Are you now, or have you ever been, a member of any religious group or church?

   If so, what is the name of this religious group or church?

11 Do you have a personal concept of God?

   If so, could you explain your concept of God?

12. What exposure have you had to Christianity in your home country?
13. What exposure have you had to Christianity while in the United States?

14. Have you read any part of the Bible?
    Which part?

15. In your opinion, who is Jesus Christ?

16. In your opinion, *how* does a person become a Christian?

Exhibit 20

Survey Record

Caller:

Date:

City:

Address (Dorm, house, apt.)	Name *	NOT HOME	NOT INTERESTED	SHARED 4 LAWS	RECEIVED CHRIST	SHARED MINISTRY-HOLY SPIRIT	PRAYED TO BE FILLED	LEFT VAN DUSEN	LEFT JESUS & THE INTELLECTUAL	LEFT COLLEGIATE CHALLENGE	LEFT TRANSFERABLE CONCEPT	SEND INTRODUCTORY STEP	SEND STEP #3	SEND FOLLOW-UP LETTER	CALL BACK	OTHER	Comments

*Request name only if person is interested or prays to receive Christ. Always get the address.
BE SURE to turn in this record. You will want to copy any information you need for your own personal follow-up ministry.

Exhibit 21
Survey Codes

CODE FOR SURVEYS

Interpret the code at the bottom of the surveys as follows:

Abbreviation	Interpretation
RC	Received Christ.
N	No decision.
AC	Already Christian.
WP	Will pray.
NO	No opportunity.
HS	Appropriated filling of Holy Spirit.
FP	Follow-through personally.
FL	Follow-through by letter.
FC	Follow-through by church.
FT	Follow-through by Transferable Concepts.

Exhibit 22

Sample Testimony #1

Nancy Thien
University of Illinois, Urbana
Senior, Elementary Education

I began my gymnastics career with a cartwheel through my parents' living room picture window. To keep me from destroying the rest of the house, they shuffled me off to a YMCA gymnastics camp.

From the time I began the YMCA classes, I felt that gymnastics was a challenge I could reach by myself. I enjoyed having my own identity.

But gymnastics is such a mental sport. You really have to concentrate, and it's easy to burn yourself out—to buckle under the strain. I looked at everything I did in a negative manner—"What did I do wrong? What will the judge take points off for?" My coach was a staunch perfectionist, and if I didn't perform the right way, I felt like a heel. I was so eager to please, and so uptight about competing.

In 1973, when I was a sophomore in high school, I spent a week at a gymnastics camp, rooming with two other girls from Seattle. It soon became evident that they were really enthusiastic about Jesus Christ. I guess I had always been aware of God and had tried to rely on Him for my strength. But making a personal commitment to Christ—realizing that He had died for my sins and wanted to be not only my Savior and Lord but also be my best friend—that was something no one had ever shown me before. So during camp I trusted my life fully to Christ, saying, "I want to know what it is to walk with You, to be more like You."

Once I committed myself to Christ, I found I could put all my feelings and anxieties in His hands. It was almost like taking a deep breath and letting all the tensions come out of me because I knew that Jesus Christ had everything under control.

Of course, saying God is in control and then believing it when the going gets rough are two different things, and I was put to the test this year during the Nationals Competition of college athletes. I trained and trained for the Nationals, working extra hard to make up for three weeks I had been down with a strep throat.

Gathered with the other gymnasts for the final practice session the day before the competition, I was amazed when all the others stopped their own workouts and applauded my performance. In fact, everyone told me I was sure to win the meet. But that dream didn't last long. On my very last practice event I landed funny and tore every ligament in my foot.

Strange enough, even lying there in a heap, I could still thank God. I know that many athletes are afraid of being seriously injured, and I used to talk about my "good luck" that kept me healthy. But in a relationship with Christ, it's not a matter of luck, it's a matter of purpose—His purpose for my life. He kept me healthy for a long time, and when it came time to be injured, He did it royally.

But I knew He hadn't let me down. God promised that if He takes something away He will return it one hundredfold. He took away my chance at the Nationals, but He gave me a peace that holds up under any kind of human disaster.

I've found that God doesn't stand on the wayside watching your life go by. He's intimately involved. I've learned to have patience. I've learned to trust. As I've learned that, everything works out for good.

Exhibit 23
Sample Testimony #2

Larry Burkett
Financial Counselor
Decatur, Georgia

My first real disillusionment in life came soon after I graduated from college in 1967. I realized that after six years of attending school in the evenings to get a degree in marketing and finance, I was totally disgusted with a system that didn't teach me what I thought I should have learned. My personal goals had always been to achieve education, position and money—in that order—but my education didn't seem to add anything valuable to my life.

Consequently, I set out to achieve my next goal—position. I tried to control everything I came in contact with, including my business, my wife and my family. I refused to take advice or direction from anybody. Confident that I could do a good job, they left me alone for fear of incurring my wrath. But even with position, my life was characterized by an alarming lack of peace and meaning. When I became vice president of a manufacturing company, feelings of rejection and depression put me in even worse shape emotionally.

I went on to achieve my third goal of accumulating money. A hoarder by nature, ever since the first dollar I ever made, I have always saved half of what I earned. But even financial status left me more and more depressed and, in conquering all three of my life goals, I discovered that nothing I had done was meaningful.

Meanwhile, as I looked around at the so-called Christians I knew—the avid church-goers—they seemed as depressed and miserable as I was. And I thought, "What good would Christianity do me?" when the Christians I saw lived the same way I did?

Then seven years ago, during a dental appointment, my dentist explained what Jesus Christ had done in his life. "I have perfect peace," he said. "I don't have to seek after new things to give my life meaning. I love my wife and my children, but most of all, I love my Lord."

God used that experience to spark an interest, and I joined the dentist's Bible study specifically to argue with him and shatter the credibility of his faith. But as I questioned everything he said during the next three or four months, I noticed wisdom in the doctor that I had not seen in anyone else. He never argued back, but took me right into the Bible. "Well, God said . . ." he would begin, giving me answers from Scripture. After six months of being confronted with the authority of God Himself, I asked Christ to come into my life, cleanse me of my selfish attitudes and actions, and inject my life with meaning.

After receiving Christ, I found that my old attitudes were conquered. I began to love people, especially my family. But the greatest change during the last seven years is that, day in and day out, my life is characterized by peace—the peace that comes from Christ, and not from trying to attain wealth and status.

Exhibit 24
Testimony Worksheet

A beginning, attention-getting sentence:

My first encounter with dynamic Christianity:

My honest reactions to it:

Why I decided to yield my life to Christ and how I did:

After I yielded my life to Christ, these changes took place:

Exhibit 25

Sample Four Spiritual Laws Talk

Just as there are physical laws that govern the physical universe, so there are spiritual laws which govern your relationship with God. The first describes something about God, the second something about man, the third something about Christ and the fourth tells you what to do with the other three.

The first law states that: "God loves you and offers a wonderful plan for your life."

There's often a great contrast between the conditional nature of human love and the unconditional nature of God's love. Human love is often selfish at its root. It says, "I love you *because* you love me," or "I will love you *if* you return my love."

But God's love is unconditional. He loves and accepts us just as we are. It's this type of unconditional love that makes human relationships work.

God's love is described in John 3:16: "For God so loved the world, that He gave His only begotten Son, that whoever believes in Him should not perish, but have eternal life."

God's plan is described in John 10:10 when Christ said: "I came that they might have life, and might have it abundantly"—in other words, that it might be full and meaningful.

But most people are not experiencing the abundant life.

For instance, O.J. Simpson, a football superstar and millionaire, was quoted in an issue of *People* magazine as saying, "I sit in my house in Buffalo and sometimes I get so . . . lonely it's unbelievable. Life has been so good to me. I've got a great wife, good kids, money, my own health—and I'm lonely and bored . . . . I often wondered why so many rich people commit suicide. Money sure isn't a cure-all."

Law Two states the underlying reason that many people like O.J. don't experience a life of abundance.

Man is *sinful* and *separated* from God. Therefore, he cannot know and experience God's love and plan for his life.

You see, man's basic problem is that he is sinful. The apostle Paul wrote: "For all have sinned and fall short of the glory of God."

Man was created to have fellowship with God; but, because of his own stubborn self-will, he chose to go his own independent way and fellowship with God was broken.

This self-will, characterized by an attitude of active rebellion or passive indifference, is evidence of what the Bible calls sin.

The word *sin* comes from a Greek word that means "to miss the mark." When someone would shoot at a target and miss the center—the bull's eye—the distance from the arrow to the bull's eye was called "sin." In the same way, we do good things, but we still miss the mark of God's perfect standards. What are the consequences for this?

The apostle Paul stated them this way: "For the wages of sin is death" or spiritual separation from God.

Because of this separation caused by sin, man is unable to reach God and the abundant life, even though he might live a morally good or religious life.

The third law explains the only way to bridge this gulf . . . .

Law Three says that Jesus Christ is God's *only* provision for man's sin. Through Him you can know and experience God's love and plan for your life.

Romans 5:8 says, "But God demonstrates His own love toward us, in that while we were yet sinners, Christ died for us."

A modern story illustrates what Christ has done for us. One day a man who was a judge tried his own son who was brought into court on a traffic violation. The judge was faced with his responsibilities to pass sentence on the guilty one, but he was also full of compassion, since the guilty one was his son. The boy was penniless, but the judge passed sentence on him. Then, he took off his robe, came down from his place of authority, stood beside his son and paid the fine himself.

Because we were helpless to pay the penalty for our sin, God, after passing the sentence of death on us, stepped down from heaven, became man and paid the penalty.

This love that Jesus showed for us when He died on the cross is more than an idea. The love of Christ lives because Jesus lives. Because Jesus is alive we can relate to a living person who loves us right now.

Not only did Christ die, but He also rose from the dead. In describing this, Paul wrote, "Christ died for our sins . . . . He was buried . . . . He was raised on the third day, according to the Scriptures . . . . He appeared to Peter, then to the twelve. After that He appeared to more than five hundred . . . ."

His resurrection is conclusive proof of His claim that He was God. In speaking to Thomas, "Jesus said to him, 'I am the way, and the truth, and the life; no one comes to the Father, but through Me.'"

You know, man has tried many ways to reach God—drugs, philosophy and even religion. But his search goes on as these attempts leave him unfulfilled. Religion and philosophy have been defined as man's best attempts to reach God. Christianity has been defined as God's best effort to reach man.

So, in summary we can see that God has bridged the gulf which separates us from God by sending His Son, Jesus Christ, to die on the cross in our place to pay the penalty for our sins.

Consider the previous illustration of a judge who had to hand down a guilty verdict against his son. Imagine the son's crime as having been more serious than a traffic violation. Let's say instead that he'd been convicted of murder. Again, the judge would have had no choice but to pass sentence. In this case he would have had to pronounce his son "guilty" and sentence him to death.

But, let's say the judge then rose and walked down to where his son stood weeping. He turned to the crowded courtroom and said, "My son is guilty and the demands of the law must be met. But because I love my son, I will pay the penalty for him." The judge took off his judicial robe and offered himself to the police officers who led him away to die for the crime of his son.

We would all agree that this is a story of great love. And it is also a picture of God's love for us. We are guilty of sin, and the penalty of sin is death. But because God loves us, He volunteered to pay our penalty by offering Himself (in the person of His Son) to die for us.

Law Four describes what we must do in light of the other three laws. It states: "We must individually *receive* Jesus Christ as Savior and Lord; then we can know and experience God's love and plan for our lives."

We must receive Christ. "But as many as received Him, to them He gave the right to become children of God, even to those who believe in His name."

We receive Christ through faith. "For by grace you have been saved through faith; and that not of yourselves, it is the gift of God; not as a result of works, that no one should boast."

There are two important words in this verse, *grace* and *faith*.

Grace refers to God's love for us, which He demonstrated by sending His Son to die for us when we didn't deserve it. God offers His grace, His gift of salvation, to us as a gift. But it is not enough to know that a gift is being offered; it must be *received* before it becomes ours.

Faith is a decision to accept the gift being offered and to trust the word and character of the person offering the gift.

A story illustrates this. In 1830 George Wilson was tried by the U.S. court in Philadelphia for robbery and murder and was sentenced to hang. Andrew Jackson, President of the United States, granted him a presidential pardon. But Wilson refused the pardon, insisting that it was not a pardon unless he accepted it. The question was brought before the U.S. Supreme Court, and Chief Justice John Marshall wrote the following decision: "A pardon is a peer, the value of which depends upon its acceptance by the person implicated. It's hardly to be supposed that one under sentence of death would refuse to accept a pardon, but if it is refused, it is no pardon. George Wilson must hang." And he was hanged.

When we receive Christ into our lives, we are actually born again. Just as being born of physical parents gives us the ability to live in this world, so being born spiritually into God's family gives us the ability to live in the spiritual realm. It's this second birth that enables us to have a relationship with God.

Finally, we receive Christ by personal invitation. Christ is speaking and says:

"Behold, I stand at the door and knock; if anyone hears My voice and opens the door, I will come in to him . . . ."

The promise Jesus makes is that He will come into our lives if we want Him to. Like marriage, receiving Christ involves two "yes" answers—one from the bride and one from the groom. One "yes" is not enough. Christ has already said "yes" to us. Now it remains for us to say "yes" to Him.

How do you say "yes" to Christ and receive Him? Receiving Christ involves turning from self to God (repentance) and trusting Christ to come into our lives to forgive our sins and to make us the kind of people He wants us to be. Just to agree intellectually that Jesus Christ is the Son of God and that He died on the cross for our sins is not enough. Nor is it enough to have an emotional experience. We receive Jesus Christ by faith, as an act of the will.

Imagine two kinds of lives:

1. The first is the self-directed life. Self is on the throne of this person's life. Christ is outside the life. This person's interests are directed by self, often resulting in discord and frustration.

2. In contrast, the second life is the Christ-directed life. Christ has come into this person's life. Self is yielding to Christ, and this individual's interests are directed by Christ, resulting in harmony with God's plan.

Which one would you say best represents your life? Which one would you like to have represent you life?

You can receive Christ right now by faith through prayer. Prayer is talking with God. God knows your heart and is not so concerned with your words as He is with the attitude of your heart. If you have never invited Christ into your life, you can do so by repeating silently in your heart the prayer I am going to say aloud in a moment. The prayer I am going to pray goes like this:

"Lord Jesus, I need You. Thank You for dying on the cross for my sins. I open the door of my life and receive You as My Savior and Lord. Thank You for forgiving my sins and giving me eternal life. Make me the kind of person You want me to be."

If this prayer expresses the desire of your heart and you would like to invite Christ into your life as Savior and Lord, just repeat the words silently as I pray them aloud.

Let's pray.

REPEAT THE ABOVE PRAYER ONE PHRASE AT A TIME. PAUSE AFTER EACH PHRASE IN ORDER TO GIVE THOSE IN YOUR AUDIENCE A CHANCE TO PRAY.

If you prayed that prayer, you can be assured of two things right now. First, Christ came into your life as He promised He would.

In Revelation 3:20, Christ did not say, "I *might* come in," "I *sort* of will come in" or "*maybe* I will come in on alternating Sundays." No, very forthrightly He said, "I *will* come in to him." So, if you repented of your sin and invited Him to come into your life, then Christ is there. You don't need to *hope* He is in your life; you can *know* He's there on the basis of His promise.

Second, you can know for sure that if you were to die right now you would spend eternity with God in heaven.

John wrote in 1 John 5:11-13: "And the witness is this, that God has given us eternal life, and this life is in His Son. He who has the Son has the life; he who does not have the Son of God does not have the life. These things I have written to you who believe in the name of the Son of God, in order that you may *know* that you have eternal life" (italics added).

The condition for having eternal life is having the Son. So, if you *know* that you have the Son, you can also *know* that you have eternal life. Note that John wrote this letter specifically to drive home this point to his friends. He says, "These things I have written to you who believe in the name of the Son of God [that is, to those who have received Him as Savior and Lord] in order that you may *know* [not hope so, feel like or wish, but *know*] that you have eternal life."

I'm really interested in what you think of the things I've shared tonight (today). To get some feedback from you, I have asked some friends to pass out some cards and pencils so that you can write down your comments or questions for me.

HAVE A COUPLE OF ASSISTANTS HAND OUT THE PENCILS AND CARDS. A HELPFUL STRATEGY IS TO ASK THE PERSONS IN THE FRONT ROW: "Would you help me out?" THIS GETS THE JOB DONE MORE QUICKLY AND INVOLVES THE AUDIENCE.

So, take a minute to let me know what you think. Just write down your name, address and phone number and any comments or questions you have.

Then, if tonight, for the first time you prayed and invited Christ into your life as Savior and Lord, place a check mark in the box after your name.

The reason I want you to do this is I have some material I'd like to get to you which I personally found helpful when I made the decision to receive Christ.

Then, if you're just interested in more information about what I shared, check that box. I promise your name won't be published as one of the 10 most religious men and women in town. I have some literature that covers the kind of issues that were addresed tonight (today), and I'd just like to get it to you.

WHILE INDIVIDUALS ARE FILLING OUT THE CARDS, SIT DOWN AND IGNORE THEM. THEY DON'T NEED DISTRACTIONS AT THIS POINT. LET THEM CONCENTRATE; AFTER THREE OR FOUR MINUTES, ANNOUNCE THAT YOU WILL GIVE THEM ANOTHER MINUTE SO THAT THEY WILL BEGIN TO WRAP UP THEIR COMMENTS. AFTER THE MINUTE IS UP, SAY:

As you finish the cards, please fold them in half and pass them in.

AFTER ALL THE CARDS ARE COLLECTED, SAY:

Thanks so much for this opportunity to be here and to share with you.

Exhibit 26

Tapes

Josh McDowell

1. "Maximum Dating" shares principles of how to enjoy an exciting dating life and gives practical ideas on how to be creative on a date. Fun talk with helpful insights.

2. "Maximum Love" answers such questions as "How do I know if I'm in love?" and "Am I ready for the responsibility of a dynamic love and sex relationship?"

3. "Maximum Sex" exposes prevailing attitudes in society that rob people of the fulfillment God intended in this crucial area. In a frank and reverent way, Josh outlines proper attitudes toward sex and explains how to develop them.

4. "The Great Resurrection—Hoax?" documents the historical evidence for the resurrection of Jesus Christ that Josh discovered when, as an unbeliever, he set out to make an intellectual joke of Christianity. The talk includes Josh's personal testimony and is excellent for sharing with non-believers.

Dick Purnell

Developing Dynamic Relationships

1. "How to Know When You Are in Love." Ever have questions about this? Here's a thought-provoking analysis of the differences between infatuation and real love.

2. "Why Couples Break Up." Dick gives four major reasons dating and marriage relationships often fail. Then he offers helpful suggestions to develop long-term commitment.

3. "Sex and the Search for Intimacy." Most of us desire that special closeness with a person of the opposite sex. Why, then, are our experiences often painful and fleeting? Discover how to have lasting love and intimate sharing in a relationship.

4. "How to Be Happy Though Single." Enjoying life to the maximum doesn't depend on your marital status. Learn the real source of

happiness. Begin to develop some inner qualities that will make you a more fulfilled person, whether you're single or married.

5. "What Is a Man?" Men: What three qualities should you develop to make you a better person? And women: What are you looking for in a man? Does he possess the attributes that make a good relationship?

6. "Commitment—The Key to Loving." The divorce rate in America is 50 percent. How can you prevent becoming part of that statistic Learn the ingredients to a marriage that lasts a lifetime.

Improving Your Life

7. "How to Handle Hassles" (5-tape set). Insecurity, family conflicts, broken relationships—these and other circumstances can make you discouraged and depressed. This study in Ephesians shows you how God can give victory, no matter what situation you find yourself in.

Solving Difficult Problems

8. "Reality of the Resurrection." Did Jesus really rise from the dead What is the historical evidence to show that the resurrection actu ally occurred? How can it make you a different person?

9. "How to Know God's Will." Can you know what God wants for you concerning your job, marriage, school, important decisions, etc.? Here are four principles that will guide you in discerning th will of God.

For information on other tapes and ordering, contact:

Liberation Tapes
P.O. Box 6044
Lubbock, TX 79413
(806) 792-3868

Exhibit 27
Films

"Football Fever"

Coaches and players from teams across the League powerfully share their personal faith and commitment to Jesus Christ. The picture unfolds with outrageous football comedy, non-stop gridiron action, and in-depth inspirational interviews with the best of the NFL.

To order, contact:

> Church Service and Supply Co.
> 1787 28th Street
> Long Beach, CA 90806
> (213) 426-6401
> (800) 421-3771
>
> (If you are involved in a Campus Crusade for Christ *campus* ministry, let the distributor know this when you order the film.)

Josh McDowell

"More Than a Carpenter"

> The story centers around Mark, a young archaeologist, and his questions regarding Christ's identity. Josh answers those questions.

"Givers, Takers, and Other Kinds of Lovers"

> Focusing on three couples, Josh deals with some painfully felt questions on relationships.

"The Secret of Loving"

> Josh discusses some pitfalls and misconceptions about love, sex and dating. He then shares God's perspective. An invitation to receive Christ is given.

"What's Up, Josh?"

> When a college student begins to struggle with the various prob-

lems and complexities in his life, his Christian roommate explains the difference Christ can make. The student becomes more and more interested as he listens to Josh lecture on campus.

André Kole

"World of Seance"

Is there a spirit world? Can we communicate with the dead? World-famous illusionist, André Kole, explains how the person of Christ is life's ultimate reality. He closes with an invitation to receive Christ as personal Savior.

"World of Illusion"

Offering a clear presentation of the gospel and an opportunity to receive Christ as personal Savior, André challenges his viewers to abandon the world of illusion for the reality of Jesus Christ.

To order, contact:

Media Distribution Services 60-00
Campus Crusade for Christ
Arrowhead Springs
San Bernardino, CA 92414
(714) 886-9711

(If you are involved in a Campus Crusade for Christ *campus* ministry, let the distributor know this when you order the film.)

Exhibit 28
Sample Evangelistic Socials

An evangelistic social is a group social gathering designed for fun and fellowship and as a platform for presenting the gospel. An evangelistic social can take many forms: popcorn party, make-your-own-sundae party, pizza party, evangelistic make-up party or a student leadership breakfast. Evangelistic socials add variety, draw students together and promote the local ministry.

A. Biblical Basis.

Jesus used social situations as a platform for demonstrating the truth of the good news. Examples: Wedding in Cana (John 2:1-11) and Matthew's dinner (Mark 2:15-17).

B. Benefits of an evangelistic social.

1. A social confronts many students at one time with the claims of Christ.
2. The environment at a social gathering is often less threatening than during one-to-one evangelism.
3. It provides a good opportunity to meet new people in a relaxed atmosphere.
4. It takes advantage of natural groups: students invite their friends.
5. It creates momentum and high visibility.
6. It shows non-Christians that Christians can have fun and are well-rounded; i.e., that they have "secular" interests.

C. Ideas for pre-evangelistic socials.

1. *Popcorn party*

   At any gathering, popcorn draws students. Make sure they can smell it down the halls of the dorm.

2. *Make-your-own-sundae party.*

    a. Have your testimonies, speaker, etc.

    b. Serve ice cream with fixings for sundaes and floats. Have vanilla ice cream, chocolate syrup, butterscotch syrup and other toppings, nuts, whipped cream and some carbonated beverages. You can ask your students to bring these things "pot luck." Or you can buy them yourself and charge 50 cents admission.

    c. Have a contest to see who can come up with the most outlandish concoction.

    d. During the refreshment time, have the Christian students "divide and conquer" (present the Four Spiritual Laws to the new students).

3. *Pizza party.*

    a. Have the students either bring pizzas or make them at the party.

    b. If possible, have special entertainment.

    c. End with testimonies, speaker, etc.

4. *Student leadership breakfast.*

    a. Invite school leaders from different classes and clubs. Send written invitations.

    b. Hold an evangelistic breakfast, using students to emcee and give testimonies.

    c. Have a staff member or a Christian dignitary speak on leadership, motivation, time management, etc.

5. *Evangelistic make-up parties.*

    a. Plan to have someone from a cosmetic company come in and demonstrate her line of make-up (Mary Kay, Jafra, Redkin, etc.). Be sure to tell her that you plan to have a speaker give a message on "Inner Beauty" after the demonstration.

b. Have the speaker give a message on "Inner Beauty." The message, designed to give non-Christians an opportunity to receive Christ, can give qualities of inner beauty, a presentation of the Four Spiritual Laws and an invitation to receive Christ.

c. Close in prayer, giving the women an opportunity to invite Christ into their lives. The women will then have an opportunity to indicate their decisions for Christ on comment cards or 3″x5″ cards (provided for each woman).

d. Have your Discipleship Group follow up the women who indicated decisions for Christ.

D. Format of the event.

1. Use the following or a similar outline.

   a. Welcome those who attend.

   b. Play ice-breaker games.

   c. Have a special feature (optional).

   d. Possibly have one or two students share their testimonies.

   e. Give a message and possibly a pray-with-me invitation.

   f. End with refreshments and fellowship.

2. Emphasize Jesus Christ throughout the program, especially in your personal interaction with students.

3. Let it be the students' social, not your own. Put them in charge of the welcome, games, testimonies, refreshments, etc.

E. Follow-up of the social.

See Chapter 13, "How to Follow Up."

Exhibit 29

Follow-up Correspondence

The correspondence Ministry at Arrowhead Springs sends follow-up materials to those who have recently accepted Christ or who prayed in faith to be filled with the Holy Spirit. The following gives the basic content of the follow-up series:

Follow-up sent to new Christians.

1. Assurance of salvation letter.

   Enclosures: Four Spiritual Laws and "Jesus and the Intellectual."

2. Presentation of the ministry of the Holy Spirit.

   Enclosure: Holy Spirit booklet.

3. Introduction to the Transferable Concepts and an invitation to receive additional study letters and Transferable Concept booklets.

   Enclosure: "How to Experience God's Love and Forgiveness."

Follow-up sent to Holy Spirit Decisions

1. Holy Spirit assurance letter.

   Enclosure: Holy Spirit booklet.

2. Introduction to the Transferable Concepts and an invitation to receive additional study letters and Transferable Concept booklets.

   Enclosure: "How to Experience God's Love and Forgiveness."

After the reader completes the initial series and sends in the reply card, he will receive the remaining Transferable Concept booklets and Dr. Bright's study letters. These materials will be sent at two-week intervals without charge or obligation.

In sending names of those who would like to receive this follow-up, please furnish the name, address, city, state and ZIP. Also, please indicate whether you would like us to send new Christian follow-up or Holy Spirit decision follow-up.

Send all names to Follow-up Department 70-00, Campus Crusade for Christ International, Arrowhead Springs, San Bernardino, California 92414.

Exhibit 30

How to Achieve a Balance Between Evangelism and Discipleship

by Bill Bright

One of the biggest concerns of my ministry during the first couple of years at UCLA was, "How does one find the proper balance between evangelism and discipling?"

Scores, and soon hundreds, of students were indicating decisions for Christ, and I didn't know what to do with all of them. Dawson Trotman, a warm personal friend and founder of The Navigators, graciously responded to my plea for help and took time from his own busy ministry to teach a class of new converts each Saturday morning. I did everything I knew to do, and just about everything anyone else suggested that I do, to help the scores of new Christians become established in their new-found faith.

Among other things, day after day I met from early in the morning until late in the evening in scheduled hour-long appointments with men who were beginning the great adventure with Christ.

Investing life

It all began with such great excitement and promise. Where else could I possibly invest my life where the dividends were so great? Think of the privilege of meeting regularly with many of the leaders of the student government and social and athletic life of the campus community to assist in their Christian growth.

Soon, however, some of these new converts failed to show up for appointments. Then rumors began to drift back to me that different students were engaged in questionable conduct that compromised their testimony for our Lord. My heart was broken. How could they—after what Christ had done for them and after all of my efforts to help them? I earnestly hoped and prayed that someone had made a mistake and the rumors were not true.

But, the rumors were true, and some of the most promising Christians, both men and women, began to miss appointments with both Vonette and me. Others missed scheduled group meetings and Bible study sessions. Finally they drifted away altogether, and some of them I have never seen again.

I went to my knees. "Oh, God, what is wrong with me? How have I failed these students? Surely, I have done something wrong. Help me to do a better job." I even prayed for those young men and women who had become like my own flesh and blood. I loved them. I longed for them to become men and women of God. Now some had gone from us. It was in this period of spiritual anguish and heartbreak that God directed my reading one day to the Parable of the Sower. It reads as follows:

"A farmer was sowing grain in his fields. As he scattered the seed across the ground, some fell beside a path, and the birds came and ate it. And some fell on rocky soil where there was little depth of earth; the plants sprang up quickly enough in the shallow soil, but the hot sun soon scorched them and they withered and died, for they had so little root. Other seeds fell among thorns, and the thorns choked out the tender blades. But some fell on good soil, and produced a crop that was thirty, sixty, and even a hundred times as much as he had planted . . . .

"Now here is the explanation of the story I had told about the farmer planting grain: The hard path where some of the seeds fell represents the heart of a person who hears the good news about the Kingdom and doesn't understand it; then Satan comes and snatches away the seeds from his heart. The shallow, rocky soil represents the heart of a man who hears the message and receives it with real joy, but he doesn't have much depth in his life, and the seeds don't root very deeply, and after a while when trouble comes, or persecution begins because of his beliefs, his enthusiasm fades, and he drops out. The ground covered with thistles represents a man who hears the message, but the cares of this life and his longing for money choke out God's Word, and he does less and less for God. The good ground represents the heart of a man who listens to the message and understands it and goes out and brings thirty, sixty, or even a hundred others into the Kingdom" (Matthew 13:3b-8, Living Bible).

This parable enabled me to better understand why some had turned away from following our Lord. Though some had gone from us, hundreds had remained and scores longed to be true diciples.

For example, in the first years, from the Phi Delta fraternity house alone, 13 young men were called into Christian service full time. Scores of others dedicated themselves to serving Christ in the pulpit, on the mission field and in the business and professional world. By the third year of this ministry, nine of the eleven first stringers on UCLA's football team (number 1 in the nation), were active in Campus Crusade and "were playing ball for Christ."

My desire to build disciples and my concern for follow-up of new converts have increased through the years, until now I am absolutely convinced that the Great Commission can never be fulfilled apart from "spiritual multiplication" which is a result of the proper balance between evangelism and discipleship. The discovery of the Parable of the Sower led me to a more careful examination of the Scriptures as I searched for a biblical basis for a balance between evangelism and follow-up.

Scriptural truths

The following thoughts represent some of the scriptural truths which I have learned about evangelism and discipling through the years:

1. Though Jesus was a greater leader, teacher and example—the greatest of all the centuries—He came to this earth primarily to seek and to save the lost (Luke 19:10).

2. The greatest thing that has ever happened to any Christian is knowing Christ; the greatest thing he can do for another person is to introduce him to Christ.

3. The one thing dearest to the heart of our Lord, assuming that we are living under the control of the Holy Spirit, is that we tell others about Him. Though not everyone has the gift of evangelism, every believer is chosen and appointed to go and bring forth fruit (John 15:16). In other words, every Christian is to witness for Christ as a way of life.

4. There is no way one can become, and remain, a truly vital and vibrant Christian without sharing his faith continually as a way of life. Not to do so is to be disobedient, and disobedient Christians cannot experience a life of victory and power.

5. If you do share your faith regularly, as a way of life, in the power of the Holy Spirit, you will inevitably be a fruitful Christian. If you have difficulty leading students to Christ on your campus, why not use the telephone survey or share Christ with people door to door or in other places such as a shopping center. Give copies of the Van Dusen letter to 10 people, ask them to read it and give you their response.

6. You can be an authority on the Word of God and still be spiritually impotent and defeated if you do not share your faith in Christ freely and faithfully.

7. Success in witnessing is sharing Christ in the power of the Holy Spirit and leaving the results to God. It is God who produces the fruit. He requires only that we be faithful in the sharing.

8. Jesus said, "Follow Me, and I will make you fishers of men" (Matthew 4:19). It is our responsibility to follow Jesus; it is His responsibility to make us fishers of men.

9. According to John 15:8, we prove that we are following Jesus when we bear much fruit, when we are actively involved in introducing others to Him. Thus, according to Jesus, we do not prove that we are following Him just because we live good lives, read the Bible, pray, and are active in the church, though all of these are important.

10. Many people in every part of the world are ready to receive Christ. Don't think that God is depending on you to earn the friendship of others before you witness to them. For example, Colossians 1:6 and 1 Thessalonians 1:6 both indicate that the Colossians and the Thessalonians responded to the gospel as soon as they heard it. There are many—in fact, multitudes—around us whose hearts are seeking after God.

11. Love for God and for others should be our motivation both in evangelizing and discipling others. The apostle Paul said, "The love of Christ constrains me." In 1 John 3:18, John writes: "Little children, let us stop just saying we love people; let us really love them, and show it by our actions" (Living Bible). How can we demonstrate that we love those whom we are seeking to introduce to Christ—those whom we are seeking to disciple? By taking a personal interest in them; by loving them by faith; by asking God to enable us to communicate a genuine compassion and concern; by spending special time with them, individually and in groups. You may want to invite them to your home for informal fellowship.

12. Sow abundantly and you will reap abundantly (2 Corinthians 9:6). The more people to whom you talk about Christ, the more there will be who receive Him.

13. The more people who receive Christ, the more there will be who will become disciples.

14. Jesus said, "No one can come to Me, unless the Father who sent Me draws him" (John 6:44). Men are born into the kingdom of God through the work of the Holy Spirit, not as a result of gimmicks, arguments or high-pressure techniques. At the same time, experience has demonstrated that to be a truly fruitful Christian, you must first be sure you are filled with (controlled and empowered by) the Holy Spirit. Second, you must be trained to communicate the gospel simply and clearly. Keep the presentation of the gospel simple. The Four Spiritual Laws were written for that purpose. In a spirit of love, with sensitivity to the leading of the Holy Spirit, always seek to bring men to a personal commitment to Christ. Encourage them to pray with you whenever possible. If they are unwilling, encourage them to pray privately and to inform you of their decision. (Exercise care to avoid arguments or high pressure that might result in a premature decision.)

15. It is an insult to the Holy Spirit to say or believe that we should not talk about Christ to men whom we cannot follow up, lest, by hearing the gospel and responding and later falling away because of a lack of follow-up, they will build up a spiritual immunity to the gospel. Ask God for creativity in new ways to witness for Christ.

16. Essentially, our responsibility in follow-up is summarized in 2 Timothy 2:2: "And the things which you have heard from me in the presence of many witnesses, these entrust to faithful men, who will be able to teach others also." The question then is: How do you find those who are faithful among the many who indicate an initial response to the gospel?

17. It is important to ask all new converts to study the Parable of the Sower and tell you with which kind of soil they wish to identify.

18. Those who want to be true disciples and fruitful followers of Christ can be followed up through:

    prayer
    personal contacts
    taking them witnessing with you
    the ministry of the local church
    Bible studies
    Discipleship Groups
    Institute of Biblical Studies

Christian literature
tapes
Ten Basic Steps toward Christian Maturity
Leadership Training Classes
Transferable Concepts
The Discipleship Series

(Through all of the above means and many more, Campus Crusade for Christ has one of the most extensive follow-up programs I know of. I enocurage you to use these materials faithfully rather than looking for new material.)

19. There are two areas of follow-up—primary and secondary—which incorporate the above means and other methods. Primary follow-up involves building people in a person-to-person situation, or in small groups. Secondary follow-up employs other methods, including most of those listed in Point 18. The secondary method should be applied to everyone. The primary method would be applied to those who are eager to proceed and who respond to the secondary follow-up.

20. Among your converts, the cream will rise to the top. Spend time with the "movers," as they are most likely to become disciples and spiritual multipliers.

21. We should not be satisfied with spiritual addition. Our ultimate objective should be spiritual multiplication. Ask yourself, "How many spiritual great grandchildren can I name?"

22. The key to building many disciples is a strong emphasis on evangelism.

23. We must keep on emphasizing the importance of the church in follow-up. For those who say the traditional church has lost its relevancy and that real meaning and fellowship are experienced only in small group fellowships in the home, I would remind you that thousands of vital churches have Bible studies, discipleship groups, fellowships and similar meetings as they seek to minister to the spiritual needs of man.

    In recent years I have personally worked with thousands of pastors and tens of thousands of laymen. The same enthusiasm we witness with students on high school and college campuses, we witness with pastors and laymen who are filled with the Holy Spirit and have learned to share their faith. The church represents the greatest source of manpower for fulfilling the Great Commission. Never criticize the church.

24. Prayer is one of the most important factors in successful evangelism and successful follow-up. The scripture gives our basis for prayer: "You do not have because you do not ask" (James 4:2). "The Lord . . . is not willing that any should perish" (2 Peter 3:9, Living). God wants all of His children to be more and more like Christ in every way (Ephesians 5:1). According to 1 John 5:14,15, we know God will hear and answer if we pray for multitudes to become Christians and for many disciples in all nations because we know that we pray according to God's will. Prayer played a major role in the lives of our Lord, Paul and other followers. Prayer must saturate every attitude and action. Encourage early morning daily prayer meetings for staff and students—wherever possible 24-hour prayer chains should be organized. Ask godly older people to join with you in praying for evangelistic meetings and follow-up of new converts by name.

25. We should not fear repetition in follow-up. Most Christians' greatest need is to understand how they can experience an abundant life in the power of the Holy Spirit and share their faith effectively. Repetition aids learning. The Holy Spirit keeps old truths fresh and meaningful through repetitions if our hearts are right with God.

26. We should not be deceived by critics who say, "Campus Crusade for Christ is shallow and superficial; we need to spend more time in 'deep Bible truths.'" First, we need to ask, "What are these so-called 'deep truths'?" Second, are these "truths" producing holy, Spirit-controlled Christians who have a vital, fruitful witness for Christ? Many years of good Bible and theological training in the best Bible schools and seminaries do not ensure victorious and fruitful lives for Christ; whereas, understanding the truths of Romans 6-8 and Galatians 2:20, depending on the Holy Spirit and sharing one's faith as a way of life will ensure a victorious and fruitful life. What "deeper truth" is there that is more important?

27. Most Christian leaders I know have not been followed up personally on a one-to-one basis, though I think this is desirable wherever possible. Some years ago I was participating in a seminar devoted to "follow-up." Many Christian leaders were

present. All of us were concerned with the need for better follow-up of new converts. Suddenly, it occurred to me to ask each of these leaders, "Who followed you up?" Not one of these men, including myself, had been followed up personally. Most had been followed up in the fellowship of various church meetings, Sunday school, Bible studies, etc. Both group and personal follow-up are important, but a vital group can be much more effective in following up new converts.

28. Philippians 1:6 is a reminder that the Holy Spirit, who produces the new life in the believer, will continue to help the believer grow. But verse 6 follows and depends on verse 4, which states, ". . . always offering prayer . . . ." This emphasizes our responsibility to pray for those with whom we work.

29. Belief in the sovereignty and power of God is essential for discipling men. The heart of the matter is whether we can believe that the Holy Spirit is able to finish what He has begun according to Romans 8:28,29, which tells us: "And we know that all that happens to us is working for our good if we love God and are fitting into His plans. For from the very beginning God decided that those who came to Him—and all along He knew who would—should become like His Son, so that His Son would be the first, with many brothers" (Living).

30. Never forget the absolute necessity of the Holy Spirit's power. After years of being discipled personally by Jesus, most of the disciples deserted Him at the cross and one betrayed Him. It was Pentecost that made the ultimate difference! Filled with the Holy Spirit, these disciples went out to change the world.

31. The Holy Spirit is the only one who can adequately follow up and help the new convert to grow and mature in his faith. Encourage the new convert to depend upon the Holy Spirit and not on your clever ideas or on excellent follow-up material alone.

32. Too much "man-centered" follow-up grieves the Holy Spirit. Too often we depend upon the Holy Spirit to produce the new birth and then we personally assume all responsibility for the follow-up.

33. While Jesus was evangelizing the multitudes, He was discipling His twelve. We, too, are commanded to evangelize the multitudes and make disciples in all nations. But don't be dis-

appointed if every Christian with whom you work does not respond to the challenge to be a disciple.

34. Not everyone is ready or "ripe" to receive Christ at the same time; neither is everybody ready to grow spiritually at the same pace. We don't force fruit to ripen (pressure people to receive Christ); neither should we try to force new Christians to grow. Encourage, but never pressure. Allow the Holy Spirit to be as original with others as He has been, and is, with you. Again, praying for the new Christians is the most important thing we can do for them.

35. Many new converts who have drifted away come back to Christ at a later time in life. Naturally, you will want to do what you can, but don't be discouraged when some of your newer or older Christian friends drift away. Many will come back to Christ months or years later.

36. "A follower is dependent upon man for growth; a disciple is dependent upon Christ for growth."

In summary, then, the basic philosophy of Campus Crusade for Christ regarding evangelizing and discipling should include the following principles:

1. Make individual and group prayer the basis for all evangelizing and discipling.

2. Sow abundantly—tell men about Christ whenever you get the chance, individually and in groups (see Romans 1:5; Colossians 1:28, Living).

3. Make spiritual growth opportunities available to all who respond to Christ.

4. Trust the Holy Spirit that disciples will emerge through the many growth opportunities afforded by Campus Crusade (personal counseling and leadership, Bible studies, discipleship groups, College Life, Leadership Training Classes, Institute of Biblical Studies, tapes, films, activity and worship in local churches). Remember, the cream will rise to the top.

5. Move with the movers. Applying the 2 Timothy 2:2 methods, disciple those who are most responsive.

6. Emphasize spiritual multiplication rather than addition.

7. Don't get "hung up" and spend valuable time on people who are not ready to receive Christ, or with Christians who are slow to move. Pray for them to "ripen" and in the meantime keep evangelizing and following up those who are responsive.

8. Take new and older Christians with you as you share your faith and get them involved in the cause of Christ in other ways.

I am confident that, as you apply these principles to your life, God will abundantly bless your ministry as He has mine—and will continue to unite us as we seek to help fulfill the Great Commission.

Exhibit 31
Steps in Becoming a Disciple

Motivation

Can you identify with this scene? It's 6:00, you just got back from an afternoon class, and your discipleship group starts in 30 minutes. You burst into your room and ask your roommate if he has any tapes you can use for your meeting tonight.

When leaders lack prayerful preparation for their Bible studies and discipleship groups, the inevitable result is a weak movement on campus. It seems that the term *leader* has been left out of "discipleship group leader." Dr. Howard Hendricks, professor at Dallas Theological Seminary, gives two qualities of a leader:

1. He knows where he is going.
2. He can persuade others to come along with him.

A leader needs both clear-cut objectives and the ability to motivate people. Unfortunately, some discipleship group leaders have vague objectives and are doing a poor job of motivating others to be a part of building multiplying disciples who want to help reach the world for Christ. The Scriptures say that "without a vision the people perish." Your vision affects all that you do in your ministry. One definition of vision is: "Vision is seeing in your mind's eye a *God-given objective* for the future so that you are *motivated to action* in the present. Our movements will perish if we don't learn to establish clear-cut objectives and motivate people to follow us in reaching those objectives."

This does not mean that discipleship consists only of clear objectives and "how to's." *Discipleship is primarily what the Holy Spirit does* in a person's life, but you have to *equip* people to do what Christ commanded us to do. If you don't equip a disciple, he becomes demotivated and loses his direction. That's why Jesus spent so much time teaching and training. In Luke 9, He told them exactly what to take, what to wear, what to say and how to respond to negative responses from people. He gave them clear-cut training.

Objective

The ojective of this material, "Steps in Becoming a Disciple," is to show you *exactly what you need to know and what training you need to receive* in order to disciple other people. Another objective is to help you become much more effective as a leader who is able to: 1) *put people in a place of success* rather than failure; 2) *help your disciples understand exactly what you expect of them* and what their specific goals are in each step of building multipliers. As a result of using the "Steps . . .," your Bible studies and Discipleship Groups will be meeting specific needs, your one-to-one time will be easier to plan and prepare for because you will know that we are trying to accomplish in that time, and *you will be more effective in motivating your students* to do the things that God has called them to do as disciples.

NOTE: The length of time it takes a student to move from one step to the next will vary according to the maturity of the student.

Teaching this to others

In teaching this material to a group, begin by brainstorming with the group members for a few minutes, answering the question: "What are some of the things that need to happen after a person prays and receives Christ to help him become a multiplying disciple?" Second, put those steps in order and discuss what happens between each step. Look at the following sheets entitled "Steps . . .," and in each step answer the question, "What does the person need to *know* and what does he need *training in*?"

NOTE: A person might know *all* the things he needs to understand and be well trained, yet not do anything about it. When you present this material to students, especially to discipleship group leaders, they need to understand that if a student is not having a quiet time, is not walking in the Spirit, or has some emotional blocks that keep him from following through in his growth as a disciple, he will not be able to progress through these steps!

Overview of the "Steps in Becoming a Disciple":

1. A person prays and receives Christ as Savior and Lord.
2. You go through basic follow-up with him.
3. You invite him to be in your discovery group.
4. You take him witnessing.

5. You challenge him to your discipleship group.
6. Someone prays and receives Christ with him.
7. He follows up that person.
8. He invites him to be in a discovery group.
9. He takes him witnessing.
10. He challenges him to be in his discipleship group.

The following chart explains the steps in the discipleship process and answers two questions: 1)What does he need to *know* at each step, and 2) What does he need to be *trained in*? Blank worksheets are provided to use as a checklist.

Steps in Becoming a Disciple

Steps	What Does He Need to Know?	What Does He Need Training In?
1. A person prays and receives Christ.	( ) 1. The gospel—Four Spiritual Laws.	
	( ) 2. Assurance of his salvation.	
	( ) 3. Read John 3.	
	( ) 4. He needs to get back with you several times to learn how to grow in his relationship with Christ.	
	( ) 5. Your phone number.	
2. You go through follow-up with him.	( ) 1. Assurance of his salvation.	1. How to have a quiet time (have a quiet time with him for several days in a row, if possible).
	( ) 2. How to walk in the Spirit.	

	( ) 3. What a quiet time is.	
	( ) 4. Other content in the "Beginning Your New Life" follow-up series.	
3. You invite him to be in your Discovery Group (D.G.)	( ) 1. Why he should be in a Discovery Group.	1. How to prepare for the Discovery Group study—show him!
	( ) 2. What is expected of him.	
	( ) 3. How he should prepare.	
	( ) 4. What time it starts.	
	( ) 5. Where it meets.	
	( ) 6. That he is accepted by the group.	
4. You take him witnessing.	( ) 1. Why you are going.	
	( ) 2. What you expect of him—that he is to pray silently for the person as you present the gospel.	
5. You challenge him to be in your Discipleship Group (D.G.)	( ) 1. What a Discipleship Group is.	1. How to prepare for Discipleship Group.
	( ) 2. What multiplication is.	2. Everything in 6-10 below (how to lead someone to Christ, etc.).
	( ) 3. The biblical basis for a Discipleship Group.	

	( ) 4. Why he should be a part of a Discipleship Group.	
	( ) 5. Where and when the Discipleship Group meets.	
	( ) 6. That he is committing himself to a specific amount of time.	
6. Someone prays and receives Christ with your disciple.	( ) 1. The gospel—Four Spiritual Laws.	1. How to present the booklet.
	( ) 2. Spirit-filled life.	2. How to make the issue clear.
	( ) 3. "How to's" of witnessing.	3. How to give "pray with me"/assurance of salvation.
	( ) 4. The biblical basis for evangelism.	4. How to motivate the person to get back together.
	( ) 5. Reasons the Four Spiritual Laws booklet is an effective *tool.*	5. How to get evangelistic contacts (team meetings, films, *Collegiate Challenge, Athletes in Action* magazine, use of surveys, randoms.
		6. How to share the Spirit-filled life.
7. Your disciple follows up that person.	( ) 1. The content of follow-up.	1. How to explain the content of follow-up.
	( ) 2. What materials to use.	2. How to motivate.

	( ) 3. How to build relationships.	3. How to set up follow-up meeting.
	( ) 4. The need to clearly set a time and place.	4. How to establish rapport.
		5. How to ask good questions.
		6. How to establish him in quiet time and Scripture memory.
8. Your disciple invites the new believer to be in Discovery Group (D.G.)	( ) 1. Content of Bible study challenge.	1. How to use the "Four Soils" parable as a challenge.
	( ) 2. Materials to use.	2. How to share the "whys" in Bible study.
	( ) 3. Why a person needs to be in a Bible study.	3. How to teach
	( ) 4. How to lead a Bible study.	4. How to ask good questions.
	( ) 5. How to set the right atmosphere.	5. How to develop a quality atmosphere.
	( ) 6. How to develop relationships.	6. (Take him to your group.)
9. Your disciple challenges his disciple to his Discipleship Group. (D.G.)	( ) 1. The biblical basis for evangelism.	1. How to witness (biblical basis).
	( ) 2. Two key questions (What is the greatest . . .).	2. How to use the two questions.
		3. How to take someone witnessing (appointment, not a random; how to include him via testimony; debrief).

10. Your disciple challenges his disciple to his Discipleship Group (D.G.)	( ) 1. Content of Discipleship Group challenge.	1. All of the above.
	( ) 2. Materials to use.	2. How to challenge.
	( ) 3. Why a person needs to be in a Discipleship Group.	3. How to teach.
	( ) 4. How to lead a Discipleship Group.	4. How to train.
	( ) 5. How to set atmosphere.	5. How to ask good questions.
	( ) 6. How to develop relationships.	6. How to develop relationships.
		7. How to lead others.

Exhibit 32

How to Teach Each Section in Your Lesson Plan

Each lesson contains four sections:

A. Sharing
B. Bible study
C. Training
D. Prayer

A. Sharing: This section is designed to open the lesson with an opportunity for the group members to share what God is doing in their lives.

1. Read or review Exhibit #34, "How to Lead a Sharing Time," when you prepare for the meeting.

2. Make this as informal and challenging as possible.

3. Seek to create an atmosphere in which everyone wants to share.

4. Don't prolong the sharing time. When it "dries up," move on to the next section.

5. View your sharing times as a thermometer for the evangelistic activity in your group. If the members rarely share about their evangelism ministries, then you will need to provide more ministry leadership for the group.

B. Bible Study: The observation, interpretation, application method of Bible study is used. This section normally centers around two main passages of Scripture. Other passages are also noted, but usually only as backup references.

1. Keep an open Bible before you. Emphasize what is in the Bible, not what is written in the leader's guide.

2. As you become a more experienced teacher, prepare for each lesson by making notes on the outline in your study guide. Then simply carry the notes to the group and leave the rest of your leader's guide at home. However, don't forget to take along any necessary training.

3. Don't be mechanical. Strive for informality and a relaxed atmosphere.

4. As you teach, be available to help meet changing needs as they arise. (Example: One of your group members has just failed an exam or lost his job and needs help in dealing with the problem.) You are not obligated to finish all the content every week, though you should not become irresponsible about it and forget your objectives.

5. Use your own illustrations. Sharing personal examples is the greatest thing you can do to build rapport in the group.

6. Do not skip the Application and Training.

7. Seek to make direct applications to the group members' present situations. The more specific you can be, the better.

8. Allow plenty of time for discussion. This is not a lecture.

9. To pace yourself, estimate the time you want to spend on each question and write it in the margin.

10. Remember: "The content you present is less important than the atmosphere you create!" (Howard Hendricks).

C. Training.

1. Primarily the training included here is to provide an exposure to the use of Campus Crusade for Christ materials in a group setting. Read the section entitled Training and follow the instructions. Not all sessions will include training.

2. Throughout the week when you meet with your group members individually, review and apply the training you learned in your group meeting.

3. The best training serves to build the confidence of those with whom you are working. Therefore, *demonstrate* the use of the training in a group setting where questions can be asked and discussed. Then *demonstrate* in a live setting during an appointment the appropriate use of the tool. Suggest they use the tool for the next appointment. Allow your group members to move at their own pace but be an encouragement to trust God with new training situations. *Communicate* the strengths of their presentation as you observed them. Try to remember that the best training serves to build the confidence of those with whom you are working.

D. Prayer Section

1. Expect this to be one of the richest times of the group meeting. If prayer goes longer than the allotted time, don't worry.

2. Pray about group members' needs as well as ministry strategy. Seek to build faith through prayer.

3. Show the group how to pray for those people whom they are or will be discipling.

Exhibit 33

Guidelines for Conducting a Discipleship Group

When you use the Discipleship Series session plans, observe the following guidelines.

1. Meet in an informal atmosphere and be enthusiastic (but not phony).

2. Have the Bible open at all times. Extensive use of the Scriptures will be required. If your group members are new Christians or are unfamiliar with the Bible, they may need help in finding Scripture passages.

3. Maintain eye contact with the members.

4. Allow enough time for sharing and building rapport at the beginning of each meeting. Don't be afraid to laugh and joke.

5. Listen for the group members' needs and seek to help meet them, either in the group or later. It is not wrong to stop in the middle of the content to pray for a specific need if you sense it would be appropriate.

6. Be sure to prepare the group for witnessing during discovery group. They should be paired up with an experienced person. You can go with only one of them, so you may need to recruit several people who are experienced in sharing their faith to go with the others.

7. Above all, be yourself. Nobody expects you to be "super spiritual," so don't try to be. Just walk in the Spirit and relax.

Remember, as you lead the group members, you are seeking to build their commitment to the point that they will want to learn how to develop their own ministries of discipleship and evangelism.

Exhibit 34

How to Lead a Sharing Time

A. The purpose of group sharing.

Group sharing was an element of the Lord's ministry with the early disciples. For example, we read in Luke 10:17 that "the seventy returned with joy, saying, 'Lord, even the demons are subject to us in Your name.'" Such spontaneous sharing is the natural result of God's working in the lives of your group members, as He had been doing in the case of the seventy recorded in Luke 10:17.

Early in the book of Acts, we read that interactions among the Christians played just as vital a role as Bible study and prayer. "And they were continually devoting themselves to the apostles' teaching and to fellowship, to the breaking of bread and to prayer" (Acts 2:42).

One sign of a healthy, vital group is a quality time of sharing and interaction among the members. This should become a matter of prayer for you as you plan your group time together. You will not be able to force group members into sharing. However, through prayer and the use of proper techniques, God will use you as a catalyst for quality sharing times. In addition to other results, a good sharing time:

1. Stimulates a sense of spontaneity.
2. Creates a sense of informality.
3. Encourages a greater freedom to speak out.
4. Develops a sense of freedom to be one's self.
5. Creates an assurance that others in the group, especially the leader, care about the group members' personal lives.
6. Enables group members to get to know one another better.
7. Allows group members to encourage one another as they share what God has done in their lives.
8. Enables group members to challenge one another to greater things as they share how God has used their lives.
9. Creates a sense of excitement and group momentum.

B. Conducting a sharing time.

1. Pre-arranged sharing.

   Pre-arranged sharing requires that the leader be aware of what is taking place in the lives and ministries of his members. As he learns of a person's needs and victories, as well as the lessons God is teaching him, the leader can then ask the person to share these things with the group the next time they meet together.

2. Spontaneous sharing.

   Spontaneous sharing may occur in two ways:

   a. The group naturally becomes involved in a sharing time during the normal course of conversation before the meeting begins. In this case, the leader need not do anything to stimulate sharing, although he may wish to ask specific questions to help guide it. Perhaps his biggest problem in this situation will be to make the transition from sharing to the Bible study or prayer time.

   b. The group becomes involved in sharing in response to simple questions posed by the leader. Some examples of questions are:

      1) "What has God been teaching you this past week?"
      2) "What has God been doing in your life this past week?"
      3) "Has anything happened this past week that you would like to share with the group?"
      4) "Does anybody have anything to share?"

3. Sharing by topics.

   Ask the members of your group to share about specific areas of their lives. Some examples are:

   a. Their favorite Bible verses and why they have become their favorites.
   b. How they came to know Christ.
   c. Something God has taught them from the Word.

d. Something they've learned from circumstances.

e. Their ministry of evangelism and discipleship.

f. The person who has influenced their lives the most (outside their families).

g. What they want to see when they are 70 years old and look back on their lives.

h. What they want to be doing five years and 10 years from now.

i. The time when God seems closest to them.

j. How they would spend a "perfect" day.

4. Providing the example for sharing.

The leader can help stimulate group sharing by becoming a model to the group members. As the leader shares freely from his own life, others will be encouraged to share.

Exhibit 35

How to Evaluate a Group Meeting

As soon as possible after the meeting, evaluate the meeting using the following form. For the first few times, it will be helpful for you to write out your evaluation.

1. Was everyone at the meeting who should have been there? What do you need to do to contact anyone who was absent?

2. Did you begin and end on time? What do you need to do to improve on this?

3. Were you thoroughly prepared for the session? What will enable you to be better prepared for subsequent sessions?

4. What was your goal for this particular session? Was the objective of the session reached in *each person's* life? Why or why not?

5. Did everyone participate in the discussion? Did certain people tend to dominate or to be left out of the discussion? What can be done to produce a better balance?

6. Did people open up to share or did you have to carry the discussion? Were you able to draw the correct answers out of the group rather than giving them the answers? What could be done to improve in this area?

7. Did the group get off on unprofitable tangents? How can you better keep the discussion on target?

8. Was the discussion theoretical or was it practical and related to the lives of the people involved? How could you have better related it to practical Christian living?

9. Did everyone reach the desired conclusion, or did some go away with unresolved questions? Are there people in the group that you should meet with for personal counsel before the next session?

10. What other suggestions can you make that will enable you to do a better job in your next session?

Exhibit 36
How to Ask Good Questions

Have you wondered what makes one question provoke seemingly unlimited discussion, while another "perfectly good" question falls on deaf ears of a group? A number of factors can cause these varied responses, but one of the most important is the quality of the questions. Good questions are phrased to provoke and stimulate discussion. Questions raised by your group members during the discussion can also be used to increase learning.

A. Types of questions:

There are four basic types of questions. Each has important and valuable uses in various situations, but not all are useful in a group discussion. They are:

1. *Leading*—A leading question implies the answer that the leader expects.

   Example: "Paul says we are to rejoice always, doesn't he?"

   Value for a discussion: *None.* It's great for a lecture, but it can kill a discussion because a response is not even required. These questions should be used only as a last resort to bring out a critical point that the group has failed to discover through more open questions. Try to get along without these.

2. *Limiting*—A limiting question limits the answer to specific details desired by the leader.

   Example: "What are three great truths in this passage?"

   Value for a discussion: *None.* It begins a mind-reading competition with the leader because it is clear that you have an exact answer in mind.

   Exception: The type of limiting question that requires a "yes" or "no" answer may be valuable to use in finding out the attitudes of other members of the group. Example: "Would the rest of you agree?"

3. *Open*—An open question allows the group to explore the passage. It clearly indicates that there may be a variety of acceptable responses.

   Example: "What are some truths you see in this passage?" Value for a discussion: *Much.* It allows complete freedom to discover one, two, or more "truths." The emphasis is on discovery, not on finding "the answer."

4. *Wide-open*—A wide-open question draws the group into continued discussion after someone has expressed an opinion, or has answered or asked a question.

   Example: "Any other ideas?"

   Value for a discussion: *Very much.* It keeps the topic of discussion on the floor.

   Of these four types of questions, your discussion should contain about 90 percent open and wide-open questions. A limiting or leading question should be used only as a last resort, when the group cannot see a point crucial to understanding the content under discussion. In this case, it is better to ask a limiting question than to tell them the answer. One caution about asking open questions: They must clearly indicate that a variety of responses is possible. Otherwise, they may be interpreted as limiting questions. For example, you may ask, "What did Paul say to Timothy?" thinking that there are at least six things in your passage. However, your group may hear, "What one important thing did Paul say to Timothy?" The question would be better worded, "What are some things Paul said to Timothy?"

B. How to use questions.

In a discussion in which five or six people are talking and asking questions while the rest of the group is silent, what should you do? Here is a brief guideline on how to use good questions to control and draw out discussion:

1. Leader-initiated questions.

   a. Direct: A direct question is aimed at one individual. Use these either to draw out silent members of the group or to direct the discussion away from someone who may be dominating the group.

b. General: A general question is one directed to the whole group, which anyone may answer.

2. Leader's response to member-initiated questions.

a. Reverse: A reverse question is returned to the one who raised it. It is particularly useful when you are asked a leading question.

b. Relay: A relay question is returned to the whole group. It enhances the discussion because it keeps the leader from being the final authority on questions raised by the group.

You should use the "clarifying questions" that are provided in your leader's guide only if the members do not give the suggested answers in response to the main question.

CAUTION: Use clarifying questions *only* if necessary. Your objective is to help the group members to discover spontaneously for themselves the right answers from God's Word.

This sense of discovery happens most often when members are responding to open or wide-open questions from the leader. In many cases, members will state the essence of the suggested answers in response to the main (numbered) question. If the members do not come up with something close to the suggested answers or the leader feels the point needs to be amplified, then (and only then) the leader can use one or more of the clarifying questions.

Generally, the first clarifying question is either wide-open ("Any other ideas?") or open (a rephrasing of the original question). In the second or third clarifying question you will often find a limiting or even leading question. These are given as a last resort and should be used sparingly and only if you feel the point is critical to continuing the discussion. The more experience you gain as a leader, the less you will need to resort to using these limiting and leading questions.

Beginning with Lesson 13, you will need to develop many of the clarifying questions yourself. Basically, these questions should follow the same pattern as above and should be used in leading the discussion only when necessary. In some of the later lessons you will also need to develop main questions from general ideas or statements. In this way, you will be developing your skill in asking effective questions.

Exhibit 37
Paul Brown Letter

CAMPUS CRUSADE FOR CHRIST INTERNATIONAL

Arrowhead Springs, San Bernardino, California 92414, U.S.A. • Telephone 886-5224 • William R. Bright, President

Though not actually written to Paul Brown, this letter contains the basic counsel which Dr. Bright gives students and adults concerning, "How to know the will of God for your life":

Mr. Paul V. Brown
The Graduate House
University of California
Los Angeles 24, California

Re: How to Know the Will of God for Your Life,
According to the "Sound-Mind Principle" of Scripture

Dear Paul:

Thank you for your recent letter sharing some of the exciting experiences which you are having in your new and adventuresome life with Christ.

When I read that part of your letter in which you expressed the desire to invest your life fully for Christ, I paused to give thanks to the Lord: first, for His great love and faithful direction of the lives of all who will trust Him: and second, for your response to His love and your willingness to trust Him with every detail of your life.

It is at this crucial point that many Christians deprive themselves of the full, abundant and purposeful life which the Lord Jesus promised in John 10:10. Failing to comprehend the true character and nature of God--His absolute love, grace, wisdom, power and holiness--many Christians have foolishly chosen to live according to their own plans rather than to consider and do the will of God. Some have such a distorted view of God that they think of Him as a tyrant whom one must either appease or experience His wrath, as those who worship a pagan god. Since they are afraid of Him, they cannot love and trust Him. This is sometimes true of individuals who have transferred to God their fear of an earthly father who may have been overly strict, unduly demanding, or even tyrannical.

In all fairness I should say that there are many sincere Christians who want to do the will of God but do not know how to go about discovering His will for their lives.

A choice young college graduate came recently for counsel concerning God's will for his life. "How can I know what God wants me to do?" he asked. Briefly I explained the safest approach to knowing the will of God--to follow what I have chosen to call the "Sound-Mind Principle" of Scripture. In less than an hour, by following the suggestions contained in this letter, this young man discovered what he had been seeking for years. He knew not only the work which God wanted him to do, but the very organization with which he was to be affiliated.

Now you may ask, "What is the 'Sound-Mind Principle' of Scripture?" In II Timothy 1:7 we are told that "God has not given us the spirit of fear; but of power, and of love and of a sound mind." The sound mind referred to in this verse means a well-balanced mind--a mind that is under the control of the Holy Spirit--"remade" according to Romans 12:1, 2 (NEB): "Therefore, my brothers, I implore you by God's mercies to offer your very selves to Him, a living sacrifice, dedicated and fit for His acceptance, the worship offered by mind and heart. Adapt yourselves no longer to the pattern of the present world, but let your minds be remade and your whole nature thus transformed. Then you will be able to discern the will of God and to know it is good, acceptable, and perfect."

There is a vast difference between the inclination of the natural or carnal man to use "common sense" and that of the spiritual man to follow the "Sound-Mind Principle." The first depends upon the wisdom of man for understanding, without benefit of God's wisdom and power; the other, having the mind of Christ, receives wisdom and guidance from God moment by moment through faith.

Are your decisions as a Christian based upon unpredictable emotions and chance circumstances--upon the "common sense" of the natural man? Or do you make your decisions according to the "Sound-Mind Principle" of Scripture?

Through the years, as I have counseled with many Christians, the question most frequently asked has been, "How can I know the will of God for my life?" Inevitably, the majority of Christians who come for counsel are looking for some dramatic or cataclysmic revelation from God by which they will know God's plan. Without minimizing the importance of feelings, which Jesus promised in John 14:21 as a result of obedience, more emphasis needs to be placed upon the importance of the sound mind which God has given. Multitudes of sincere Christians are wasting their lives, immobile and impotent, as they wait for some unusual or dramatic word from God.

The Scripture assures us that "God has not given us a spirit of fear, but of power, and of love, and of a sound mind." Thus, a Christian who has yielded his life fully to Christ can be assured of sanctified reasoning, and a balanced disciplined mind. Also, God has promised to give His children wisdom, according to James 1:5-7. Further, we can know with "settled and absolute assurance" that, when we pray according to the will of God, He will always hear and grant our petitions (I John 5:14, 15). Since the Christian is to live by faith, and faith comes through an understanding of the Word of God, it is impossible to overemphasize the importance of the Scripture in the lives of those who would know and do the will of God.

If you would like to know the will of God for your life, according to the "Sound-Mind Principle" of Scripture, may I suggest that you follow this bit of logic. Consider these questions: "Why did Jesus come?" (He came "to seek and to save the lost"--Luke 19:10.) "What is the greatest experience of your life?" (If you are a Christian, your answer quite obviously will be, "To know Christ personally as my Savior and Lord.") "What is the greatest thing that you can do to help others?" (The answer is again obvious: "Introduce them to Christ.")

Jesus came to seek and to save the lost, and every Christian is under divine orders to be a faithful witness for Christ. Jesus said, "Herein in My Father glorified, that ye bear much fruit; so shall ye prove that ye are My disciples." It logically follows that the most important thing I can possibly do as a Christian is to allow the Lord Jesus Christ in all of His resurrection power to have complete, unhindered control of my life; otherwise He cannot continue seeking and saving the lost through me.

Thus, every sincere Christian will want to make his God-given time, talents and treasure available to Christ so that his fullest potential will be realized for Him. For one Christian, this talent which God has given him may be prophetic preaching, evangelism or teaching; for another, it may be business; for another, the ministry or missions; for another, homemaking, as expressed in Romans 12:5, I Corinthians 12, 14; Ephesians 4; and other Scriptures.

As you evaluate the talents that God has given you in relation to your training, personality, and other qualities, may I suggest that you take a sheet of paper and make a list of the most logical ways through which your life can be used to accomplish the most for the glory of God. With the desire to put His will above all else, list the pros and cons of each opportunity. Where or how, according to the "Sound-Mind Principle," can the Lord Jesus Christ through your yielded life accomplish the most in continuing His great ministry of seeking and saving the lost? Like my young friend, you will find that such a procedure will inevitably result in positive actions leading to God's perfect will for your life. But note a word of caution: the "Sound-Mind Principle" is not valid unless certain factors exist.

Campus Crusade		Teaching		Church Ministry		Business or Profession	
Pro	Con	Pro	Con	Pro	Con	Pro	Con

1. There must be no unconfessed sin in your life; following I John 1:9 takes care of that: "If we confess our sins, God is faithful and just to forgive us our sins and to cleanse us from all unrighteousness."

2. Your life must be fully dedicated to Christ according to Romans 12:1, 2 and you must be filled with the Holy Spirit in obedience to the command in Ephesians 5:18. As in the case of our salvation, we are filled and controlled by the Spirit through faith.

3. In order to know the will of God, you must walk in the Spirit (abide in Christ) moment by moment. You place your faith in the trustworthiness of God with the confidence that the Lord is directing and will continue to direct your life, according to His promise that the "steps of a righteous man are ordered of the Lord." For "as you have therefore received Christ Jesus the Lord, so walk in Him." How? By faith--placing your complete trust in Him. Now, you must go on walking by faith. Remember, "that which is not of faith is sin," and "the just shall live by faith," and "without faith it is impossible to please God." Faith is the catalyst for all of our Christian relationships.

The counsel of others should be prayerfully considered, especially that of mature, dedicated Christians who know the Word of God and are able to relate the proper use of Scripture to your need. However, care should be taken not to make the counsel of others a "crutch." Although God often speaks to us through other Christians, we are admonished to place our trust in Him. In Psalms 37 we are told to delight ourselves in the Lord and He will give us the desires of our hearts, to commit our ways unto the Lord, to trust Him and He will bring it to pass. Also, in Proverbs 3 we are told, "Trust in the Lord with all thine heart: and lean not unto thine own understanding. In all thy ways acknowledge Him, and He shall direct thy paths."

God never contradicts Himself. He never leads us to do anything contrary to the commands of His Word; for, according to Philippians 2:13 (Phillips): "It is God who is at work within you, giving you the will and the power to achieve His purpose."

Through the centuries sincere religious men have suggested spiritual formulas for discovering the will of God. Some are valid: others are unscriptural and misleading. For example, a young seminary graduate was investigating various possibilities of Christian service and came to discuss with me the ministry of Campus Crusade for Christ. Applying the "Sound-Mind Principle" to his quest, I asked, "In what way do you expect God to reveal His place of service for you?" He replied, "I am following the 'closed door' policy. A few months ago I began to investigate several opportunities for Christian service. The Lord has now closed the door on all but two, one of which is Campus Crusade for Christ. If the door to accept a call to a particular church closes, I shall know that God wants me in Campus Crusade." Many sincere Christians follow this illogical and unscriptural method, often with most unsatisfactory and frustrating consequences. Don't misunderstand me. God may and often does close doors in the life of every active, Spirit-controlled Christian. This was true in the experience of the Apostle Paul. As recorded in Acts 16:6-11, he was forbidden by the Spirit to go into Bithynia because God wanted him in Macedonia. My reference to "closed door" policies does not preclude such experiences, but refers to a careless hit or miss attitude without the careful evaluation of all the issues.

This approach is illogical because it allows elements of chance, rather than a careful, intelligent evaluation of all the factors involved, to influence a decision. It is unscriptural in that it fails to employ the God-given faculties of reason that are controlled by the Holy Spirit. Further, the "closed door" policy is in error because it seeks God's will through the process of elimination rather than seeking God's best first. It should be understood that true faith is established on the basis of fact. Therefore, vital faith in God is emphasized rather than minimized through employing Spirit-controlled reason. In making decisions some sincere Christians rely almost entirely upon impressions, or hunches, fearful that if they use their mental faculties they will not exercise adequate faith and thus will grieve the Holy Spirit.

There are those who assume that a door has been closed simply because of difficulties that have been encountered. Yet, experience has taught and Scripture confirms that God's richest blessings often follow periods of greatest testing. This might include financial needs, loss of health, objection of loved ones and criticism of fellow Christians. God's blessing is promised, however, only to those who are obedient--who demonstrate their faith in God's faithfulness. The apparent defeat of the cross was followed by the victory of the resurrection.

An acceptable consideration for discussing God's will contains four basic factors somewhat similar to the "Sound-Mind Principle": (1) the authority of Scripture; (2) providential circumstances; (3) conviction based upon reason; and (4) impressions of the Holy Spirit upon our minds. However, such an appraisal is safer with a mature Christian than with a new or carnal Christian, and there is always danger of misunderstanding "impressions."

You must know the source of "leading" before responding to it. To the inexperienced, what appears to be the leading of God may not be from Him at all but from the "rulers of darkness of this world." Satan and his helpers often disguise themselves as "angels of light" by performing "miracles, signs, foretelling events," etc. The enemy of our souls is a master counterfeiter.

Remember, just as turning the steering wheel of an automobile does not alter the car's direction unless it is moving, so God cannot direct our lives unless we are moving for Him. I challenge you to begin employing the "Sound-Mind Principle" today in all your relationships. Apply it to the investment of your time, your talents and your treasure; for this principle applies to everything you do in this life. Every Christian should take spiritual inventory regularly by asking himself these questions: Is my time being invested in such a way that the largest possible number of people are being introduced to Christ? Are my talents being invested fully to the end that the largest possible number of people are being introduced to Christ? Is my money, my treasure, being invested in such a way as to introduce the greatest number of people to Christ?

Every Christian is admonished to be a good steward of his God-given time, talents and treasure. Therefore, these investments must not be dictated by tradition, habit or by emotions. Every investment of time, talent and treasure, unless otherwise directed by the Holy Spirit, should be determined by the "Sound-Mind Principle" of Scripture, as described in II Timothy 1:7.

Regarding the questions asked by your girl friend, the same principle applies to her. How does this "Sound-Mind Principle" apply in the case of a secretary, homemaker, an invalid, or one who, because of circumstances beyond her control, does not have direct contact with men and women who are in need of Christ?

First, each Christian must be a witness for Christ; this is simply an act of obedience for which one need not possess the gift of evangelism. If normal day-to-day contacts do not provide opportunities to witness for Christ, an obedient Christian will make opportunities through personal contacts, church calling, letter writing, etc. Two of the most radiant, effective and fruitful Christians whom I have known were both bedridden invalids who, though in constant pain, bore a powerful witness for Christ to all--stranger and friend alike. "That which is most on our hearts will be most on our lips," was demonstrated in their lives. Second, a careful evaluation should be given to determine if God may not have a better position for one. Again, the "Sound-Mind Principle" applies. For example, a secretary in a secular organization may not have much opportunity to make her life count for the Lord. It may be that God wants to use her talents in a Christian organization. One should be very careful,

however, not to run from what appears to be a difficult assignment. A careful appraisal of one's present responsibilities, with this new understanding of God's leading, may well reveal a great potential for Christ.

For example, I know that there is a great scarcity of qualified secretarial help in many Christian organizations, including Campus Crusade for Christ. Quite obviously, members of an office staff do not have as much contact with men and women who are in need of our Savior as those who are actually working on the campus or conducting evangelistic meetings. However, according to the "Sound-Mind Principle," if their lives are fully dedicated to Christ, they can make a vital contribution to the effectiveness of any Christian ministry. By relieving others who have the gift of evangelism without the talent for business or secretarial responsibilities, the overall ministry for Christ in such an organization is strengthened greatly. In this way, they can more fully utilize their talents in helping to seek and to save the lost.

Obviously, therefore, a dedicated member of the secretarial staff of the world-wide ministry of Campus Crusade for Christ is just as vital to the success of this campus strategy as those who are working on the campus. My own personal ministry has been greatly increased by the dedicated efforts of several secretaries who are more concerned about winning students to Christ than with their own personal pleasure.

One further word of explanation must be given. It is true that God still reveals His will to some men and women in dramatic ways, but this should be considered the exception rather than the rule. God still leads men today as He has through the centuries. Philip, the deacon, was holding a successful campaign in Samaria. The "Sound-Mind Principle" would have directed him to continue his campaign. However, God over-ruled by a special revelation, and Philip was led by the Holy Spirit to preach for Christ to the Ethiopian eunuch. According to tradition, God used the Ethiopian eunuch to communicate the message of our living Lord to his own country.

Living according to the "Sound-Mind Principle" allows for such dramatic leadings of God. But, we are not to wait for such revelations before we start moving for Christ. Faith must have an object. A Christian's faith is built upon the authority of God's Word supported by historical fact, and not upon any shallow emotional experience. However, a Christian's trust in God's will, as revealed in His Word, will result in the decisions which are made by following the "Sound-Mind Principle." The confirmation may come in various ways--depending upon many factors, including the personality of the individual involved. Usually, the confirmation is a quiet, peaceful assurance that you are doing what God wants you to do, with expectancy that God will use you to bear "much fruit."

As any sincere Christian gives himself to a diligent study of the Scripture and allows a loving, all-wise, sovereign God and Father to control his life, feelings will inevitably result. Thus, the end result of a life that is lived according to the "Sound-Mind Principle" is the most joyful, abundant, and fruitful life of all. Expect the Lord Jesus Christ to draw men to Himself through you. As you begin each day, acknowledge the fact that you belong to Him. Thank Him for the fact that He lives within you. Invite Him to use your mind to think His thoughts, your heart to express His love, your lips to speak His truth. Ask Jesus to be at home in your life and to walk around in your body in order that He may continue seeking and saving souls through you.

It is my sincere prayer, Paul, that you may know this kind of life, that you may fully appropriate all that God has given to you as your rightful heritage in Christ. I shall look forward to hearing more from you concerning your personal application of the "Sound-Mind Principle."

Warmly in Christ,

Exhibit 38

Statement of Faith

The sole basis of our beliefs is the Bible, God's infallible written Word, the sixty-six books of the Old and New Testaments. We believe that it was uniquely, verbally and fully inspired by the Holy Spirit, and that it was written without error (inerrant) in the original manuscripts. It is the supreme and final authority in all matters on which it speaks.

We accept those areas of doctrinal teaching on which, historically, there has been general agreement among all true Christians. Because of the specialized calling of our movement, we desire to allow for freedom of conviction on other doctrinal matters, provided that any interpretation is based upon the Bible alone, and that no such interpretation shall become an issue which hinders the ministry to which God has called us.

We explicitly affirm our belief in basic Bible teachings, as follows:

1. There is one true God, eternally existing in three persons—Father, Son and Holy Spirit—each of whom possesses equally all the attributes of Deity and the characteristics of personality.

2. Jesus Christ is God, the living Word, who became flesh through His miraculous conception by the Holy Spirit and His virgin birth. Hence, He is perfect Deity and true humanity united in one person forever.

3. He lived a sinless life and voluntarily atoned for the sins of men by dying on the cross as their substitute, thus satisfying divine justice and accomplishing salvation for all who trust in Him alone.

4. He rose from the dead in the same body, though glorified, in which He lived and died.

5. He ascended bodily into heaven and sat down at the right hand of God; thus, he was alienated from his Creator. That historic fall brought all mankind under divine condemnation.

6. Man was originally created in the image of God. He sinned by disobeying God; thus, he was alienated from his Creator. That historic fall brought all mankind under divine condemnation.

7. Man's nature is corrupted, and he is thus totally unable to please God. Every man is in need of regeneration and renewal by the Holy Spirit.

8. The salvation of man is wholly a work of God's free grace and is not the work, in whole or in part, of human works or goodness or religious ceremony. God imputes His righteousness to those who put their faith in Christ alone for their salvation, and thereby justifies them in His sight.

9. It is the privilege of all who are born again of the Spirit to be assured of their salvation from the very moment in which they trust Christ as their Savior. This assurance is not based upon any kind of human merit, but is produced by the witness of the Holy Spirit, who confirms in the believer the testimony of God in His written Word.

10. The Holy Spirit has come into the world to reveal and glorify Christ and to apply the saving work of Christ to men. He convicts and draws sinners to Christ, imparts new life to them, continually indwells them from the moment of spiritual birth and seals them until the day of redemption. His fullness, power and control are appropriated in the believer's life by faith.

11. Every believer is called to live so in the power of the indwelling Spirit that he will not fulfill the lust of the flesh but will bear fruit to the glory of God.

12. Jesus Christ is the Head of the Church, His Body, which is composed of all men, living and dead, who have been joined to Him through saving faith.

13. God admonishes His people to assemble together regularly for worship, for participation in ordinances, for edification through the Scriptures and for mutual encouragement.

14. At physical death the believer enters immediately into eternal, conscious fellowship with the Lord and awaits the resurrection of his body to everlasting glory and blessing.

15. At physical death the unbeliever enters immediately into eternal, conscious separation from the Lord and awaits the resurrection of his body to everlasting judgment and condemnation.

16. Jesus Christ will come again to the earth—personally, visibly and bodily—to consummate history and the eternal plan of God.

17. The Lord Jesus Christ commanded all believers to proclaim the gospel throughout the world and to disciple men of every nation. The fulfillment of that Great Commission requires that all worldly and personal ambitions be subordinated to a total commitment to "Him who loved us and gave Himself for us."